ARIEL SHARON

ADDITIONAL BOOKS BY URI DAN

Sharon's Bridgehead

The Mossad
(with Dennis Eisenberg and Eli Landau)

90 Minutes at Entebbe
(with William Stevenson)

To The Promised Land

Blood Libel

Kippur: An Album of Photographs of the Yom Kippur War

The Secret War: The Spy Game in the Middle East
(with Yeshayahu Ben-Porat)

The Eichmann Syndrome
(with Edward Radley)

Eli Cohen: The Spy From Israel
(with Yeshayahu Ben-Porat)

Lansky: Mogul of the Mob
(with Dennis Eisenberg and Eli Landau)

ARIEL SHARON
AN INTIMATE PORTRAIT

Uri Dan

ARIEL SHARON: AN INTIMATE PORTRAIT
Copyright © 2006 Michel Lafon Publishing S.A.
English language translation copyright © 2006 Palgrave Macmillan
All rights reserved. No part of this book may be used or reproduced in any
manner whatsoever without written permission except in the case of brief
quotations embodied in critical articles or reviews.

First published in France by Michel Lafon as *Entretiens Intimes avec Ariel Sharon*
First English-language edition published in 2006 by
PALGRAVE MACMILLAN™
175 Fifth Avenue, New York, N.Y. 10010 and
Houndmills, Basingstoke, Hampshire, England RG21 6XS.
Companies and representatives throughout the world.

PALGRAVE MACMILLAN is the global academic imprint of the Palgrave
Macmillan division of St. Martin's Press, LLC and of Palgrave Macmillan Ltd.
Macmillan® is a registered trademark in the United States, United Kingdom
and other countries. Palgrave is a registered trademark in the European Union
and other countries.

ISBN-13: 978–1–4039–7790–8
ISBN-10: 1–4039–7790–9

Library of Congress Cataloging-in-Publication Data
Dan, Uri.
   [Ariel Sharon. English]
   Ariel Sharon : an intimate portrait / Uri Dan.
      p. cm.
   Includes bibliographical references and index.
   ISBN 1-4039-7790-9 (alk. paper)
   1. Sharon, Ariel. 2. Generals—Israel—Biography. 3. Israel. Tseva
haganah le-Yisra'el—Biography. 4. Israel—History, Military. 5. Prime
ministers—Israel—Biography. I. Title.

DS126.6.S42D3613   2006
956.9405'4092—dc22
[B]
                                                              2006050664

A catalogue record of the book is available from the British Library.

Design by Letra Libre

First edition: October 2006

10 9 8 7 6 5 4 3 2 1

Printed in the United States of America.

To my wife Varda and my son Oron,
who supported me all these years
during my battle for Ariel Sharon

CONTENTS

Photosection appears between pages 143 and 144.

ACKNOWLEDGMENTS

Marching beside Ariel Sharon for more than 50 years in the long and critical struggle for Israel's defense and security required the support of many friends in Israel and around the world. I beg them not to be insulted if they were not mentioned in the book, and I wish to acknowledge them here.

I want to thank Eric Fettmann of the *New York Post* for his real friendship and warm support during more than a quarter of a century. This mutual friendship, with both Ariel and myself, developed in the United States and later in Israel, where he was managing editor of the *Jerusalem Post*. He has always been there around the clock to give advice, to explain the American political and media scenes, and now to put the finishing touches on this book.

Since the earliest days of Sharon's political struggle, he enjoyed the deep friendship of journalist and author Lucinda Franks and her husband, Manhattan District Attorney Robert Morgenthau. In recent years, Lally Weymouth of *Newsweek* and the *Washington Post* also stood beside us.

In France, my friend Patrick Wajsman, editor-in-chief of the significant quarterly *Politique Nationale*, backed Sharon during the darkest days and always urged me to interview him as much as possible. This enabled me to keep an ongoing record of Sharon's thinking and actions after he became prime minister.

I will always remember our meetings with the late A. M. "Abe" Rosenthal, former executive editor of the *New York Times*. After becoming a columnist for the paper, his was one of the strongest and most important voices supporting Israel during Sharon's lonely crusade for peace.

Above all, Rupert Murdoch was there beside Sharon ever since they first met at the old offices of the *New York Post* on South Street in Manhattan in 1982, when Arik was defense minister. A warm friendship developed, based on mutual respect. Rupert instantly appreciated Sharon's outstanding leadership, so he opened up the pages of the *Post* (and, later, Fox News Channel) for special interviews, all before Sharon was recognized, in his 2005 speech at the United Nations, as one of the world's most important political leaders.

Seth Lipsky, during his years with the editorial pages of the *Wall Street Journal*, could always be counted on as a friend and supporter; he has remained so, first as editor of the *Forward* and now as publisher and editor of the *New York Sun*.

Al Ellenberg introduced me to American audiences on the pages of the *SoHo Weekly News* and later as the Israeli correspondent of the *New York Post*. Through it all, he has been not only a great editor, but also a great friend.

The same holds true for Sidney Zion, whom Arik and I first met during the Six-Day War. Throughout the coldest days for Sharon, Sidney always had a warm place for him in his column—and, more importantly, in his heart.

It would take an entire book to thank my son Oron, but I need to acknowledge here all his characteristic hard work to prepare this manuscript.

Finally, my deepest thanks to Catherine Spencer, who translated the manuscript from French into English, and to my editor at Palgrave Macmillan, Alessandra Bastagli, without whose encouragement and help this book would not have been possible.

FOREWORD

In Israel, it is easier to make history than to write it. It is not unusual for an order to become a historic act. Or a historic error.

Throughout Israel's existence there have been so many noble and extraordinary acts, executed at such a stupefying rate, that it is very difficult to relate them afterward. That is, however, what I have attempted to do in writing this book. I have been Ariel Sharon's friend for half a century, and for more than 40 years I regularly kept a journal of our conversations, recording the secrets and musings that he chose to share with me. I have always believed that Sharon was the man who most embodied Israel's destiny—even his adversaries today compare him to a biblical hero. To preserve his reflections and his opinions represented, in my mind, a civic duty. As well as including private conversations that were recorded then and there, sometimes when the event was still taking place, this book includes exclusive interviews that Ariel Sharon gave me during these decades.

In this book, the reader will discover 50 years of the thoughts and actions of an extraordinary leader. Most important to me, I would be very happy if he, too found in it the story of my deep, constant and unconditional friendship. He once wrote to me: "Above all, you are a true friend who has always been there." I am still here.

Uri Dan, Paris, Tel-Aviv, May 2006

ראש הממשלה
Prime Minister

ד' אלול, תשס"ה
8 ספטמבר, 2005

לאורי ידידי ורעי במלאות לך שבעים,

יש אנשים שאפשר לספר את מסכת חייהם כרצף של תמונות מרגעים בלתי נשכחים כפי שנקלטו
בעין המצלמה.
ויש כאלה שאפשר לתאר את מסכת חייהם בכמה אלפי מילים.
לך אורי, נפלה הזכות שבמשך למעלה מיובל שנים המילים שכתבת והתמונות שצילמת הם תיעוד
מרתק של מסכת חיים שאין רבים שחוו אותם. אבל יותר מכך : הם תעודה מאלפת של רגעים
היסטוריים שהנצחת ותיעדת בתהליך ההיסטורי של תקומתה המחודשת של האומה היהודית
במולדתה.

עבורי היית ותמיד תהיה – עיתונאי חרוץ ורב תושייה, סופר ויועץ, איש מקצוע "ללא מורא וללא
משוא-פנים". אך יותר מכל – אתה לי חבר וידיד אמת שתמיד היה שם, ברגעי השמחה והתעלות;
בשעות הקשות של כאב וטרגדיה אישיים ; בימים של שמחת הניצחון ובלילות חשוכים תחת אש
צולבת "בחצר", או בפעולות התגמול ובשאר שדות הקרב שתקצר היריעה מלפרטם.

אבל יותר מכל אני זוכר לך שהיית עמי באותם שעות שלפני הכרעות גורליות, ברגעים המיוחדים של
"בדידותו של המפקד" – היית שם ושתקת, אבל היית וזה החשוב.

אתה איש העולם הגדול. תמיד התפעלתי מהמידע הרב שלך ומהההערכה הרבה שרוחשים לך ברחבי
העולם.

ואחרי כל מה שנאמר, תמיד נשארת הרעות, שזר לא יבין אותה ועליה רציתי לומר לך מילה אחת :
תודה.

שלך, לנצח רבה
אריק
אריאל שרון

Jerusalem, Israel

To Uri, my friend and companion,
on the occasion of his seventieth birthday

There are people whose lives can be unfolded like a succession of unforgettable moments, as if they had been caught through the objective lens of a camera. There are others whose existence can only be described with thousands of words.

You, Uri, have had the privilege of seeing how the words you have written and the images you have taken over the course of 50 years recount in the most absorbing way an experience that few others have lived through. Better still: you have captured forever the decisive moments of the historical rebirth of the Jewish nation in its homeland.

For me, you have been and you always will be a thorough and resourceful journalist, a writer and an adviser, a professional "without fear or prejudice." Above all, you are a true friend who has always been there, in moments of laughter and celebration, in difficult times of pain and personal tragedy, in the luminous joy of victory as well as during the dark nights of heavy fire in the court of death, or during reprisal operations and other battles too numerous to mention.

More than anything else, I remember your presence at my side in the moments that preceded fateful decisions, moments that belong to the "solitude of the leader." You were there and said nothing: you were there, and that was what mattered.

You are a man of experience who is open to the world. I have always admired the breadth of your knowledge and the fact that you are appreciated everywhere. All said, there remains a complicity that a stranger could never understand and for which I want to say just this: thank you.

With all my friendship, Arik.

ISRAEL TODAY

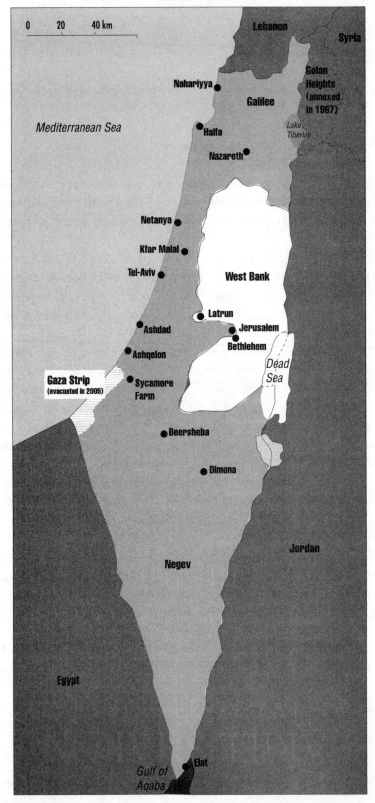

0   20   40 km

Lebanon

Syria

Nahariyya

Galilee

Golan
Heights
(annexed
in 1967)

Mediterranean Sea

Haifa

Lake
Tiberias

Nazareth

Netanya

Kfar Malal

Tel-Aviv

West Bank

Latrun

Jerusalem

Ashdad

Bethlehem

Dead
Sea

Ashqelon

Gaza Strip
(evacuated in 2005)

Sycamore
Farm

Beersheba

Dimona

Jordan

Negev

Egypt

Elat

Gulf of
Aqaba

INTRODUCTION

1954: MY FIRST MEETING
WITH ARIEL SHARON

The first time I met Ariel Sharon, at his headquarters in Tel-Nof, south of Rehovot, in 1954, neither he nor I suspected that a friendship would develop between us, a friendship that we would enjoy without interruption for more than 50 years.

A young soldier of 19, I arrived at headquarters without having asked for permission. I didn't know that the existence of Sharon's regiment, the 890th Paratroopers—the only parachute unit in Israel—was a secret and that even Sharon's name was a secret, too. Everything was a secret in this newborn country that had been created barely six years earlier, in 1948. At the time, I knew nothing about military laws, state secrets, censorship and security rules; I did not understand that an ordinary soldier had to ask for special authorization to get on a base. Nevertheless, the guard on duty brought me into the commander's small office. A red beret lay on his table, which was covered with a dark green cloth. A bulb suspended from an electric wire dangled above the table.

"Well? What has the cat dragged in?" Sharon called out in his clear, thundering voice. He stood tall in his impeccable dark uniform, the stripes of a lieutenant colonel on his shoulders. He scrutinized me suspiciously; I soon learned that this was a habit of his. The higher in rank he rose, the more suspicious he became. His brown hair was mixed with white, making him appear much older than his 26 years. He had fought in the war of independence, and this gave rise to both respect and fear in me since I knew how much blood had been shed in that war.

Born in Palestine under the British Mandate on February 26, 1928, Ariel Sharon was the son of Shmuel and Vera Scheinerman, a

Russian and a Belorussian, respectively, who had moved to Kfar Malal moshav,* north of Tel Aviv, in 1922. Like many of his companions in arms, Sharon had swapped his original surname for a Hebrew one, choosing the name of the region where he was born, Sharon.

I remained standing in front of Lieutenant Colonel Sharon and explained that I was the correspondent of the military weekly *Bamahané:* "I heard that you were carrying out military operations beyond enemy lines. I'd like to accompany your unit onto the battlefield."

"Who talked? Who couldn't keep his mouth shut?" Sharon exclaimed. His eyes, red with lack of sleep, glowed with anger.

Uri Avneri, the editor of the weekly *Haolam Hazé,* had taken me on during the previous year. My childhood dream of becoming a reporter had come true. When the time came for me to put my uniform back on, Avneri recommended me to General Zvi Zur. Avneri had even written an article about me in his newspaper. I had blushed with pride at his words: "One day Uri Dan will be one of the greatest journalists in Israel."

Thanks to the backing of General Zur, after the usual military training I was appointed a correspondent at *Bamahané,* the official army paper. Chasing every bit of news, I had heard a rumor about a secret unit led by a certain Ariel Sharon. It was said that these men infiltrated Gaza and the West Bank to carry out reprisals whenever terrorists killed Jews in Israel.

"Who talked?" he asked again.

"Colonel, I can't remember," I stuttered, hanging on to the journalist's golden rule: never reveal your sources.

"Well, if I were you I'd try to get my memory back. . . . We have all night."

After a long pause, Sharon invited me to sit down. Keeping military, political and personal secrets was his golden rule. He never trusted someone who did not understand this principle.

Sharon explained that the paratroopers' operations had to remain secret and that he could not talk about them to me—even if I worked for a military newspaper—unless the chief of staff, Moshe Dayan, himself gave authorization. Sharon added that if I gained such an au-

---

*   Agricultural cooperative (plural, "moshavim").

thorization, I would have to undergo officer training, as well as para-trooper, commando and combat training, before I could accompany his unit. Only then could I come back to see him.

"Is it true what Uri Avneri wrote about you in the paper?" he asked suddenly. "That one day you would be one of the greatest journalists in Israel?"

"I don't know, sir!"

How could Sharon remember an article that had appeared months before—and, on top of that, had appeared in a paper that had declared open war on the government of Prime Minister David Ben-Gurion? Thus ended our first conversation, a conversation that was to have repercussions on my entire personal and professional life.

Did Uri Avneri's praise play a part in Sharon's eventual decision to let me accompany his commando unit? How ironic if it did, for this same Uri Avneri later became Yasser Arafat's principal supporter and spokesman in Israel. Many years later, Sharon told me that his friendship for me began that night, when I had refused to reveal my sources. He liked that.

FORTY YEARS LATER, AUGUST 1994

The telephone rang in my room at the Taranne hotel, Boulevard Saint Germain, Paris. It was Ariel Sharon.

"Do you always stay in the same hotel when you're in France?" he teased me.

"Always! From the window of my room I can see, as usual, the church of Saint Germain des Prés, the Flore and the Deux Magots. I haven't decided yet where I'll be going for my coffee and croissant."

"I'm in my office in Tel Aviv. The atmosphere in Likud is so rotten that I'd rather be walking around Paris. Is the Brasserie Lipp still there?"

"Of course! It's very close to my hotel."

"Here," he complained, "Yitzhak Rabin and Shimon Peres continue to give everything away to the Palestinians. And in Likud, Netanyahu is boasting that he's going to be the next prime minister." He was joking, but I detected bitterness in his voice.

"Don't be surprised—it's quite likely that he will be prime minister," I said. "Bibi is very popular. It's not in your best interest to stand in his way; you'll risk tripping yourself up."

Sharon resented this confrontation with Bibi—Sharon had done so much for Israel in wartime, and had created Likud, and was now being eclipsed by a cocky young greenhorn. Benjamin Netanyahu had only recently entered national politics, as deputy minister of foreign affairs, after his successful stint as Israeli ambassador to the United Nations.

Sharon interrupted me: "I'm not calling about that. *Haaretz* wants to do an article on our friendship. One of their correspondents has just called me and I want your permission."

"Orit Galili? She also contacted me. But *Haaretz* hates you so much that I'm reluctant to do the interview."

"That's why I want to ask you whether it wouldn't be wise to do it, to accept the interview to redress the balance."

"And how!"

"Good. Now you can go and have your coffee at the Deux Magots."

✡

On my return to Israel, the article appeared on several pages of the *Haaretz* supplement, with the title, "The Start of a Wonderful Friendship." It was a pleasant surprise, coming from this paper that had announced the end of Sharon's political career not without joy. The following is an extract from the article:

> In the eyes of politicians and journalists, the connection between Sharon and Dan seems to be an alliance of interests. Sharon was an excellent source of information for Uri Dan when he was a military correspondent, and Dan repaid him by crowning him in the press with the title of "Arik, king of Israel." Over the years a deep friendship has developed, which no one would call one-sided. "There is no point-scoring between us," Uri Dan declared. And yet it is clear that the journalist plays the role of an acolyte who looks up to Sharon as a spiritual father, while Sharon supports him like a son, even though their age difference is only eight years: Ariel Sharon is 66, and Uri Dan is 58. Ties of absolute loyalty have formed between them. There is no one, outside his family, whom Sharon trusts as much, and the same goes for Dan. . . .
>
> For two years, Uri Dan took part in all the reprisal operations under Sharon's command. He was with the paratroopers at Houssan,

Kalkilya and Kinnereth. And during the Sinai war he parachuted with them from Mitla Pass. On Sharon's instigation, Uri Dan even underwent military training so as to cover combat from the front lines. Sharon confirms: "Uri is one of the few military correspondents who experienced war. Many have written about battles but he saw them while fighting in the trenches."

In 1973 Uri Dan made the now-famous statement that "Those who didn't want Sharon as chief of staff will have him as minister of defense. Those who don't want him as minister of defense will have him as prime minister."

He would repeat the second part of this prediction 10 years and a war later, when Sharon left the ministry of defense after the investigation of the massacres of Sabra and Chatila. Did Sharon like that statement? At first, not too much.

I asked him what he thought of it today. "What worries me," he replied, smiling, "is that Uri Dan's political predictions have always turned out to be true; I don't want to talk about his personal predictions."

Sharon appreciated Dan's originality: "Uri is one of the rare journalists who writes original material. When I read other military reporters, I know exactly who they have talked to. All Uri's information, however, is first-hand. More than once he gave me vital news before it was officially released."

"I have never allowed professional ethics to make me write an article critical of Arik," explains Uri Dan, "because I didn't want to play the objective journalist. At least my subjectivity is known and openly declared: I am on Sharon's side."

Sharon adds, "Uri has immense talent and because of me he has unjustly had to go through numerous trials. Certainly we have had occasional differences. Several times I have said to him, 'If you don't agree with me, why don't you say so? Why don't you write about it? If you occasionally attacked me a little, you would be one of the most popular journalists in Israel.'"

Uri Dan refused to give an example of an issue on which he and Sharon were in disagreement. "But that doesn't mean that we agree about everything. My friendship with Arik is based on total honesty," he explains.

For his part, Sharon agrees to divulge two big areas of disagreement between them: "Uri was opposed to the withdrawal of the settlements in Yamit, in the Sinai. He feared that it would cause long-term problems, as well as creating a precedent. My response to him at the time was that if there was no withdrawal there could be no peace with Egypt. Several years earlier, he had also criticized me for believing that Arafat was someone one could have genuine dialogue with. At the time, I thought he was wrong; now, I think he was right."

The day Ariel Sharon and Uri Dan left the ministry of defense, *Time* magazine published an article claiming that Sharon had encouraged the Christian falangist leaders in Lebanon to massacre Palestinians in Sabra and Chatila. Sharon decided to sue *Time* for defamation; he experienced one of the most difficult periods of his career but was never abandoned by his faithful friend Uri Dan. For 23 months, they fought the case together. When the court decided in his favor, Sharon thanked Dan, without effusiveness as was his wont. He said to him simply: "Without you, I wouldn't have come through."

1948

THE WAR OF INDEPENDENCE

On November 29, 1947, the U.N. General Assembly voted on Resolution 181, which stipulated the division of Palestine into two separate states, one Jewish and one Arab, with Jerusalem under international control. The Arab countries' rejection of this plan led to the first Israeli-Arab war, unleashed on May 15, 1948, the day after the proclamation of the independent state of Israel. The armies of Transjordan, Egypt and Syria, aided by Lebanese and Iraqi troops, attacked Israel.

I was only 12 at the beginning of the war of independence, but I know how brutal the battles were. I trembled when the Arabs of Jaffa attacked in 1948, and I cried when Jerusalem's Old City, and with it the Wailing Wall, fell into the hands of the Jordanians.

At the time, Sharon led an infantry regiment. On the Latrun road, the formidable Arab Legion had inflicted a crushing defeat on the Israeli Defence Forces (IDF). On the 50th anniversary of the creation of the state of Israel, Sharon told me about the lessons he learned from this episode:

✡

Ariel Sharon, exactly 50 years ago, in May 1948, you were seriously wounded during the battle of Latrun, undertaken to force the blockade of Jerusalem and to take back the police station that the Jordanians were occupying. How does your memory of that episode—your frantic race across a burning battlefield, in the scorching summer, dressed in shorts and sandals and shaking with pain—influence you?

Shoes, not sandals. In shorts, yes. And I wasn't running, but was crawling with great difficulty. Yes, that battle had a lasting influence on me in many ways, particularly regarding the treatment of the wounded.

How so?
Not everyone managed to escape. Some soldiers remained on the battlefield. Men from my group. I was commanding the assault section of the division charged with opening the road to Jerusalem and liberating the village of Latrun. We then had to descend to the Trappist monastery and if possible continue to the police station. That was the goal of the mission. We attacked at dawn on May 26, 1948.

At dawn?
Yes. We were supposed to attack during the night, but disagreements within the general staff held us up. The bus that was to transport my section was parked near the army encampment north of Kibbutz Hulda, and I saw senior officers having an animated discussion inside. Time passed. Obviously I didn't know the reason for their disagreement; I only knew that I had to take the left side of the village and go down to the monastery of Latrun. What I feared most of all was being stuck down there in the middle of the day without having completed my mission. And the discussions went on and on . . . Many years later, I learned that there had been a bitter debate between the heads of the newly formed 7th Brigade and the battalion commanders. The latter were against the attack because of the Jordanians' numerical superiority. In the final analysis, it was Ben-Gurion who insisted on the attack—he has said as much in his diary. He was afraid that a cease-fire would be implemented before we had succeeded in reaching defendable borders. It was a constant cause of discord between him and the chief of staff office. Several times, conscious of the passing time, he demanded more combativeness.

And it was only later that you discovered all that?
Oh yes, much later. That night, between May 25 and 26, 1948, I was just waiting impatiently for the order to leave. We had been at war for almost six months and my section had already taken part in several operations, with numerous losses. Time was running out, when we wanted to move and act. I also began to worry when I learned that we would have two 65-mm Mexican cannons. I had never seen a cannon

in action, and I had the feeling that we would have no choice but to use them! I had explained to my men the importance of this operation in forcing the blockade of Jerusalem. No one questioned the relevance of our mission, despite the losses we had sustained since the beginning of the conflict. Ten men in one place, 15 in another, 40 in another still. All the time, painful losses. However, throughout that war I never had the feeling—and I think this was characteristic of my generation—that we were powerless against the Arabs. I don't remember a single instance of despair.

Even when you faced the best prepared army of all, the Arab Legion?
Yes. In fact, we didn't know much about them—only that the Legion had already conquered the Old City of Jerusalem.

What happened during this battle that influenced your military philosophy?
It was a terrible battle. We didn't arrive until five in the morning. A thick fog covered the fields. Just as we began advancing, the fog lifted all at once and we were in a hail of gunfire. The whole hill opposite erupted in fire. That hill . . . When you go down from Jerusalem toward Tel Aviv you can hardly see it, but if you come from the south, you clearly see the olive grove planted on the side that goes up to the village.

What were you armed with?
We had just received Czech weapons. Until then, half my men—my section consisted of 35—had firearms, and the other half only had grenades. The Russians had allowed us to secure Czech rifles. We also had submachine guns, Israeli-manufactured Stens, and Bren machine guns and other similar weapons. We suffered casualties from the beginning of the conflict. It was impossible to advance under sustained fire. Some units of the Arab Legion were commanded by British officers, and I met one of them nine years later, during my course at the Staff and Command College in Camberley, England.

I gave the order to fire the 52-mm mortar. A boy from my moshav, Azriel Ratzabi, got up to put a shell into the mortar. A bullet went through his lungs and killed him. I managed to bring my section up to a little path, beneath Latrun. It was impossible to go any further. From eight in the morning, the Jordanians began rushing down the hill. They crossed the road and went into the olive trees, issuing shouts that froze the blood. We shot at them, they withdrew and then advanced again. It didn't stop.

Were they villagers or soldiers?
Legionnaires. We remained stuck at the foot of the hill until midday. Every time we tried to climb, they shot at us. Around noon, Iraqi planes entered the battle. Everything around us was burning. We were dying of thirst: the *khamsin* (a hot desert wind) exacerbated the dry, scorching heat, and we had not brought any water.

Not even gourds?
We had nothing. Absolutely nothing. I had been wounded at midday. A bullet in the stomach, which came out at the thigh. I also had an arm in plaster, a souvenir from an accident that had happened a month earlier.

Did someone look after your wounds?
No. We also had no bandages.

Were you losing blood?
Yes, but luckily no vital artery was affected and I remained fully conscious. Getting out of that sticky situation seemed impossible to me. Of our men, 15 were already dead, 11 were wounded and 5 had been taken prisoner. Of the whole section, only 4 men were still fit. After we had pushed back the enemy offensive, we were stuck with a broken radio transmitter, without means of communication or the possibility of withdrawing. The Jordanians approached from time to time, and we would shoot and throw grenades. That went on from eight in the morning until noon. Then our two cannons opened fire. I thought that the offensive against us would resume and that enemy reinforcements would arrive, but at one o'clock there was a sudden and total silence. Enemy fire had ceased. I lifted myself up a little and suddenly saw behind us, from the east, Arabs advancing silently. They weren't soldiers. They were coming down the hill that had been occupied by our forces, Hill 314, which today overlooks the district of Neve Shalom. I understood that the artillery fire was meant to cover their retreat. Faced with this new situation, I gave the order to withdraw,

telling my men not to move toward the evacuation point for the wounded at the village of Beit Joz—the current site of Kibbutz Harel—and also to avoid the Latrun road, where the Jordanians had a mechanized unit with cannons. I was half dead of thirst, exhausted, and the withdrawal seemed to demand a superhuman effort. I saw the four fit men of the section go ahead of me, and I didn't even resent them for it.

They didn't help their injured commander?
They passed ahead of me and the other wounded, very simply because there was no way of evacuating us. We were in a critical situation—all our forces had beaten a retreat and we had been abandoned. I feared that Arab villagers would come to kill the wounded, as was their custom. Gathering the last of my strength, I began to crawl, on all fours, on the ground covered with hot ash. As I was wearing only shorts, my knees were covered with burns; my hands were, too. Another wounded man, a soldier who had joined my section two days before, was crawling beside me. He had a smashed jaw and was a terrible sight. But at that moment it was the arms and legs that counted, particularly the legs. He was moving several feet away from me, to the left. I could not remember his name. He couldn't talk because of his broken jaw, and I didn't have the energy to speak. It was a strange race between us—climbing as best we could—and the villagers who were coming down the hill. The Jordanians held the whole line of Latrun: the police station, the monastery, the village of Dir Eyub and its surroundings. The soldier who was crawling beside me took another hit, a bullet in the shoulder, although the Jordanian fire had stopped. The people of Beit Soussin were attacking from their village, south of the old Jerusalem road that goes through Shaar Hagai.

They descended slowly, looking for wounded men to finish off and for possessions to loot. The way in which the Arabs dealt with our wounded certainly spurred us on; no need to deny it. Still crawling silently, we had reached the first terrace. My companion in misadventure helped me climb it, and we continued dragging ourselves along to the second terrace. Again he helped me get over it, and in this way, terrace by terrace, we arrived at the other side of the hill. What a relief. There I found the rest of the company, who were beating a retreat.

The company's second in command, Moshik Lanczet, who was also wounded but less severely, tried to haul me onto his back. I weighed only 68 kilos at the time, but I was still too heavy. I could nonetheless lean against him, and we hobbled across the burning fields, avoiding the road to the west and the hills to the east. We wanted to get to Kibbutz Hulda, several kilometers away. To this day, I cannot understand why I was so upset that I could not remember the name of the soldier who had helped me escape.

Suddenly, I saw a jeep coming with a moshav girl, Rivka Bugin, at the wheel. She had come to see what was happening at the front. Rivka had served in the British army, driving trucks in the Libyan desert. She was a wonderful girl who, sadly, died afterward. She was accompanied by her brother, Shmulik Bugin, the famous driver of *Infernal Tiger*, the IDF's only armored vehicle, taken from the Jordanians. Seeing them coming and going, looking for wounded, I suddenly remembered the name of my soldier: Yacov Bugin, their cousin.

Despite everything that's happened to me since, I still remember the shudder that went through me. Arriving near what is today the Nachshon crossroads, I almost collapsed. Someone took me in their arms and put me in an armored car.

Had you fainted?
No, but I had a moment when everything went fuzzy. I don't remember exactly. There was smoke everywhere. At Kibbutz Hulda, I was laid out on a stretcher. It was a long drive to the Hadassah hospital in Tel Aviv. My face was covered with a towel, and I heard people talking about me:
  "Yet another goner!"
  "Who is it?"
  "Arik."
  "Where was he hit?"
  "In the genitals."
  I was happy to still be alive, but what a blow!
  From Hulda we went to Mazkeret Batia. The convoy of ambulances stopped next to the synagogue. The women of the moshav brought jugs of milk to quench our thirst. I couldn't drink because of the wound in my stomach. I still remember the image of those women

solicitously taking care of us while I worried frantically about the injury to my genitals. The convoy set off again, passing through Naan, and arrived at Bilu camp, transformed into a military hospital, where the injured were gathered. My stretcher was placed on the ground, and a charming volunteer nurse asked me to urinate. I couldn't. She asked for a catheter to be brought, and I said, "Wait, I'll try again." This time I succeeded. She kissed me on the mouth, and then I realized that my wound was not where I had feared.

Later we took the road to Tel Aviv. We had just reached the entrance to the Hadassah hospital in Balfour street when Egyptian planes attacked the area. Everyone who could jumped out of the ambulances, while the wounded lay inside them until the bombing was over.

In 1967, after the Six Day War, I accompanied you to the site of the battle of Latrun, and you told me that that event had marked you.
A lot, yes, and in many ways. In fact, there wasn't a single senior officer on the ground, and that was what was lacking at the critical moment. I was commanding a section, but there was no one there to analyze the situation and make decisions. For example, if our forces had received the order to keep on until nightfall while their evacuation was organized, we would have saved a lot of men, including some wounded. An officer capable of understanding the situation would have ordered, "We won't leave, even if there are more losses." In the end there would have been fewer losses, and the wounded who stayed on the ground would not have been killed.

Could the officer also have given the order to withdraw?
But withdrawal was impossible!

One thing has concerned me since Latrun: the need for a commanding officer in the theater of operations who is capable of making decisions according to the real evolution of the situation, rather than relying on occasional radio-transmitted messages.

The question of the wounded is the second thing that has haunted me since Latrun, and which has never given me peace. The Arabs massacred the wounded. They didn't take prisoners, even in the Legion units under British command. Now the wounded remained on the battlefield at Latrun . . .

How did that influence you later, when you commanded paratroopers and armored vehicles, during the Six Day War and after the crossing of the Suez Canal?

It became an unbreakable rule for me: the wounded are not to be abandoned on the battlefield. That also applies to prisoners, even if you have to take hostages. The IDF never broke this rule. That is why, on October 7, 1973, arriving at the canal front with my division, I insisted on rescuing the surrounded men in the fortifications of the Bar-Lev line who were calling for help—and it was still possible. Some of them said to me afterward that they had recognized my voice, sure that I would save them. I managed to get some of them out, despite the categorical opposition of the senior command.

The command center at the front?

Yes. For me, the question of the wounded and of prisoners is a moral one of the greatest importance. It is unthinkable to evaluate it in terms of figures and statistics.

I believe you acted in this way in the case of Sergeant Yitzhak Jibli, a prisoner in Jordan in 1954?

Exactly. And also in 1952, when we captured two Jordanians to exchange them for two soldiers from the Givati brigade who had crossed the border by mistake during a patrol in the region of Kalkilya. The Jordanians refused to give them back. I was then an operations officer in the northern command.

What did you do to make your paratrooper and armored vehicle units aware of the fate of the wounded?

The order was categorical: the wounded are not to be left on the ground. Never. Not in any circumstances.

Because of what you experienced during the battle of Latrun?

Not only that. I didn't react to what I experienced but to what I saw. Fifty years have passed since Latrun, and the fate of the wounded has continued to obsess me. I can still see those youngsters, 17 to 20 years old, and also men who were older than me.

You were 20?
Yes. I remember their faces. I knew them all, without exception. At the time, the structure of the army was still regional.

They all came from your region, from Sharon?
Yes.

The IDF had just been created and it suffered a loss that day. How did you feel?
During the war of independence, we had victories and some crushing defeats. Nonetheless, despite the heavy losses, I never experienced the slightest feeling of despair or powerlessness. I don't remember a single moment when I lost confidence, and I think that was the same for everybody. I lived through several of the IDF's brutal defeats— Latrun, the attack against Iraq El-Manshiyeh, the Faluja Pocket— without ever losing the certainty that we would triumph in the end. Sure, we sometimes failed, and that meant many lost comrades, but I never saw soldiers in tears.

Unlike what we saw during the 1990s?
Yes. That didn't exist at the time. In 1948 our soldiers were absolutely convinced that our reasons for combat were just, and they didn't experience the slightest doubt about this. They knew that it was a war of survival. The war of independence cost us more than 6,000 men and women, the elite of our youth, of a Jewish population of 600,000. Not everyone fought. As usual, it was a small number who defended the people.

1956
THE SUEZ CAMPAIGN

Since 1955, I had covered several commando operations with Sharon and his paratroopers. Being a war correspondent bears little resemblance to its depiction in action films or novels: it is a terrifying job, a job in which death and danger are constant companions.

Moshe Dayan, then number two to the chief of staff, had given permission for my articles to be published in the military weekly *Bamahané*. The press, in Israel and abroad, reprinted my descriptions of operations on the ground. I was, however, forbidden from giving names, and was particularly forbidden from using pictures of Sharon and his men. Apart from those who were killed at the front, I could identify people only by their nicknames. I didn't even have permission to use the word "paratrooper."

Motivated by an insatiable curiosity, I have been a journalist for 50 years, and I have had the privilege of accompanying the spearhead of the IDF in its toughest combats. I covered missions against bases harboring Palestinian fedayeen in the Gaza Strip, against Egyptians who supported fedayeen in the Sinai desert, against Syrians who machine-gunned Israeli fishermen at Lake Tiberias, and against the Jordanian army and police who were protecting terrorists in Transjordan. As a young citizen of Tel Aviv, I met the bravest soldiers, most of whom had come from kibbutzim* and moshavim. I knew Meir Har Tzion, a 20-year-old officer whom Sharon respected deeply; Rafael Eitan, known as "Raful" (Israelis love diminutives); "Katcha," Shimon Kahaner, one of the most remarkable soldiers of the 101st Commando

---

* Plural of "kibbutz."

unit, and Yitzhak Jibli, as well as many others whose names have become legendary.

Above all, there was Colonel Ariel Sharon, "Arik." I always preferred to call him "Ariel," which means "lion of God," because the name Arik didn't seem to convey his stature. After intensive training and scouting incursions, he would send his combatants behind enemy lines. He knew how to maintain the excitement of battle—his unit always waited for the next operation with unabated impatience.

Scouts provided information about Egyptian and Jordanian bases so that when Palestinian terrorists committed murderous acts against Jews, Sharon had access to complete dossiers that determined the objectives of Israeli retaliation. Sharon explained, "I had to propose a plan of operation in the hours immediately following an attack; that's the only time the government authorized a raid behind enemy lines, in Gaza or the West Bank."

In fact, the government followed the wishes of a single man, David Ben-Gurion. Some historians claim that it was Ben-Gurion who unleashed reprisal actions after terrorist attacks by Arabs. The truth is completely different. The initiative for these reprisals came from Sharon. More than once I found myself at his headquarters in Tel-Nof when he learned that Palestinians had killed a Jew in Kfar Saba or in Raanana. He would immediately call Moshe Dayan, who had since been promoted to chief of staff: "Moshe, why do we do nothing against these assassins? We are ready to carry out an action in Jordan or in Gaza tonight."

Moshe Dayan would then go to Ben-Gurion to present the proposals for retaliation. Ben-Gurion would ask, "Who will lead the action?"

"Arik and Har Tzion."

These two names were enough, for they represented a guarantee of success. Meir Har Tzion, seriously wounded in 1956, was Sharon's most gifted lieutenant. When he lost his young sister Shoshana, killed by bedouin in the Judean desert in 1955, Har Tzion had avenged her death by killing the five men responsible for the crime.

Before Sharon, no officer had taken the initiative of proposing "immediate" operations to the defense minister or the chief of staff. The responsibilities that Sharon assumed at such a young age, as well as his repeated victories against terrorism, gave rise to a wave of jealousy among his senior officers in the IDF. Every time Ben-Gurion went to visit him in his office—an unusual gesture on the part of the prime minister—Ariel would say to me, smiling, "This is going to cost me dearly!"

From 1956, General Moshe Dayan himself tried to hold back Sharon's career. Dayan feared that he would be eclipsed by this lieutenant colonel, who was much younger. Dayan, a brilliant and original commander, tried to take credit for all the reprisal operations. At the time, Sharon was up for promotion and was to lead a parachute division. Internal rivalry scotched the plan, however, and he remained a simple unit commander. Sharon explained the political calculations that had led to this situation: "They refused to let me be promoted to colonel, which involves the command of a brigade. And so my 'brigade' was christened Unit 202."

Without doubt Dayan was also wary of Sharon's charisma. When Sharon explained to his soldiers the strategic details of an operation beyond the border, he always managed to give them a feeling of security, as well as the certainty of success.

I like history, and I admire the Bible as a history book—an immense history book about the Jewish people. When Sharon, full of life, humor and energy, climbed into his jeep with his soldiers headed for the battlefield, I saw historical figures: the Jews fighting for their freedom against the Greeks, Romans and others; David confronting Goliath; the Judges of Israel; Gideon and Samson. Sharon came right out of one of those stories. And 50 years ago I predicted that a book—or even several books—would be written about him.

✡

During the summer of 1956, following an assassination by Palestinians who had infiltrated Israel from Jordan, Sharon received the order to carry out a punitive operation that same evening. He was to capture the Jordanian police station at Gharandal, in the valley of Arava, and destroy it, before returning to Israel.

Sharon got to his headquarters in Tel-Nof in the afternoon of Shabbat. He was wearing khaki trousers, a sky-blue shirt and sandals. Without even putting his uniform back on, he ordered his soldiers to push into the Negev, 180 kilometers south, and he deployed jeeps, command cars (vehicles for transporting troops) and trucks all along the route to Eilat, a small village at that time. Access by sea was impossible because the Egyptians controlled the Straits of Tiran. As for the road, perhaps one car an hour would pass in the middle of the night.

The chief of the reconnaissance unit, Meir Har Tzion, reconnoitered the Jordanian police station and then led the troops toward Gharandal. For night missions, Sharon trusted only himself and Har Tzion. They had the natural gift of being able to make their way across an unknown terrain in complete darkness. They needed only to look at a map or to have inspected the place beforehand. Even Moshe Dayan knew of this talent: "When Sharon studies a map, he studies it like a conductor studies a concert score."

I was walking at night beside Sharon and Colonel Rehavam Zeevi, known as "Gandhi,"* who was Moshe Dayan's envoy. None of the soldiers had spoken a word or made a sound, even when our feet got stuck in quicksand. We moved along in silence until we were 200 meters away from the police station. The building towered above us on the hill, its menacing shadow standing out against the star-filled sky. And then Gandhi, Dayan's man, looked at his watch: "Moshe said that if you hadn't managed to take the building by two o'clock in the morning, you mustn't go ahead with the operation."

There was barely a quarter of an hour left before the attack would start. Sharon insisted that the operation should be carried out, but Gandhi interrupted him: "Moshe worries that if you return at dawn, you'll be a target for the Jordanian air force."

Despite the darkness, I could sense that Sharon was trying to control his anger, knowing only too well how his rivals in the general staff would exploit a dereliction of duty. He gave the order to his men: "Turn back!"

It was only a postponement, however; six weeks later Sharon went back to Gharandal after a second Palestinian attack and razed the Jordanian police station to its foundations.

---

* One year, for the festival of Purim—the Jewish carnival—Colonel Zeevi, who was very thin, dressed up as Mahatma Gandhi, wearing a white cloth and holding a goat on a leash. The nickname was ironic, for Zeevi was never known for his nonviolent methods.

The battle against terrorism poses thorny moral questions: How does one target armed men who deliberately take refuge among civilians? What kind of response can be delivered when one is not faced with a regular army?

Since its creation, Israel has enshrined the immutable principle of "purity of arms"—the ethical use of military force—and has tried as much as possible to protect civilians from attacks. Despite this real concern, tragic errors were committed, which reinforced the national consensus that Arab terrorists should in no case be followed into their own terrain. After the crisis of Kibya, the Israeli government restricted itself to targeting police and military locations, even if these operations proved more costly in terms of its own soldiers' lives.

At that time, Sharon was in charge of the secret Unit 101. On the night of October 12, 1953, a Jewish inhabitant of the village of Yehud, Suzanne Kanias, and two of her children—Shoshana, aged three, and a one-year-old boy—were killed in their sleep by terrorists. Those responsible for the murders had left a trail that led to the village of Kibya in the West Bank. Moshe Dayan ordered the destruction of the village's principal houses. Sharon recounted this secret reprisal expedition, carried out on October 14, 1953, and called "Operation Shoshana":

"At the headquarters in the forest of Shemen, I told Moshe Dayan, 'We will raze that village.' We set off, carrying almost 700 kilos of dynamite. Israeli fighters had taken the village and neutralized the Jordanian forces. Equipped with loudspeakers, our soldiers went through the streets and, speaking in Arabic, urged the inhabitants to evacuate their homes. They came out, and we didn't touch a single hair on their heads."

The soldiers then blew up the houses, as Sharon had promised Dayan.

"Then, completely exhausted, I went to bed," Ariel went on. "When I woke up, I heard on the radio that the Jordanians had announced that we had massacred around 60 civilians. I couldn't believe it."

Some of the villagers had preferred to hide in their cellars, despite the soldiers' instructions to evacuate. Israel was condemned by the

United Nations, and Israeli leaders placed the responsibility entirely on Sharon. Ben-Gurion published a communiqué declaring that the destruction of Kibya was the work of irregular Israeli forces acting under the influence of the anger provoked by the Palestinian attacks. Sharon repeatedly explained, in vain, that the deaths were a regrettable tragedy but that his unit had done everything they could to protect the civilians.

Six years after the operation, Ben-Gurion called Sharon to his office in Tel Aviv to interrogate him:

"Who gave the order to carry out the raid against Kibya?"

"I don't know, but I know who I made my report out to."

"Who?"

"You."

"I was ashamed of that action," declared the elderly Ben-Gurion.

Sharon laughed as he recounted the conversation, adding, "Ben-Gurion is the one with white hair that sticks out? Then it was to him that I made out my report on Kibya. I was never afraid of Ben-Gurion; I respected him. But Moshe Dayan feared him."

✡

The loss of life during reprisal operations was sometimes heavy. In particular, I remember October 22, 1956. The night before, at Raanana near Kalkilya, Arabs had killed a farmer in his field and cut off his ears. We left from Kibbutz Eyal, near the Israeli-Jordanian cease-fire line. Through binoculars, Sharon examined the target: the large police station of Kalkilya. He turned to the young tank commander, Zvi Dahab: "Can you strike the building to cover the paratroopers?"

"Just tell me which window I should hit."

Before the raid, Sharon spoke to his officers: "Do you know what keeps us commanders alert, as we approach an enemy target when we are worn out after a long march? What motivates us to carry out the attack? The feeling of responsibility to our soldiers. We know that they are looking at us. We know that they are waiting for our signal and that they are fighting with us."

It was very important for Sharon that he and his officers be first in the line of fire.

Ariel also didn't take military rules of confidentiality lightly, so he forbade a noncommissioned officer from participating in the Kalkilya operation. He reproached him: "You spend your time at Cassit* and you chat away, talking about our operations to *Haolam Hazé* journalists."

The officer, deeply hurt by this remark, insisted on taking part in the operation despite Sharon's words. He died during the battle. The Kalkilya police station was entirely destroyed, but 18 paratroopers were killed and 60 were wounded. The next day, Sharon and I returned to the headquarters at Tel-Nof in an army Ford.

Moshe Dayan, the chief of staff, urged Sharon to go posthaste to the defense ministry in Tel Aviv to have an "off the record" meeting with the editors of the Israeli press. It was the first time that Sharon was presented to journalists, and he asked me to accompany him. He knew why Dayan required his presence at this meeting: three years after the beginning of the reprisals, this was the first time that there had been as many as 18 Israeli casualties. Sharon explained: "The editors will ask questions and will no doubt be critical. That's why Dayan would rather that I explain the unfolding of events and shoulder all the responsibility, so I will be implicated."

Sharon called this atmosphere "the war of the Jews." And then he uttered these memorable words: "I would prefer 100 wars against Arabs to one battle against Jews. In a war against Arabs, the battle is certain and clearly defined—quite quickly. But the internal struggle among Jews has no end. You think you control them, but in fact it's they who control you."

The editors of the main Israeli publications looked on with curiosity as Moshe Dayan introduced them for the first time to the man who was going to make headlines in the Israeli press for the next 50 years: "You have doubtless already heard his name. Lieutenant Colonel Sharon directed the operation that destroyed the police station at Kalkilya, and for which we paid a heavy price."

✡

---

* A well-known café in Tel Aviv's Dizengoff street.

On Friday, October 25, 1956, I rushed to the office of the deputy chief
of staff, General Meir Amit, in Tel Aviv. There had been extreme tension in the Near East since the Egyptian president Gamal Abdel
Nasser had signed a military agreement with the Soviet Union and
nationalized the Suez Canal. Moshe Dayan and Shimon Peres, then
head of the defense ministry services, were looking for an opportunity
to start a preemptive war. The Egyptian army had to be broken before
it managed to get to the Soviet arsenal.

Peres won the support of the French socialist government under
Guy Mollet, from whom he managed to buy arms in secret, in defiance of the embargo imposed by the United States—which had refused to sell any arms to Israel since Israel's creation in 1948 so as to
try to preserve good relations with the Arab world.

Ships discharged French AMX 13 tanks on the beaches of Ashdod
and Ashkelon, while the Israeli air force had acquired Marcel Dassault
fighter planes. In addition, rumor had it that there would be a general
mobilization of reservists.

"What is happening?" I asked Meir Amit.

"Go and see your friend Arik at Tel-Nof. Next Monday you can
parachute with his unit behind enemy lines."

"What enemy?"

The general did not reply, and I remained ignorant until my arrival at Tel-Nof on Sunday, October 28. The young leader of the
890th, Major Rafael Eitan—"Raful"—assembled the men and announced that we would leave for combat the next day at 1700 hours.
Our target was situated 30 or 40 kilometers from Suez, in the very
heart of the Egyptian desert on the Sinai peninsula, east of Mitla Pass.
Some 400 paratroopers were gathered in Shekem Hall, the military
cooperative, when Raful declared, "We are going to parachute for the
first time in 2,000 years." As if there had been Jewish paratroopers two
millennia ago, fighting against the Romans at the time of the destruction of the Temple in Jerusalem! Paratroopers started to sing their
lucky song, "Why Didn't You Tell Me Before?"

The following day, I saw a French officer for the first time. Colonel
Simon was wearing a magnificent red beret, decorated with a beautiful
ribbon that fell to his shoulders. An interpreter translated his words
into Hebrew as he explained to our paratroopers how to work the 106-
mm recoilless rifles. Simon announced that the French troop-transport

planes would land at night at Mitla Pass. They would take off from the air base at Akrotiri in Cyprus, and we should tell them where to parachute new guns, jeeps and provisions.

Toward noon, Sharon emerged from the operational center of the 202nd Brigade headquarters. He paused on the threshold with Raful and other officers of the brigade.

"Are you ready, you and your men?" Sharon asked Raful with a big smile.

Sharon had recruited Raful himself. He had absolute faith in him, for Raful, too, came from a family of farmers.

"You will have to cope by yourself for a day, until I rejoin you," continued Sharon.

Our offensive was to begin by parachuting 270 kilometers behind enemy lines. When Lieutenant Colonel Sharon advanced with his men on the road to Sinai on Monday, October 29, 1956, in order to take three Egyptian positions, he did not doubt the success of the mission that Ben-Gurion and Dayan had entrusted to him. Sharon was aware that the secret accord signed with the French and British governments meant that the Israeli attack would above all serve as a pretext for a Franco-British "peace making" invasion of the canal. But his main concern was to weaken an enemy that had been newly armed by the Soviets.

The spirit of bravery inspired by this 28-year-old officer caused the parachutists to squabble over who would be included among the 380 men to board the several French planes. In the afternoon, for the first time in our lives, we saw the impressive spectacle of 16 transport planes—Dakotas and Nordes—lined up on the base at Tel-Nof. I felt very proud as I clambered into a Dakota with Raful. "Mystère" fighter planes flew around us to ensure our protection. When we received the command to jump, I gazed at a magnificent spectacle: the Suez Canal running through the desert like a long blue band in the light of the setting sun. All around me in the sky hundreds of white blossoms were scattered. That first parachute jump was truly spectacular.

On the ground the next day, our unit was holding its own in spite of the Egyptian Migs and the attack of a tank regiment. In the early evening—just six hours later—Sharon arrived at the head of his men, wearing a khaki army sun hat and his face covered with dust. He was as happy as a child.

The following day at dawn, Sharon inspected the positions that we had dug out on the hills. He was so proud of his soldiers that he kept repeating, "Every one of you will get a paratrooper star as big as a sheriff's to commemorate the jump." He sometimes added, laughing, "I've got a clean, dry uniform in my bag in case they ask us to enter Cairo." His confidence was contagious, and everyone believed that a march on Cairo might actually happen.

Alas, on Wednesday, October 31, death struck Mitla Pass. Sharon had sent 200 paratroopers as scouts to the pass, 30 kilometers from the Suez Canal. The intelligence officer Gideon Mahanaimi had reported that the Egyptian soldiers had deserted the zone. In fact, they were looking out for us from behind the rocks, armed with heavy machine guns, and they began sniping at us relentlessly.

At noon I took my place in a caterpillar track vehicle with Mota Gur, the regiment commander. We were surrounded by the wounded and the dead. At 2100 hours we left in a yellow Egyptian armored vehicle, manufactured by the Soviets, that we had taken from the enemy. Sharon had tried everything that he could think of to get everyone out of the pass safely. He directed the evacuation of the wounded with the same determination. Immediate medical attention was given by the light of campfires, which also served as beacons for landing planes— Dakotas that touched down in the middle of the desert to take our soldiers to safety. At the time, we didn't have helicopters. In the deep voice of a commander who had already fought for independence in 1948, Mota Gur said to me, "Uri, that was a close call today."

Ariel Sharon was not a man who often indulged in affectionate gestures, so I was surprised when he placed his hand on my shoulder that evening of October 31, 1956, in the Sinai desert. By the light of the campfire he asked me, "Was it hard?" He knew what I was experiencing without my having to say a word. We had survived the terrible Egyptian ambush, but 38 Israeli paratroopers were killed and 120 were wounded. It was only when I saw Sharon staring at my right cheek that I realized that shrapnel had damaged my ear and that my cheek was covered with congealed blood.

That day, for the first time in my life, I prayed to God. It was then that I persuaded myself that God exists. Who else would have been able to save me so often, against all kinds of attacks? At Mitla, I even called on Rabbi Meir Baal Haness, known as the "master of miracles," to intercede on my behalf with the Almighty.

1957

AN OUTSTANDING OFFICER

Encouraged by his military success, Sharon made it a point of honor to be seen as the representative not just of the Israeli population but of the Jewish people. He measured geopolitical risks in the light of a question that seemed primordial to him: *Is it good for the Jews?* As for the retreat in March 1957 from Sinai and the Gaza Strip, under heavy pressure from the Americans, Sharon considered it "bad for the Jews," and bluntly said as much to Ben-Gurion.

In autumn 1957, the Tel Aviv district chief of police invited me to Martef Rishon, a good restaurant in Allenby Street, a stone's throw from the sea. As the young war correspondent covering military operations on the ground for *Ma'ariv*, then Israel's largest daily newspaper, I already enjoyed a certain reputation. The chief of police, Amos Ben-Gurion, was none other than the son of the prime minister. He wanted to talk to me about our mutual friend, Ariel Sharon, and asked me to tell Sharon to stop criticizing his friends and the IDF hierarchy: "People already envy him his military success; this jealousy could turn to hatred if he continues to show contempt for his superiors. On the other hand, if he can hold his tongue he has a good chance of being promoted to chief of staff by my father."

The meal over, I went to Tsahala, a residential neighborhood of Tel Aviv allocated to IDF officers, to warn Arik. He was not perturbed: "Amos already said that to me, but I think the only way to improve the situation in the army is by telling the truth without flinching, even when it hurts. The truth is that it's my direct relationship with Ben-Gurion that is causing this jealousy."

Shortly thereafter Sharon was sent for senior officer training at Camberley, England. Was this a move to keep the rather frank officer out of the high echelons of IDF for a while? This gave me the opportunity, during a stopover in London, to encounter a dashing Ariel Sharon wearing a very British three-piece suit and carrying the requisite black umbrella.

In 1961, Lieutenant Colonel Sharon learned that his telephone had been bugged by order of General Zvi Zur, the chief of staff. Zur hoped to gather proof for Ben-Gurion that Sharon was confiding military secrets to a journalist friend—who happened to be me. However, I was always careful not to transform Sharon's confidences into "scoops." Defense secrets were the IDF's sacred cow at that time. Israel consisted of barely 1.25 million Jews, almost half of whom were recent immigrants, and therefore the constant fear was that spies had slipped in among them. If the lowest-ranking civil servant at the ministry of defense had contact with a journalist, he would be suspect. Putting Sharon under surveillance was likely a roundabout way of both punishing him for his outspokenness and holding back his career. He was relegated to secondary functions and could only chomp at the bit.

During this period of marginalization, Sharon took comfort from his wife Margalit and their son Gur. Ariel and Margalit had fallen in love in 1947, when he was 19 and she was 16. Margalit, her parents, three brothers and three sisters had all survived the Shoah. While watering the orange trees at Kfar Malal, Ariel had set eyes on a good-looking girl, with golden curls cut like a boy's and a dazzling smile, working in the next field. He had climbed over a fence to be with her. The war of independence overturned the plans of the young sabra* and the Romanian refugee, and they married in 1953. Their son, Gur, Ariel's lion cub, was born in 1956.

I had met Margalit in March 1955. Ariel and I had arranged to meet in the offices of the chief of staff in Tel Aviv because he wanted to read the full version (before it was censored by the military authorities) of the article I had written on the first large-scale Israeli raid in the Gaza Strip, which was occupied by the Egyptians at the time. His wife, who had become a psychiatric nurse, was with him and asked to read the text afterward. She was passionate, concerned and moved by everything involving Ariel. I know that during that

---

* An Israeli born in Israel.

daring operation she had waited anxiously on a kibbutz near Gaza for her husband's return.

One day in 1956 I was in Sharon's headquarters, several months before the Suez campaign when he was still commander of the 202nd Brigade, and I met Lily, a pretty brunette with a sensual mouth and bright eyes. I was eager to get to know her better.

"You're mad!" a lieutenant said to me. "You can't chat up the commander's sister-in-law!"

MAY 1962
ADIEU MARGALIT

The friendship that bound Ariel and me together made me a permanent member of his household. I spent long evenings in the company of his wife, Margalit, and their son, the adorable Gur, in their apartment in Tsahala (the residential quarter in Tel Aviv allocated to IDF officers). Ariel and Margalit cast a tender and watchful eye on my private life as a young bachelor, grilling me mischievously on my friendships, as well as on my love affairs. When I finally announced that I intended to marry my latest conquest, with whom I was madly in love, they celebrated the news.

Soon thereafter, my world collapsed: I read in the press of my beloved's engagement to the CEO of Marks & Spencer. Heartbroken, I disappeared.

Ten days later I returned to my bachelor pad on the third floor of a building in Tel Aviv. A note was waiting for me on my door. I recognized Ariel's handwriting: "I have been looking for you for several days. I've searched everywhere, even in the nets of the Yarkon* fishermen. I'm glad I haven't found you. Don't do anything stupid."

No sooner had I begun to feel cheerful again, when another crisis, far more serious, struck our group. On May 2, 1962, General Aharon Doron from the military headquarters called me to the editorial offices of *Ma'ariv*. He told me that Arik's wife had died in a car accident on the road from Jerusalem to Tel Aviv and asked me to go and break the news to Sharon. I arrived at Tsahala with a heavy heart. The door of the house was open. Going in, I saw a lieutenant colonel of the Israeli air force, Moti Hod, who had arrived before me. Standing in

---

* River that crosses north Tel Aviv.

front of Hod, Sharon was squeezing his right fist in his left hand, as though to stifle a gesture of despair. Hod did not know the details of the accident; he knew only that a truck had crashed into Margalit's car on the Abou Gosh heights and that she died instantly. Gur called to his father to come and play with him, which Sharon always did when he got home early. Without a word, Ariel went up to his son. He had to tell his son, barely five years old, that he would never see his mother again.

During the week of mourning, without revealing his pain, Sharon welcomed the friends who came to offer comfort. His parents had taught him not to show his emotions. But when we were alone, he let his tears flow freely, and he talked to me with anguish about Gur, who was inconsolable at the loss of his mother. Fortunately there was Lily, Margalit's sister—as pronounced a brunette as her sister was a blonde. Employed in the judicial identity department of the police, she asked for prolonged leave to look after her nephew. She never went back to her job.

Lily took over the reins of the household and comforted Gur and his father. It is still common in Israel for a wife's sister to assist her sibling's family when death strikes. A year later, the chief military rabbi of the IDF joined Lily and Ariel in marriage, and I attended the wedding at the headquarters of the army rabbinate. Sharon rediscovered happiness, and Gur once again had two parents. At the end of the year, Lily gave birth to Omri, followed a year later by Gilad. The Sharon family now had three sons.

In the meantime, I had finally met the woman I was to marry, and she still shares my life today. Colonel Rehavam ("Gandhi") Zeevi organized our wedding reception at his new house at Ramat Hasharon in September 1963. My wife Varda and I were honored by the presence of Ariel Sharon and the minister of agriculture, the former chief of staff Moshe Dayan. According to the notes in my diary, between toasts to the young bride and groom, Dayan, Sharon and Gandhi spoke at length about the various strategies of opening up the road leading to Mount Scopus. Half of Jerusalem was still occupied by Jordanian forces. Four years later, Jerusalem would be reunified after the Six Day War.

1967

THE SIX DAY WAR

You were lieutenant colonel in command of the northern sector when you began fighting to save Israel's water supply.

In 1964, neighboring Arab countries decided to divert the three sources of the Jordan—not because they needed the water but because they wanted to cut off Israel's supply. Of these three tributaries, the Banias has its source in Syria, the Hatzbani has its source in Lebanon, and the Syrians claimed that the Dan's northern bank adjoined their border. On the ground, Syria should have been the principal actor in this joint operation. The water from these sources supplied a third of Israel's needs; it was literally a question of life or death.

The whole business resulted from negligence. To the east of the Dan kibbutz, in the heights called Banias Hill, lies a territory situated inside Eretz Israel.* Conquered by the Syrians during the war of independence, it was restored to us as a demilitarized zone after the armistice agreement of 1949. Shortly afterward, however, the Syrians tried to regain control of the demilitarized territories. They didn't always succeed, but that didn't stop them from trying. So, in the zone of El Hama, which wasn't conquered by the IDF during the war but which came back to us under the terms of the armistice agreement, Israeli soldiers wearing police uniforms carried out occasional patrols. In 1951, a police patrol was ambushed. Seven were killed. We didn't go back to El Hama, and the Syrians seized it. The second strategic territory was the zone of Metulla. It took several tough clashes and many losses before we managed to regain control.

---

* The whole land of Israel as assigned to the Jews by God.

The third zone was Banias Hill. Since the end of the war of independence, the attempt to settle Khan Ad-douar had failed because of its inhospitable nature, and the commander of the northern sector had to content himself with installing a permanent observation post there. A settlement is in essence an ordinary place: visits to the doctor, children on the way to school, a woman about to give birth, the delivery of goods—its daily life needs to be protected. The moment there is nothing more than a military presence in a region, there is no need to protect it. Run risks every day? Pointless. You go there now and again. Until you find the place has been occupied. Sometimes, it seems insignificant. You say to yourself: never mind, small violations of the agreement can happen, it's no big deal. But when it comes to agreements, you should *never* give up *anything*.

One day, the Syrians captured two of our men, Yehuda Dayan from Kibbutz Beit Alpha and Gideon Gretz, now a renowned sculptor in Italy. They released them after several months, largely because of the Americans' intervention. After this incident, the post at the settlement remained empty; we sent in only occasional patrols to show our presence, until the day our men saw Syrians on the hill. Israel didn't react. As well as the Golan Heights, Syria had now occupied Banias Hill, in violation of the armistice agreements. At first glance this event seemed irrelevant. But it soon became a critical issue, because that hill was the keystone of the Arab plan to divert the sources of the Jordan River. If we had continued to guard Banias actively, then the plan to deprive us of water would never have occurred to them and the destiny of the Middle East could have been different.

Once they were masters of the territory, the Syrians dug a canal and a tunnel connecting Banias Hill to Tel el-Ahmar. In 1964, they brought enormous quantities of material there.

You think that an active Israeli presence would have avoided the tension and eventually the Six Day War?
Absolutely. Everything would have been different. This reminds me of our weakness during the cease-fire in the Sinai after the war of attrition in August 1970, when the Egyptians advanced their battery of missiles and Israel didn't bat an eyelid. After a thousand days of conflict, fatigue got the better of our wariness. We said to ourselves, "What, get mixed up in that mess yet again?" And that cost us ten un-

tenable days on the Egyptian front, in October 1973. You must therefore remain vigilant—always.

It was solely because they held Banias Hill that the Syrians were
able to act. They launched the excavation work with great zeal and advanced technical means. Their idea was to create an artificial slope so
as to divert the course of the sources toward the Yarmuk,* depriving
Israel of a third of its water supply. This was a very serious and dia-
bolic plan, put into operation by highly competent engineers. At the
time I was directing the staff of the northern command, under the orders of General Abraham Yaffe. The Syrians claimed that their border
passed along the northern bank of the body of water formed by the
source of the Dan. I proposed reducing the pond and constructing a
road along the length of its northern bank, in the dried-up part of the
basin, taking great care to build the road in Israeli land, without
touching Syrian territory.

On November 1, 1964, the day construction began, we were subjected to fire from two Syrian tanks, which our tanks did not succeed
in neutralizing. Beware: danger. I still remember the rage of Israel
Tal, "Talik," who was then commander of the armored vehicle corps.
We nonetheless decided to resume the task two days later, on November 3, and this time we were ready to respond to fire. As soon as
the Syrians started to fire, our planes got involved. It was the beginning of the deterioration of relations between Israel and Syria,
though neither country had respected the armistice agreements, anyway. From that day, we pursued our action against the diversion of
the sources of the Jordan and strongly defended Israel's rights over
the smallest piece of border territory. It's no longer a question of
keeping agricultural land; it's a question of ensuring that signed
agreements are strictly adhered to.

And how did it end?
We succeeded in interrupting the Syrian efforts. What a situation!
Dozens of machines attacking Banias Hill. It was easy to reach the
machines nearest us, but the construction taking place ten kilometers from the border posed greater problems. This was where Talik's

---

* Jordan's largest river.

genius lay: he managed to lengthen the range of our tank cannons to 12 kilometers. That was the end of the attempt to divert the water supply.

All this was going on under Syrian fire?
Yes. It was only a brief confrontation, but the greater battle continued. The Syrians stopped their work near the border to concentrate on more sheltered zones, which provoked a series of incidents during 1965. From the beginning of 1967, the Soviet Union, which was supplying arms to Cairo and Damascus at the time, rubbed its hands and started spreading the false rumor that Israel was preparing to attack the Syrian front. The Egyptians abandoned their war in Yemen and massed troops in the Sinai. That was what led to the Six Day War. Everything began with that little hill on the Banias plateau—and several seconds of Israeli distraction.

You really believe that the history of the Middle East could have been different?
In my opinion, yes. It perhaps shows to what degree, in our relationship with the Arabs and with the world in general, we should never let anything go.

In 1967, no one envisaged a war.
No. And yet war happened. Initially a member of the general staff and head of training services, I was promoted immediately to the head of the 39th Armored Division of the central command. With the general mobilization of May 1967, I went down to the Negev.

How does one go from a situation of being relatively unconcerned to a state of war?
I heard news of the mobilization in a Jerusalem stadium during preparations for the military parade to celebrate the anniversary of independence. The hardest thing for me was to see the loss of confidence in the general staff. We officers on the ground had an unshakable confidence in our men and in our capabilities. We who had prepared and trained the troops now "divorced" the highest-ranking officers. Confidence reigned in all the divisions stationed in Sinai—with me, with Abraham Yaffe, with Talik and with the sector commander, Yeshayahu Gavish—but not in the high command.

At what moment did you sense this loss of confidence?

The doubt came from below. The Israeli people's anxiety, fear and uncertainty were transmitted to the center. That is what concerned me the most, and it happened more than once. How could a country with strong military power suddenly lose confidence?

Confidence regarding what?

Regarding Israel's capacity to resist and to win if war was forced on it. I had never before seen such fearfulness among my compatriots. The prime minister, accompanied by the defense minister, Levi Eshkol, and by Yigal Allon, met three of us—Matti Peled, Abraham Yaffe and me—before naming Moshe Dayan minister of defense. We told him that we were in a position to win against the Egyptians, pointing out the dangers of a wait-and-see policy, which in the end risked costing Israel more dearly. The situation hardly left us any choice: combat was inevitable. Eshkol later took me aside and said, "Pressure was put on me to choose Dayan." I told him that as far as the forces I commanded were concerned, it made little difference to me. I had nothing against Dayan, whom everyone respected, but even if Mrs. Beba Idelson of Histadrut* had been put in Defense, my division would have fought in exactly the same way.

In hindsight, wasn't that war a mistake?

I don't think we had a choice. Accepting the closure of the Straits of Tiran, for example, which would have shut off our access to the Red Sea and therefore forced us to give up free navigation, would have meant capitulation. What could the state of Israel have agreed to? It is legitimate to wonder about the errors we may have committed *after* the Six Day War, but one thing is certain: in that context, it was impossible to avoid war. Avoiding war would have meant that Israel was giving in and that the new state could be pressured into submission, cowed. One mustn't forget Israel's status before 1956 and its international recognition after the Sinai campaign in October of the same year. Again, we didn't have to hesitate in choosing between war and

---

*   A trade union organization, the General Federation of Workers in the Land of Israel.

peace, but rather in choosing between war and the ransom we would have to pay to avoid it—the only question was what price we would be prepared to pay.

How did leaders like David Ben-Gurion and Levi Eshkol, whom you knew well, launch the Sinai campaign or the Six Day War? They were no longer young men and, moreover, they were born abroad. Now some people claim that the leaders born in the Diaspora lacked resistance and that they gave in easily.

There is no relationship between leadership abilities and place of birth. I have repeated that for decades. There is no relationship between an individual's place of birth and his national pride or his ability to hold his head up high.

You have seen sabra leaders behave like ghetto natives and vice versa?

Absolutely, all the time, throughout these 50 years. There is no connection. And no relationship between tousled mops of hair* and leadership, either.

How did Levi Eshkol behave in this war?

In my opinion, he could have come out of it victorious and strong. I even said as much to him.

When?

Just before the famous evening of the "stammered speech,"† when I explained to him that Dayan's promotion did not affect me.

---

* The trademark style of Ben-Gurion and the other early leaders of Israel.

† At the end of May 1967, Prime Minister Eshkol spoke on the radio station Kol Israel with the intention of reassuring the Israelis; in fact, he succeeded only in increasing their anxiety. Unable to decipher the text he had been given, he began stammering. This incident symbolized the uncertainty that reigned in the country's political hierarchy.

*Was Moshe Dayan already minister of defense when he undertook his tour of
duty at the front?*
He didn't have a governmental role yet.

And he offered you his services as a driver for armored vehicles?
He said, "I hope they'll keep a place for me as a tank driver." I didn't
take him seriously; in any event, we had enough drivers.

But you were sure that he was ready to take orders from a tank commander?
Dayan had a daredevil's courage and nurtured the crazy idea that
nothing could happen to him. From this point of view, he was an exceptional being, a brilliant man with an original mind. I don't know
the detail of what happened between the army and the government.
As for Yitzhak Rabin, the chief of staff, I didn't find that out until very
much later.

What they call Rabin's collapse just before the war?
Yes, I didn't know about it at the time. Just imagine: I was on the
ground, training my troops. Calm, serenity and self-confidence
reigned—until I suddenly notice incomprehensible troop movements.
Units moving jerkily, without any logic, from south to north and
north to south. Our own forces—our support! I contacted the general
staff to find out what was happening. Rabin's secretary told me that he
was ill, full stop. That day, the command passed into the hands of Ezer
Weizman,* who became chief of operations.

*Moshe Dayan was named minister of defense by Levi Eshkol on the eve of the
Six Day War, and he kept that post in Golda Meir's government during the
war of attrition and then during the Yom Kippur war. Certain circles claim,
particularly today, that these leaders turned a deaf ear to Anwar el-Sadat's
"calls for peace" at the beginning of the 1970s and that they blindly and
knowingly carried us toward the Yom Kippur war. Do you share this view?*
It's a bad way to present things. We can't judge the leaders of that period in hindsight. Behind his image as a bon vivant, Dayan hid a
deeply pessimistic temperament. As for Golda Meir, her profound

---

* Future president of Israel, from 1993 to 2000.

concern for the fate and the future of the Jewish people led her to challenge the Arabs' statements. She thought that one had to be very cautious so as not to fall into their traps. You have to understand that it was another time and another generation. When we entered peace talks with Egypt, years later, and I telephoned my mother from Cairo, she would end every one of our conversations with the same words, pronounced in the Russian accent she never lost: "Don't trust them!" Her generation didn't believe in the possibility of a negotiated peace with the Arabs.

You yourself, head of the southern command until July 1973, were you aware of the steps taken by Sadat toward Israel?
No, and yet I had fairly frequent, albeit informal, contact with our heads of government. But I only saw the cabinet for the first time in 1975, when I collaborated with Prime Minister Rabin.

Until then, despite your high military functions, you had never been invited to cabinet meetings, as is the custom today?
That didn't happen at the time.

And when Golda Meir summoned you?
That was in private interviews when she wanted to discuss a point with me or when I wanted to see her. I met Ben-Gurion dozens of times, as well as the defense ministers who came after him: Pinhas Lavon, Levi Eshkol, Moshe Dayan. No, there were no machinations, and no, Sadat's proposals were not deliberately rejected. Absolutely not.

You say that Moshe Dayan was a pessimist who was always worried. Was Golda Meir also prone to worry?
Yes, without doubt.

And Ben-Gurion?
In the original plan for the Suez campaign, the 890th Paratrooper Battalion of the 202nd Brigade was to launch the operation. Moshe Dayan and Ben-Gurion feared that, at the last moment, the French and the British would refuse to intervene on the canal, even though they had come to a secret agreement with Israel about it. Each party

had its priorities. London wanted to settle the question of the Suez Canal, and Paris wanted to end Egyptian interference in North Africa. For us, it was the serious problem of terrorist raids launched from the Gaza Strip by the Egyptian secret services, as well as the threat of Nasser's pan-Arabism.

Ben-Gurion feared that if his allies withdrew at the last minute, it would be difficult to withdraw the battalion that had already parachuted in. Dayan, chief of staff, was concerned that our forces would penetrate too rapidly through the Sinai desert to keep control of an escape route if need be. Three days before the operation, Dayan arrived at the Tel-Nof base. "In case the campaign aborts," he declared, "I'm counting on you to get our forces out of there." I replied that I was certain of our ability to complete our mission successfully.

At the time you were a 28-year-old colonel?
I was a brigade commander but a lieutenant colonel. I saw Ben-Gurion just before he announced to the government the start of the campaign. He invited me that morning and told me about his interviews in France with the Prime Minister, Guy Mollet. I was, of course, already aware of the planned operation since my men and I had been preparing for it. On that dramatic day, a secretary suddenly burst into the room to say that the education minister, Zalman Aran, couldn't find his driver. Ben-Gurion exclaimed, "So tell him to take a taxi!"

Was this in his office in Tel Aviv?
No, in Jerusalem, behind the Jewish Agency, in the old office of the prime minister. Ben-Gurion told me of his concerns regarding the British. He was wary of them, while he trusted the French, perhaps because he was dealing with a Socialist government.

After all, it's normal that a political leader, particularly in a small country like Israel, should be permanently on the alert. Perhaps you interpreted as pessimism what was only Dayan's legitimate concern?
And so what if it was? I don't see anything dishonorable in it; it wasn't fear. Not at all. I wasn't surrounded by people who were terrified but just preoccupied. Golda Meir, Ben-Gurion and Levi Eshkol sometimes worried, perhaps because they had experienced life as Jews of

the Diaspora, but I never detected fear in them. Never. Not in Ben-Gurion nor in Sharett.*

You met Moshe Sharett when he was prime minister?
Yes, two or three times, but I didn't know him very well. I also want to stress that all these leaders never acted in haste. They accomplished great things, if one considers the situation in hindsight. Sharett as well.

During its first 50 years the state of Israel produced exemplary leaders. Today, acts of heroism by Jews and Israelis are supplanted in the collective memory by exactions committed against the Palestinians. You joined the Haganah† at 14, and at 20 you participated in the war of independence. Which myths did you grow up with? What great figures of Zionism or Jewish history inspired you?
I remember my father Shmuel, after a hard day's labor, sitting beside my bed singing "Atop Mount Scopus," a song written by Avigdor Hameiri in 1930.

Did you already know the story of Joseph Trumpeldor?‡
Of course. We would sing "In Galilee, at Tel-Haï." I was perhaps ten when I first heard about the Nili§ of Sarah and Aaron Aaronson.** All these tales had a marked effect on me. I remain convinced, however,

---

* Moshe Sharett (1894–1965) was director of the Jewish Agency's political department from 1933 to 1948, when he became the first foreign minister of the newly created state of Israel. He briefly led the government as the country's second prime minister from 1953 to 1955.

† A Jewish paramilitary group at the time of the British Mandate.

‡ Joseph Trumpeldor (1880–1920), ex-officer in the Russian army, organized Jewish immigration to Palestine and founded the Pioneer movement (Hechalutz). He died while fighting a band of Arabs on Tel-Haï Hill, speaking the famous words, "It is good to die for our land."

§ Clandestine Jewish organization created by Aaron Aaronson that offered its services to the British during World War I with the aim of toppling the Ottoman Empire.

** Sarah Aaronson, Aaron's sister, was arrested and tortured by the Ottomans. She committed suicide.

that more than anything else my life was influenced by the irrigation of the orchards, the pruning of the vines and the nighttime watches in watermelon and melon fields. We left home very young at that time, but those are the memories that still accompany me.

You had bathed in the Jewish myth?
The Jewish myth, alive and authentic, surrounded us. During the troubles with the Arabs, our parents volunteered to help defend isolated localities. A childhood memory: my mother hitching up the cart, loading it with rolls of barbed wire, getting a rifle hidden in the stable, concealing it under a sack and then disappearing into the night to pull down a fence or put up another. "Neighborly" disputes with the Arabs were multiplying at that time. This notion of the "pioneer" was part of our daily lives. We mustn't exaggerate, however: the entire population of Israel was not involved. We were aware of it in places where you had to remain constantly alert, above all in agricultural communities where this myth constituted a tradition of sorts that was passed from generation to generation.

OCTOBER 1967
GUR'S DEATH

I was living in Paris, working as the western European correspondent for the Israeli newspaper *Ma'ariv*, when on the eve of the Jewish New Year, October 3, 1967, my editor called me and flatly announced, "There has been a tragedy; your friend's son Gur is dead. Arik asks you to return at once."

The first flight for Israel didn't leave Orly until the following day. I was aghast at the blow that fate had struck my friend. Two months before this catastrophe, Lily and Ariel had been basking in happiness. Lily had rejoiced at seeing her husband return unharmed from the battlefield and also enjoy national, even international, recognition for the first time. Sharon featured among the brilliant generals of the IDF who had secured a lightning victory in the Six Day War, a victory that had astounded the entire world.

Omri and Gilad were still toddlers of three and two years of age, respectively. At ten, their older brother Gur was already treated as a big boy by Lily and Arik. Father and son went out riding together and explored the growing country. Arik showed his son the landscapes of Judea and Samaria, the ancient olive trees and the terrace cultivation. He took Gur to Jerusalem and explained to him that, with the liberation of the Old City and the departure of the Jordanian occupier, the Jews could now return to pray at the Wailing Wall. Arik also described the sanctuaries that had risen from the Temple Mount and that had been destroyed, first by the Babylonians and then by the Romans.

Gur was thin, like Ariel as a boy, and his every feature resembled his father's. He had asked to be photographed with Ariel beside the Wall. This photo of the uniformed general, his hand on his son's shoulder, took center stage in the Sharons' sitting room. "Gur loves it when I tell him the ancient history of our people in Eretz Israel," Sharon explained proudly.

In their house in Tsahala, Lily and Ariel observed the week of mourning, the shivah, surrounded by friends who had come to comfort them. From time to time, one or the other would disappear to cry in private. When Lily took refuge in the bedroom, Arik followed her and came back with red eyes. For seven days their house was always full of people. Everyone came to present their condolences: Moshe Dayan, then defense minister; senior IDF officers; combatants who had fought under Sharon's command; members of kibbutzim and moshavim, some of whom had known the child. On the upper floor, helpful neighbors took turns in looking after the two little ones, Omri and Gilad.

Ariel described the tragedy to me: "That morning, I was alone in the house with the children. Lily had gone out shopping for the New Year's celebration. I was trying to shave, but I was continually interrupted by telephone calls from friends wishing me a happy New Year. Suddenly I heard a shot. I ran outside and saw Gur lying on the ground, covered with blood. His skull was smashed and there was a gun beside him. 'He fired,' said Omri, referring to a child in the neighborhood. I immediately knew that Gur was dead. I took him in my arms, and neighbors took us to the hospital, where they confirmed his death. We buried Gur beside Margalit so that this wonderful child can rest next to his mother."

For years, I saw Sharon get angry when he read somewhere or other that his son had accidentally killed himself while playing with an old rifle. He said to me several times, "Gur was a sensible boy. Ever since he was a small child, I had taught him that he must never play with weapons, and above all, I repeated, one never points the barrel of a gun at someone's head, including one's own."

Lily and Ariel asked me to stay on after the others had left, as if they were afraid to face their grief alone. One night, around 3 A.M., I was nonetheless going to call a taxi to go back to the center of Tel Aviv, when Lily and Arik insisted on driving me there. There was a thunderstorm with lightning flashes streaking the sky, from which torrential rain was pouring. Seated in the back, I heard my friends' stifled sobs and, suddenly, "Life has no meaning anymore."

"Life has no meaning anymore." These devastating words came from Ariel Sharon's mouth as he gripped the steering wheel of his military Plymouth, his body shaken by his vain attempts to stop his tears. Next to him, Lily's crying intensified as she heard the words resound in this car that was hurtling through the streets of Tel Aviv, under the first autumn rain.

It took my breath away to hear a man of Sharon's caliber falling prey to despair in this way. Upset, I took hold of my friend's large shoulders and said angrily, "How can you say such a thing? When you visit the families of paratroopers who have died in battle under your command, I have always heard you encourage them to continue to lead a normal life, for their sake and for that of their other children. Now you need to search deep inside for strength, for your sake, for Lily's sake and for the sake of Omri and Gilad, your two wonderful children."

Lily could not stop crying. We arrived at my home and I got out of the car, accompanied by Ariel, despite my protestations. I embraced him, in an attempt to comfort him.

I prolonged my stay in Israel for another week after the mourning period ended, to try to ease my friends' unbearable pain. Sharon slowly returned to his activities as head of training in the IDF, with sad eyes. His hair was streaked with new strands of silver. But I sensed that he had recovered the day that he said to me, "Levi Eshkol's government was ready to give back all the territories in exchange for peace. But peace with whom? At the Khartoum summit,* the Arabs had said no three times: no to peace, no to conciliation and no to negotiation with Israel. I have obtained Moshe Dayan's authorization to transfer the IDF's training centers to Transjordan."

It was the beginning of the Jewish settlement of Judea-Samaria.

---

* Arab summit convened following the Six Day War; the summit adopted a hard-line position that excluded all recognition of the state of Israel.

1968
REPOPULATING
THE PROMISED LAND

You have been active for over 50 years on Israel's military and political scene. Where do you think you had your greatest victories: on the battlefield or in your governmental capacity?

I had the privilege of taking part in all the wars, of seeing the state of Israel develop and of contributing to its defense and security. That is of considerable importance. Nonetheless, in my view, it is populating the land of Israel with Jews that will determine our fate in the long term. Consequently, without wanting to minimize the importance of national defense, I had the immense honor from 1977, in my functions as president of the ministerial committee on population and as defense minister, of establishing 230 settlements in Galilee, the Negev, the Golan Heights, Judea-Samaria, the Jordan valley and the Gaza Strip. In fact, Israel is waiting for new Jewish arrivals. We must encourage aliyah* and make it our number one priority.

You were already involved with managing repopulation, well before you held ministerial functions?

That is true. In 1967, at the end of the Six Day War, after having broken through the Egyptian military machine at Umm Katef, in the Sinai, and crossed the Suez Canal with my division, I telegraphed the infantry school and ordered them to transfer, completely or partially, to the Jordanian military base closest to Nablus. Then, when I resumed my functions as commander of training at the general staff, I proceeded with the

---

* The return of Jews to Eretz Israel; literally, "the ascent."

transfer of other centers. At the time, Defense Minister Moshe Dayan also envisaged installing the families of active soldiers at these new bases.

As commander of training services, you therefore made the decision to transfer the IDF bases in Judea-Samaria to the sites that had formerly been the Arab Legion's bases in Jordan.

Obviously with authorization from the minister of defense. However, Dayan could be as lacking in courage in the public arena as he was wildly courageous on the battlefield. He wasn't prepared to fight for this project, even if he spoke to me about it several times. In the meantime, I continued to transfer training bases and military schools. In fact, this formed the first wave of Jewish settlement in Judea-Samaria. There, too, it wasn't easy. There were discussions with the general staff, directed by Haim Bar-Lev. He said to me about Beth-El, "This will cost millions." I replied that it would be worth every cent.

Neither the army nor the government opposed the transfer of bases?

There was a lot of opposition, but I received a great deal of help from Matti Peled, the commander of logistical services. In 1977 these military bases received the first settlements. Kedumim was established first, and then Elkana. The movement began during the Rabin-Peres government. The transfer of military bases followed the map of settlements: a part of the recruit base at Nahal to the Jordan valley; a paratrooper base to the Sanur valley; the infantry school beside Nablus; the Horon camp; the military police camp at Kadum, today Kedumim; the artillery recruits camp at Dir Sharf, today Shavei Shomron; the instructor training school at Beth-El; a paratrooper base at Beit Sahour near Bethlehem; the military engineering base at Gush Etzion; the military engineering training camps at Adoriam, between Hebron and Dahariya, and in the Jordan valley, and then, later, the base of Golani recruits at Bezek.

Did you think at the time that you would perpetuate the Israeli presence there?

One night in 1977, 12 core members of Gush Emunim* settled in Judea-Samaria, near the military bases, marking the start of the great

---

* "Block of the Faithful," a group of the first settlers in Judea-Samaria; the group supports Jewish settlement of land throughout Eretz Israel.

settlement movement and the beginning of the Jewish repopulation of the territories.

None of that could have happened if you hadn't been at the head of the army's training services.
Someone else might have acted differently. I don't know. No one had done this before me.

But the government understood what you were doing? They were aware of it?
What a question! Nothing happened in secret.

Did Moshe Dayan not follow through with this project, although he talked about Shilo and Anatoth—the site of the Tabernacle before the building of the Temple in Jerusalem, and the cradle of the prophet Jeremiah?
In spite of his profound attachment to Eretz Israel, as I said earlier, Dayan was fearful in the public arena. I think that he felt hampered by his colleagues' lack of enthusiasm. It was nonetheless his idea to install the families of active soldiers in the bases. But he didn't see that far ahead and saw things on a smaller scale. I saw the future Jewish settlement in these places.

Were you aware of the government's decision, around June 19, 1967, to declare itself ready to give back all the conquered territories in exchange for peace with the Arabs?
At that time, I was in Australia. I was the first senior officer sent by the government to meet Jewish communities of the Diaspora and to talk to foreign officers. In any case, that decision did not concern me because at the time the army was not involved in politics. None of us dared break that rule. The chief of staff, Dayan, was a member of the central committee of Mapai,* but it was unthinkable that a soldier would dare to propose a political solution. Everyone confined themselves to their own domain.

A 39- or 40-year-old general decides to transfer all the military bases and you talk of an army that didn't get involved in politics? Isn't it a political act

---

* Party of Workers of the Land of Israel, founded by Jewish immigrants in Palestine in 1930 and the forerunner of the Labour Party.

to install army bases in Judea-Samaria? Did you follow security, political or national interests?

Historical, security and national interests all at the same time. But my primary motivation was and remains historical. One of my mistakes over the last 30 years was not to have stressed the historical dimension enough. Judea-Samaria is the cradle of the Jewish people, and the feeling of having a right to it—which is a crucial element of security—depends above all on the fact of living in a place that belongs to you. The idea that only the security aspect matters is a mistake, not only mine but certainly also mine.

What was your mistake exactly?

To have emphasized, for all those years, the security argument in justifying the need to guard Judea-Samaria and the other territories. The security question is a temporary one and is easy to debate, while the historical aspect, which is fundamental, is stronger than any other. The attraction of Eretz Israel lies in biblical stories, festivals, seasons and landscapes. Everything with us is history. The Tomb of the Patriarchs in Hebron, for example: no other people in the world possess such a monument, a memorial four thousand years old where the ancestors of the Jewish nation are buried, Abraham and Sarah, Isaac and Rebecca, Jacob and Leah. In the United States, millions of people go to contemplate with emotion Jefferson's tomb or the Lincoln memorial, which date from one or two centuries ago. Here we are talking about sites that are several thousand years old. It is a question of right and of force. Yes, I acknowledge the mistake of not having said over the years that the historical argument was in fact the primordial question—of which the security argument was only a consequence.

Does that mean that as a young general commanding Tsahal's training services you saw no contradiction between the historical, national and security dimensions?

I think they are intimately linked. But our generation was not aware of it. Take Abraham Mapou's *The Love of Zion.** He wrote that book in

---

*   Written in Hebrew, this 1853 novel tells the story of children, princesses and shepherds in the idyllic setting of Isaiah's Jerusalem.

the middle of the nineteenth century without ever having set foot in Eretz Israel, but the reader has the impression that he is exploring Samaria. Jews nourished themselves on this love. It is what kept them going in exile.

The novel contributed greatly to evoking nostalgia for Zion in eastern Europe.

1969–1973
SHARON AGAINST
THE BAR-LEV LINE

T he war of attrition for the Suez Canal began soon after the Six Day War. A few weeks after the Israeli victory, the Egyptians started firing in provocation against the forces posted on the eastern part of the canal. The Israelis felt that they had to respond, but how? There were two options, and the course of action proposed by the chief of staff, Haim Bar-Lev, took precedence. Israel would build a sort of Maginot line to protect its southern border.

A wall of sand and earth raised along almost the entire length of the Suez Canal would both allow the observation of Egyptian forces and conceal the movements of Israeli troops on the eastern bank. This defense system, called the Bar-Lev line, included 30 or so small strong points—*maozim*—stretched out over almost 200 kilometers. The two great victors of the Six Day War, Ariel Sharon and Israel Tal, "Talik," were fierce opponents of these fortifications, which they thought were both expensive and ineffective. Notwithstanding, the Bar-Lev line was completed in spring 1970.

In April 1969 you opposed the construction of a line of fortifications along the canal. Was this during the great debate that took place in the general staff, with the participation of Moshe Dayan?
The Bar-Lev line was not planned; it was the result of a convergence of circumstances. When the Egyptians began firing, the Israeli posts on the canal began to entrench themselves. This provoked more intense fire from the Egyptian side, and we began covering the trenches. The IDF's main qualities—rapid movement and skillful maneuvering— would have been much better employed in a fortified position further back rather than on an exposed line of fortifications practically at the

water's edge, 200 or 300 meters away from the enemy. This kind of fortified line demands constant coming and going—doctors, technicians, delivery of provisions and munitions and so on. It was then suggested that concealed openings should be created in these fortifications so that cannons could be fired at the Egyptians' flanks to stop them from crossing the canal. But there was no way such openings would remain secret. The whole defensive concept of the Sinai was faulty. No, we weren't forced to post ourselves along the waterline to ensure the security of the Suez Canal.

The government wanted the canal to remain closed?
Yes, but we could have built these fortifications 12 kilometers inland and deployed mobile forces along the length of the canal. Would the canal have been reopened? Of course not. But it was, apparently, "politically important to manifest a presence." Did we need to "manifest our presence" in more than 30 fortifications when it was enough to manifest it at a single point, in the place that suited us best?

On the banks of the canal?
Not necessarily. For example, on the bank of Great Amer Lake. Our forces did not have to stay immobile 200 meters away from enemy eyes.

You explained all that?
The debate began in 1968 and continued in 1969. There were two men on one side—Israel Tal and myself—and the chief of staff on the other.

And the minister of defense?
Dayan didn't get involved in the controversy.

Did you speak to him about it in private?
More than once during this period, and again during the winter of 1970.

You were already head of the southern command?
Yes. We were in the middle of the war of attrition, and I brought up the defensive doctrine of the Sinai again during a meeting with Dayan

at Rephidim (Bir-Gafgafa). I communicated my serious objections to him, as head of the southern command, and he agreed to accompany me on the ground, although he had a leg in a cast. We had hardly left our vehicle when artillery fire peppered the courtyard of the fortification that we wanted to visit. Everyone rushed toward the nearest bunker. Unable to run, Dayan lay down on the ground, and I did the same. He advised me to use my influence to modify the defense scheme on the canal. I reminded him that he could give the order himself.

He didn't want to get involved?
He said to me, "Influence them."

Is that the same thing he said to you three years later, in October 1973, after the Bar-Lev line collapsed?
Yes. On October 17, 1973, when we had already held the bridgehead on the western bank of the Suez for 36 hours and no one, apart from the forces of my division, had yet crossed the canal, Dayan told me to use my influence to bring about a wholesale crossing of the canal, assuring me that I was capable of changing headquarters' mind.

And yet he was the minister of defense?
That was Dayan. Full of daring on the tactical level but not on the ground. In fact, he didn't distinguish himself during the war of independence. Concerned about the political affiliation of the members of the general staff, Ben-Gurion wanted senior officers who were loyal to Mapai, the party in power. Dayan was named commander of the Jerusalem brigade during the second half of the war, and in that role he led the operation designed to liberate the high commissioner's palace—an operation that failed. When I was leading a battalion in that same brigade a little later, at the beginning of the 1950s, I learned why it had suffered few losses, from the mouth of the very officers who had taken part in that operation. They had received the command, "Take it if you can"—hardly a categorical order.

Was this the kind of order that Dayan gave you?
Take the Kibya operation in 1953, for example. Dayan was then chief of operations of the general staff, directed by Mordehai Makleff. He

called me to him and said, verbatim, "If the resistance is too strong, please restrain yourself and blow up only a couple of houses next to the village." I replied that we would take 700 kilos of explosives and that the village would be razed. In 1958, on my return from the military academy at Camberley, Ben-Gurion asked my opinion of Dayan. I expressed my satisfaction at seeing him in the government and said I hoped he would be elected to high office, except for that of prime minister. "Why?" Ben-Gurion asked. "Because he's not willing to assume any responsibility," I replied.

You were practically forced to leave the IDF because of your opposition to the Bar-Lev line, weren't you?
Indeed. In April 1969, Moshe Dayan took part in a particularly stormy meeting of the general staff. Instead of concentrating on my objections to the Bar-Lev line, the debate turned into a violent personal attack. I left, protesting against this atmosphere of a court-martial. The assembly immediately decided to check my military status. I never paid attention to my military pay or other details; I didn't even know if I had signed for a long term of duty. Several days later, the head of administrative services asked me under what conditions I preferred to leave the army. I replied that I had no intention of leaving. He then told me that my engagement had expired and that since I had not renewed it, I was considered demobilized; it was up to me to choose the means. Instead of discussing the issue, I asked for a form and on the spot signed a request for a ten-year prolongation of engagement. It was rejected. I was up against an insurmountable wall. Dayan stated that he could do nothing in opposition to the chief of staff, Haim Bar-Lev. Golda Meir refused to intervene and sent me back to Bar-Lev. I had nowhere else to go. It also seemed to me that, after so many years in the ranks of the IDF, I shouldn't have to beg for a prolongation of my engagement.

Then my situation changed completely. 1969 was an electoral year. After the announcement of my imminent departure, I decided to see Menachem Begin, who held a ministerial portfolio in the national unity government. Menachem and I were like family; his father and my grandfather had many ties, and my grandmother, who was a midwife, had helped his mother bring little Menachem into the world. I had also known Yosef Sapir* since my childhood, from the time when he worked the land and I accompanied my father to buy orange tree grafts from him. His family was one of the oldest of Petach-Tikva and owned a magnificent citrus fruit plantation beside the Yarkon. It was Yosef who introduced me to political life by saying, "You want to recycle yourself? Join us." I was called to meet Begin and Sapir at the King David Hotel.

You drank to your joining Gahal?[†]
I didn't join on the spot, but I had taken the bait. I wasn't scared of leaving the IDF after so many years, but it was a difficult decision. At the same time I felt hypnotized. On the way back, I picked up a young paratrooper who was hitchhiking. We chatted, and he urged me to stay in the army, which reinforced my doubts. Back home I shared my concerns with Lily. Despite my great esteem for Begin, he inspired in me a sort of instinctive fear. I who had never been frightened of anyone was trembling before the intense willpower that emanated from this slight man. His benevolent gaze could take on an implacable edge at times.

So you didn't give Begin a definitive reply?
No. I decided to wait several days. Meanwhile Pinhas Sapir, the all-powerful finance minister, the strongman of Mapai, intervened with Bar-Lev on my behalf, entreating Bar-Lev to find immediate means of reintegrating me into the army. Yoske Yariv, a senior officer in Mossad[‡] who was very close to Bar-Lev, proposed a solution: get me out of Israel and send me on a tour of the world.

---

*   Yosef Sapir (1902–1972), born in Jaffa, became mayor of Petach-Tikva (1940–1951) and then head of the general Zionist party. He was among the initiators of the movement's union with Herut in 1965, and he took the lead of the Liberal Party in 1971. Sapir occupied several ministerial posts (Health, Transport, Commerce and Industry) in the 1950s and 1960s.

†   Herut-Liberal block, the rightist party of Begin and Sapir.

‡   The Israeli intelligence agency.

Simply because of your opposition to the Bar-Lev line?
Yes. They wanted to exclude me from the IDF because of a divergence
of views on a matter of principle: I thought this static defense scheme
was catastrophic. In short, off I went on a very long journey. First to
the United States, where I toured universities and military bases, then
to South America, Japan, Korea—where I went to the 38th parallel—
Hong Kong, Iran and Australia. I was allowed to do everything, except to land in Israel.

*Meanwhile, the war of attrition around the forts of the Bar-Lev line contin-
ued interminably. Didn't you feel that you had chosen the easy route? Do you
regret not having resigned with a bang?*
No. I am not the type who likes to cause scandals. I don't remember
ever having alerted the press when I wore the uniform of the IDF. The
army is a rather closed institution and should remain so. I think that
you have to stay where you are and try to act from within. Exerting an
influence from the outside demands specific characteristics that I don't
possess. I am incapable of spending entire evenings in secret cabals
with people who do nothing but congratulate themselves. I like quiet,
music, landscapes, friends. I am not made to manipulate crowds.

What happened when you got back from your tour?
Israel was in an electoral period. Ezer Weizman, former head of the
air force, had left his post as number two of the IDF to enroll in the
ranks of Herut, and I was named head of the southern command, replacing Yeshayahou Gavish, who was promoted to head of operations.

1970
SHARON RETURNS

Ariel Sharon, nominated head of the southern command on January 1, 1970, was now responsible for Israel's most exposed border. He and Lily settled in the capital of Negev, Beersheba. This change was welcome; the house in Tsahala still bore the imprints of Margalit and Gur.

Lily busied herself with transforming their spartan lodgings into a welcoming home. She began by planting rosebushes in the tiny garden, where the couple entertained Ariel's colleagues and various political figures for dinner. In the sitting room they hung pictures painted by Shmuel Scheinerman, Ariel's father. From time to time, Lily and her husband would go to the theater or to the openings of art exhibitions. They particularly liked the work of the artist Uri Lifschitz, a former member of Sharon's paratrooper unit. Lily would not miss the concerts of the Israeli Philharmonic Orchestra, and Ariel liked to recall that as a young boy he had learned to play the violin. This memory inevitably meets with dubious looks: Sharon is associated with rather less melodious instruments.

The Egyptians were bombing the Bar-Lev line daily. Sharon, who still did not believe in the effectiveness of such a rampart, built three sites on the border of the Suez Canal that would allow armored vehicles to cross in the event of an offensive on Egyptian soil.

Sharon was responsible for the southern command until July 1973. During the summer, the chief of staff, David Elazar, retired from active duty. This time Arik, who had also left the army, lent a more attentive ear to the political sirens. The timing was perfect: it was an electoral year, and the vote was scheduled for October. The moment had come to jump in the water.

Ariel convened the press at Bet Sokolov, the Tel Aviv office of the association of Israeli journalists. He brandished his Mapai party membership card in front of the gathering and then tore it up. Reserve General Ariel Sharon had issued a challenge to his country's establishment: he would no longer accept that a single political party should have sole control of the state's economic, media, social and intellectual forces. He called for the creation of Likud ("Consolidation"), a union of the Zionist opposition parties: Gahal (Menachem Begin's Herut in association with the Liberal Party) and La'am (the regrouping of three marginal factions: the Free Center, the State Party and the Eretz Israel movement).

Sharon soon discovered the ruthless world of politics. Now that he was the campaign director of the new party, rather than just a military hero, he was no longer the darling of the press. For the first time in his life, Sharon was ripped to shreds, and even his collaboration with Menachem Begin could not save him from this fate.

The Yom Kippur war quickly overturned the electoral calendar, however; the national vote, scheduled for October 21, was postponed until December 31. And Sharon's destiny was suddenly transformed: returning to the southern front, at the head of an armored division, he led Israel to an astonishing victory.

1973
THE YOM KIPPUR WAR

On October 6, 1973, the day of Yom Kippur (the day of Atonement), at 1400 hours, Egyptian and Syrian forces launched a joint surprise offensive against Israeli troops. Five Egyptian divisions attacked the length of the Suez Canal, while the Syrian army opened a second front in the north, on the Golan Heights.

The transition from peace to war is brutal and traumatic—even for an experienced soldier like Ariel Sharon. On the eve of Yom Kippur, I met him in the Likud headquarters, where he had set up his electoral campaign base. He was the last to leave the building. From his temporary office on the twelfth floor, Tel Aviv stretched below in the calm that preceded the contemplative time of Yom Kippur. Ariel, in khaki trousers, blue shirt and sandals, was preparing the last electoral offensive before the vote at the end of October.

The following evening, as the holy day was coming to an end, we met in Sharon's home at Beersheba. It was dinnertime, but no one had an appetite. Arik was not the same man. The curtain had fallen on the political campaigner; before me stood a division commander, General Sharon, recalled hastily to serve the flag. Once more in uniform, his expression serious, somber and thoughtful, he was sitting at the kitchen table of his army lodgings.

Sharon's day had begun at dawn, in the farm that he had just bought; it was there, in the late morning, that he had received the news that war was imminent. From that moment, the mobilization of his division took place in record time. After having consulted his officers, Arik issued orders and toured the emergency supplies. Then, from his home, he gave the last directives and waited for the implementation reports.

The telephone on a stool beside him rang. Arik listened in silence, said a couple of words, hung up, began eating again distractedly and then growled: "The situation on the canal is bad." Another telephone call. Arik turned to us: "They said the Hermon fortification has fallen."

The reserve commander Zeev Amit, "Zevale," Sharon's best friend and his brother in arms, was chain-smoking. He questioned Sharon angrily: "What does that mean?" That was the question the entire population of Israel was asking at that moment: How could it have happened so quickly? Like Zevale, we refused to believe in the possibility of defeat.

Arik's reply shocked us: "What were you hoping? That things would turn out differently? You're surprised?"

"How are we going to get out of this?"

Arik immediately retorted: "You don't know? We'll cross the Suez Canal and the war will end over there." He picked up the telephone once more, gave orders to his division headquarters, listened to the reports. Delays were caused by serious organizational issues and missing pieces of equipment. Later, a reserve officer of the division headquarters described the situation in the following terms:

"The first difficulty was no transportation. From the gathering points, we heard that the buses had not arrived. The alert was given very late, and it seemed there was a dearth of drivers. General mobilization had been decreed all at once instead of in the usual stages, which meant that there was no time for proper organization. We also lacked binoculars and flashlights. We had sent someone to the police station to obtain them, but the police commander had told us, 'Telephone the owners of large stores and ask them to be here in half an hour. I will go and requisition the flashlights in person.' And we got hold of 600 flashlights. All these materials should, of course, have been found in the emergency supplies, but provisions were lacking. In fact, everyone was caught short."

OCTOBER 7, 1973:
STRAIGHT TO THE CANAL

Sharon seemed delighted when he learned that his friend, General Abrasha Tamir, had arrived at headquarters: "Ask him to wait for me; we'll leave at two o'clock in the morning." Lily appeared, apologizing for not being able to prepare a real dinner. Sick with worry, she knew her husband and realized that he would make it a point of honor to fight on the front lines. This natural fear was one that visited every household in Israel that terrible night. Arik went to kiss the children, who were already asleep. Shortly after midnight he left the house for his headquarters, which was buzzing with activity. After a brief conversation, he went out to see the men of his division.

Sharon's appearance galvanized them. They dropped whatever they were doing and gathered around him. Their faces were serious, tense. Arik spoke calmly and in a low voice. Then he inspected the other units. A group of men who had been brusquely torn from their homes had begun a furious race against time. At almost 3 A.M. on October 7, 1973, the division commander left for war in a station wagon requisitioned for the occasion. A witness recalls: "During the night, Arik gave the order to all the companies that were ready, to depart. There were no machine guns and not enough binoculars. Whoever was ready—off to the canal! The tanks rattled off. They crossed at least 200 kilometers in their caterpillar tracks, but a tank has to stop frequently to refuel so the journey took around a dozen hours."

✡

Abrasha, Zevale and Colonel Yehoshua Sagi, an intelligence officer in our division, were seated in the back seat of our vehicle while Ariel was next to the driver, his arm on the door and his red beret folded under the epaulette of his shirt. He was lost in thought and barely spoke. The car drove unnervingly slowly, even though traffic was intermittent. Now and again, the headlights met only darkness ahead. Several times Arik asked the driver to get Voice of Israel on the mobile radio. All we could hear was the end of a sentence: " . . . the enemy is attacking on all fronts."

Abrasha sighed, "So this is what you call a reserve general's car and radio. To think that later they'll say: the division commander advanced to the front."

Arik joked, "Do you want them to give me a helicopter?"

"Copters can be disastrous," replied Abrasha. "Since they were invented, certain generals see battle only from on high, like a bird. If they also have a bird-brain, that puts us in a bad spot!"

"During the Six Day War we used helicopters to drop Colonel Danny Matt's paratroopers behind Egyptian lines, and that was terrific," Sharon recalled.

The car passed in front of the Umm Ketef defenses. In the dim predawn light we could make out the damage that had been done on the ground. Arik explained how, more than six years earlier, he had directed the major breakthrough toward the canal: "Then, it was we who took them by surprise."

Now he was en route to his fourth war in the desert. In 1956, Sharon had driven in a jeep to Mitla Pass; in 1967, in a caterpillar vehicle; in 1969–1970 he was on the bank of the canal during the war of attrition. And now he was leaving for the front in a civilian car.

Taking advantage of the element of surprise, the Egyptians pushed through the Bar-Lev line easily—like its "impenetrable" French model, the Maginot line, the Bar-Lev line did not resist for even a day. The first enemy banners were planted on the eastern bank of the canal in the early afternoon, and at 1800 hours, the armies of Anwar el-Sadat were firmly planted along the former Israeli defense line. To allow armored vehicles to get through, sappers attacked the sand and earth embankments with water hoses.

On the morning of October 7, the situation was serious and the figures disastrous: almost 200 Israeli tanks had been destroyed. That night Ariel Sharon decided to assist the soldiers who were isolated by the Egyptian breakthrough and were issuing distress signals. On October 8, an Israeli counterattack failed, and Moshe Dayan ordered a withdrawal. Starting on October 9, the front stabilized, but Sharon wanted to cross the canal as soon as possible and tried to persuade headquarters to let him do so, arguing that he had prepared three sites for exactly this purpose.

OCTOBER 14, 1973:
BATTLE IN THE DESERT

At dawn on October 14, a thousand Egyptian armored vehicles unleashed a spectacular offensive. The 2nd and 3rd Egyptian armies fired tens of thousands of shells at Israeli forces; all around us, vehicles were burning and diffused the horror of death. The Sinai's most terrible day had begun. Before it disappeared on the horizon, the setting sun was unusually brilliant.

In the darkness that descended on the desert, half-tracks—armored vehicles for the transport of troops—made their way among the burning vehicles, constantly shaken by the shells that exploded near them. Shadows danced on the pale sand of the dunes. We stopped. No one spoke; the only sound came from the radios. An oasis of silence in a war-torn desert.

Suddenly, about a kilometer away, the flash of a tank cannon. All through the night the Sinai erupted with the light of flares, reflected a hundredfold by the gigantic mirror of white sand. We felt naked, vulnerable and defenseless before the projectiles raining down in that raw light. Two hundred and fifty Egyptian tanks blazed, half of them destroyed by Sharon's division. Arik had lost only five armored vehicles. With his radio network, he controlled the battle.

From that moment, Sharon's voice, full of confidence and preceded by his personal code, "This is 40," rang out from all the transmitters giving orders and demanding reports. That tireless voice was heard by thousands of fighters, boosting them in the difficult hours. Throughout the night, Sharon circulated among his armored brigades to direct the offensive. Ahead of us, combat raged.

"This is 40. I am waiting for a report!" Sharon was talking to Amnon Reshef, who was directing a scout patrol.

Reshef replied calmly, "It is a cannon-to-cannon fight. I think we have destroyed the headquarters of the Egyptian division."

Under the blazing sky, Arik's lips broke into a smile. He had finally convinced the highest command of the value of this plan. They had authorized him to cross the canal.

Amnon had been fighting since the first hours of the war. On October 6, his tanks had moved ahead to assist the fortifications and had tried to push back the Egyptians. Sharon's division had brought Amnon reinforcements, allowing him to replenish his decimated units. Amnon felt great pride at having been entrusted by Ariel with a key mission: to make a nighttime assault on the bank from which the canal would be crossed and to open the access points so that the troops could advance freely to the bridgehead. On October 15, at

1800 hours, Amnon unleashed his offensive on what would later be called the court of death.

The battle was at its height: officers were falling, and a shell struck a half-track, instantly killing ten men. From 2100 hours, the communiqués detailing losses began to flood in. Another of Amnon's units came up against enemy tanks defended by infantry. Trucks burst into flames, and stocks of munitions exploded, struck by enemy artillery. Hundreds of Egyptian soldiers were spread out through the desert. Some fled. Others entrenched themselves, using their antitank weapons against Amnon's vehicles. "The Egyptians are scattering like bees from a hive," Amnon announced to Arik.

Israeli artillery concentrated its shooting on the landing zone on the other side of the canal. Seventy tons of powerful shells were fired during one hour over a surface of 500 square meters, preparing the ground for the paratroopers.

The night before, at Tassa, Danny Matt and Sharon had together studied the details of the paratroopers' movements: how Danny's men would get across the canal, how they would seize the opposite banks and how they would protect the armored vehicles. After nine days of frustrating combat and faced with the Egyptian successes, such a mission seemed mad. But the two men had no doubt that the mission would succeed. Watching them, one was also struck by the absolute trust they had in each other.

Seventeen years after Mitla, history repeated itself: Arik sent Danny's group ahead as scouts—this time in inflatable dinghies instead of in the planes they had used in 1956. Arik's hair had gone white in the meantime, but Danny's beard was as black as it had been 20 years earlier, although his face was furrowed with lines. They were joined by several veteran paratroopers, lions from the period of reprisals who had been propelled into a modern conflict. History seems to have chosen them to fight side by side in all of Israel's wars.

The first dinghies were quickly launched into the water; only two had been damaged during the long journey across the burning desert. Artillery fire on the western bank covered the operation. It was one thirty in the morning. The boats filed silently across to the other bank without difficulty. The paratroopers landed amid palm trees, conifers and eucalyptus trees. A pale ray of light transformed the canal into a silvery ribbon. The Egyptians seemed disconcerted. They didn't fire at the half-tracks of the paratroopers as they came and went; although their tanks were very close, they remained silent.

✡

The atmosphere between headquarters and Sharon was deteriorating because of Sharon's determination to cross the canal as quickly as possible. Bar-Lev threatened "disciplinary measures" against him. While the paratroopers were crossing the canal, Chief of Staff David Elazar, Reserve General Amos Horev, Bar-Lev, Shmuel "Gorodish" Gonen, commander of the southern front, cabinet minister Yigal Allon and Moshe Dayan, the defense minister, were gathering at the command center at the front.

Around three o'clock in the morning, Yigal Allon went for a short nap. Moshe Dayan, suffering from a cold and in a bad mood, suggested withdrawing the paratroopers from the western bank because the equipment that would enable the floating bridges to be installed on the water had not yet arrived. What is more, Dayan feared that the paratroopers would be "massacred." Bar-Lev confirmed this to me after the war: "Dayan was panicking."

The defense minister's proposal was rejected. This time the command center was in agreement with Sharon, and they decided to carry out the operation despite the risks. David Elazar congratulated Danny Matt by radio, and he replied, "Yes, everything is fine. We are in good form. We are in Africa. Thank you, sir." A large smile lit up Sharon's face: "We can continue on to Cairo!" The wind of fortune had just turned in his favor. Ariel explained his strategy to his officers at 7 A.M., aided by maps. Later, Bar-Lev radioed, proposing to delay the offensive. Sharon refused: he would cross the canal, even if the necessary equipment was still far away.

OCTOBER 16, 1973:
THE ARMORED VEHICLES
CROSS THE CANAL

Shortly after midnight, on October 16, Sharon gave the following order to his mobile command center: "Ahead for Matzmed!" Thanks to his hundreds of radio conversations with all his units, Sharon was perhaps the only person to have an overview of the struggle in which his division was engaged. Now he pushed ahead toward the heart of the combat and the nerve center of the theater of operations: the bridgehead that had just been established at Deversoir, a village situated at the canal mouth on the Egyptian side. Sharon moved forward with Haim Erez's tanks to consolidate what became the key to success in this terrible battle: the crossing of the first Israeli armored vehicles onto the western bank of the canal, a crossing that was later referred to as "the invasion of Africa by Israeli forces."

It was 5 A.M. when the advanced command center penetrated into the court of death. To the left the silhouette of the fortification was outlined, while in the morning fog that rose from the canal an unforgettable spectacle could be seen: paratroopers on the embankment, their guns pointed west to cover their comrades who were already on the other bank. The orders, given in a low voice, were executed to the letter. Matzmed, north of Great Lake Amer, was one of the three sites prepared by Sharon when he was head of the southern command; there the rampart was very small, and to enable the exact point to be located, he had had red bricks scattered around, as if by accident.

A strange silence reigned. Not a shell, not a bullet. Nothing could be heard except the purring of motor vehicles. Sharon got out of a half-track. He took the engineering officers toward a hollow brick wall and ordered the driver of the first bulldozer to knock it down. Sharon personally directed the operation, even going so far at one point as to sit inside the yellow monster himself. The wall collapsed in a cloud of dust, and it fell, mixed with black earth, into the canal water. The route had been cleared.

That the bulldozer was even there was a miracle. It had been "turned back" by a battalion commander who was driving toward Matzmed with a dozen tanks. The tractors that Sharon was waiting for weren't at the meeting point, but when he passed a stray bulldozer, he ordered the driver to follow him. He was thus the last to accidentally take part in our clearing.

The dawn light made the hole in the rampart seem like a window opening onto a magic place. Everyone huddled around to look through the fog that was floating over the water, and on the other side of the canal, like a mirage, there were palm trees. Egypt!

In the early morning, Sharon convoyed Colonel Haim Erez with his tanks into the court of death. He entrusted him with a daring mission: to destroy four or five batteries of surface-to-air missiles on the eastern bank of the canal. "If you succeed," Sharon said, "we'll be able to fly our planes through that corridor." Abrasha smiled, and Sharon continued, "This will really be the first time in history that armored vehicles open up the way for the air force!"

Given the carnage that the Egyptian missiles were causing among our planes, everyone understood the importance of this mission. Haim, his black beret set at an angle as usual, replied laconically, "Alright." And he left, Arik and his officers following with their gaze the column of armored vehicles that were moving onto the floating bridges. Abrasha murmured, "So long as they let us obtain victory. We've already lost ten days."

Neither he nor Arik could imagine that high command would again waste two precious days. A column of paratroopers arrived; I recognized Israel Harel, my neighbor at the editorial office of *Ma'ariv* in faraway Tel Aviv. He had a kippa on his unshaven head and a smile on his lips. We greeted each other joyfully. Suddenly he bent down and picked a piece of parchment from the scorched debris: "They even burned the scroll of the Torah!" He placed the fragment carefully in his knapsack and rejoined his comrades, who were already crossing the canal. Soon it would be the turn of the first tanks.

Arik was hungry, but he seemed relieved. "What hell that night was!" he commented. "Did you see that barrage of antitank missiles? Everyone was shooting. In this kind of war, sometimes you are a general commanding one or two brigades, and sometimes a private handling a machine gun or throwing grenades."

At 6:45 A.M., Danny Matt's men received Haim's first tanks, which had rolled over the bridge and were hidden under cover of the palm trees. In four hours, the 28 tanks crossed the canal on floating pontoons. The meeting between the paratroopers and the tank operators was emotional: the paratroopers formed a guard of honor for their comrades and applauded them.

On their side, the Egyptians were unnerved. Danny informed Arik that he had destroyed six trucks transporting 120 Egyptian soldiers who were to help hold the canal's freshwater passage points. Probably thinking that he was talking to compatriots, an Egyptian soldier who escaped on a rowing boat insulted the Israelis, who shot at him from

THE YOM KIPPUR WAR

the western bank. Danny then hoisted the flag with the Star of David, to demoralize the enemy.

The day was calm. But the chief of staff had doubts; he thought that the bridgehead was "not secure" and that the tank and paratrooper units were dangerously isolated. When Bar-Lev told Sharon that he was surrounded, Sharon responded with an ironic monologue: "Am I surrounded or surrounding? Danny Matt is surrounding the Egyptians, but according to you, they are surrounding us. Amnon is surrounding the enemy, but according to you, the enemy is surrounding him. We are surrounded, but we are surrounding the Egyptians. When are you going to understand that in a mobile war in the desert we are sometimes surrounded and sometimes surrounding?" His expression sad, Arik climbed to the top of the rampart; from below, the soldiers gazed at his massive silhouette.

It was only on the following day that hell broke loose. On October 17, at 7 A.M., the first Egyptian shells fell on our paratroopers—the beginning of a barrage of fire that did not stop until after 5 P.M. on October 22.

OCTOBER 17, 1973:
SHARON IS WOUNDED

Until the sun rose on the second day of the Israeli forces' presence on African soil, frustration spread among Sharon's men like a disease. The mobile headquarters moved toward the eastern rampart of the court of death, the farthest from the canal. Combat began again. Perched on a Zelda tank, his head bare, Arik was examining a map. Abrasha was seated next to him lower down. I was opposite them. A thundering noise. The first shells of the day fell a few meters from our tank. Everything shook. Clouds of smoke. A bitter smell. Shouts of the wounded.

"Bazooka shells," said Abrasha. A cracking sound. Shrapnel shook the sides of our vehicle. "160-mm shells," Abrasha continued. "They seem to have gotten organized during the night. You have to admit we gave them the time."

Sharon observed the courtyard from his perch. Shells dug craters; some fell in the water or in a grove of trees on the other side of the canal, where our paratroopers were. Arik asked Danny Matt by radio to localize the source of the fire. "It's coming from Ismailia," Danny replied. Sharon asked him whether it was possible to neutralize the Egyptians. Danny announced that his men had discovered enemy observers perched in the trees and that they were liquidating them.

Every minute that elapsed seemed to last an eternity. We felt passive and powerless. Sharon gave the order to reinforce the defense of the courtyard. Half an hour passed. The fire did not diminish, and Sharon decided to move his advance headquarters. The half-tracks took off. Ours had hardly gone a few meters when shells hit the side, and we were hurled into the crater. Arik ordered the driver, "Reverse!" But the driver panicked, and instead of going back, he went forward and got us even more stuck. "I said, 'reverse,'" Arik calmly repeated.

Another shell exploded beside us. Arik's legs started trembling violently. The driver still hadn't managed to get us out. Arik was holding his head in his hands; blood ran along his chin and fell onto his trousers. Not a sound came from his mouth. Abrasha and I looked at each other, terrified. Abrasha murmured, "A head wound. He's done for. The division commander is done for."

That lasted no more than a few seconds. Arik's voice roused us from our daze: "Does someone have a bandage?" He wiped his face with a palm. Everyone breathed. Arik was alive, and his wound wasn't serious. At the moment, that was the only thing that mattered. The cloth that he wound around his forehead immediately reddened. Meanwhile the driver had finally managed to free the vehicle, and the convoy of half-tracks could move in line toward a safer shelter.

Abrasha said in a soft voice, "Without Arik, everything here would be over."

A communiqué from Danny on the paratroopers' situation mentioned numerous wounded. Sharon ordered them to be evacuated behind the front lines as quickly as possible. Danny told him cautiously that Zevale was among the wounded but did not mention that Zevale had been hit in the head by a shell and had lost consciousness, and that his state was critical. Arik wanted to know if anyone knew more; he was assured that Zevale was about to be evacuated.

An urgent message arrived: Sharon should go immediately to the front headquarters to consult with Moshe Dayan. The meeting should take place 20 or 25 kilometers east of the canal. Arik thought that he would be able to persuade the high command to cease its hesitant dance and to send reinforcements onto the western bank of the canal. It would be the first time since the beginning of operations that Sharon would find himself face to face with the chief of staff; their previous—and sterile—discussions had taken place by radio.

The half-track scaled the steep slope. It wasn't yet midday, but the heat was already unbearable among the dunes of white sand. The front commander, Haim Bar-Lev, was stretched on the ground, leaning on an elbow, one of his favorite cigars between his lips. Near him were his chief of staff and General Avraham Adan. Bottles of fresh orangeade were passed around. Taking the cigar from his mouth, Bar-Lev addressed Sharon brusquely: "Let's be frank; any resemblance between the plan you submitted to us and the one you have carried out is coincidental."

Was this the famous fraternity between soldiers that Bar-Lev delighted in after the war? Sharon didn't know yet that his dismissal had been mentioned twice in the presence of the front commander or that a press campaign was being mounted against him at home, with the collaboration of the IDF's spokesperson. Bar-Lev had just shot the first salvo in what would later be called the "war of the generals."

Not without difficulty, Sharon kept calm. He restricted himself to remarking, "You could also tell me that I have never taken part in this war."

After this exchange, each camp now in its position, Bar-Lev maintained that the bridgehead was indefensible, while Sharon insisted on pursuing the offensive. Moshe Dayan, for once, weighed in to support Sharon. The defense minister suddenly declared, "I'm with Arik. Tell the prime minister that I won't be there tonight for the government meeting." Without doubt, the fact that he would be the first member of the Israeli government to step on Egyptian soil played a part in Dayan's decision. He possessed a sort of sixth sense that always led him to make the right decision.

Dayan's reasons mattered little to Sharon. He had won his case, and that was enough for him. The worried man recovered his celebrated joie de vivre. Then Sharon jumped onto a barge with Dayan, en route for Africa.

On October 17, 1973, at 4 P.M., Ariel Sharon and Moshe Dayan disembarked on the other bank. A soldier declared solemnly, "Moses has returned to Egypt!" On October 22, the United Nations imposed a cease-fire on the Israeli and Egyptian armies. The following day, the Syrians laid down their arms on the northern front.

1974
ARIK, KING OF ISRAEL

1994. We were in the office that Sharon was renting in a Tel Aviv building. I was astounded to hear him say, in a resigned tone, "You told me I would never be a revolutionary."

"How can you remember that? It was 20 years ago."

"So I have as good a memory as you!"

We were talking about the dangerous concessions that Rabin and his minister of foreign affairs were making to the Palestinians, and I was urging Sharon to mobilize public opinion against this process. That was when he reminded me of the words that I had spoken a couple of months after the Yom Kippur war.

In 1974, the Israeli public was reeling in shock from the Egyptian-Syrian offensive and from the heavy losses that Israel had sustained. Nearly 2,500 were dead, and more than 5,000 were wounded—a catastrophe that caused the fall of Prime Minister Golda Meir and her defense minister, Moshe Dayan. Sharon was hailed as a national hero, however. People were praising "Arik, King of Israel," to the skies, even if the press was reporting claims of his insubordination. I was the only journalist to support Sharon, in the columns of *Ma'ariv* and then in a book entitled *Sharon's Bridgehead*.

The press attacks served only to strengthen Ariel and Lily Sharon as a couple. Several months earlier, Sharon and Lily had bought Sycamore Farm, an estate in the Negev, and they were gradually bringing it back to life. While waiting for it to be livable, the Sharons moved to Rehovot. Wherever they lived, Lily always created a welcoming and calm atmosphere in which Ariel could relax for a few hours—in Nahalal when he led the northern command, and in Beer-sheba when he led the southern command—but it was on this farm that Lily created the ultimate home. Sycamore Farm was not just a house, it was an anchor—a peaceful haven to which her warrior husband returned to recharge among the vines that stretched into the distance, among the roses in the garden, among the family paintings on the wall and among their sons, who were attending schools in the area. While serving him his favorite dishes, Lily would listen to Arik's impressions, ideas and problems, and advise him with the wisdom of her heart. Ariel always valued the good sense of his wife, who was his seismograph and his mine detector.

In time of war, Lily knew how to hide her anxiety, looking after the wounded in hospitals and comforting bereaved families while also waiting for the telephone to ring. If Arik didn't call, she would call him. She absolutely had to know what was happening from day to day. When Sharon left the army in 1973, she hoped that he would devote himself to farming and to his family—but then war broke out again. And just after the military victory came political combat.

✡

Sharon was elected to the Knesset as a Likud member on December 31, 1973. The left still held the majority, with Golda Meir as prime minister, but Israel criticized its leaders—Golda Meir, Moshe Dayan and the chief of staff, David Elazar—for not having anticipated the war. They resigned in the spring of 1974. Yitzhak Rabin, chief of staff during the Six Day War, and Shimon Peres, the pillar of the Labour Party, were angling for the post of prime minister. Rabin, with whom I was linked, asked me if Sharon was ready to support him. "A declaration of support from Arik matters more than one from anyone else," he explained.

That evening I met Ariel at the Tel Aviv Hilton, accompanied by his maternal uncle, Joseph, who had arrived from Paris. Sharon immediately agreed to support Yitzhak Rabin publicly, and he called several journalists from a phone booth in the hotel foyer. His declaration was on the front page of all the daily newspapers the following day.

On June 3, 1974, Rabin was elected prime minister, and the portfolio of defense was returned to Shimon Peres. Sharon, an army reserve corps general, continued to make regular trips to the Sinai to train his three armored divisions. I don't know whether his tan came from these trips to the desert or from the hours that he spent at the wheel of his tractor on his Negev farm. He got up every day at five or six when he was staying in the apartment he rented at Rehovot, and he went to work in the fields.

When we spoke, Sharon didn't hide his anxiety. According to him, the government and the IDF's general staff were trying so hard to atone for the troops' lack of preparedness in the Yom Kippur war that they refused to learn the real lesson from it and undertake the complete reorganization that the army sorely needed. Sharon was also enraged by the way that the establishment and the media minimized his role in the 1973 victory and, worse still, by their attempts to blame him for negligence when he was at the head of the southern command before the war.

Several months later, Rabin asked me to visit him on Shabbat. Whisky on the rocks at hand, he told me about an idea that he held dear: he hoped to make Sharon—even though Sharon was on the right—his adviser on defense, to raise the morale of an army still suffering from the losses of October 1973. "Tell Arik that he cannot imagine the calamitous state the army is in. I need him to restructure the IDF and to restore its confidence. Only Arik can counterbalance the influence of Shimon Peres and Motta Gur."[*]

I refrained from telling Rabin how much Ariel shared his opinion. Pointless, in any case. Peres and Gur had just forced Sharon to leave the Knesset by invoking a new law forbidding a reserve officer from taking up parliamentary office. In his resignation letter Sharon wrote, "For me, getting the IDF back on its feet is more important than playing these little political games." To my great surprise, however, Ariel refused Rabin's offer point-blank. "He's too weak," he declared. "He couldn't bring about the necessary revolution in the IDF."

Rabin was insistent, first in person and then by sending me numerous emissaries. My mission was in vain; Sharon refused to change his mind. But Sharon did finally consent to meet the prime minister. I went to pick Sharon up in his Rehovot apartment at 6 A.M. one morning in June 1975. While pouring me a coffee, Sharon exclaimed, "I'm going to tell him no. So stop plaguing me about it."

Lily and the children were still sleeping when we took the road for Jerusalem in Sharon's little Alfa Romeo. "Rabin is making you an offer you can't refuse," I insisted. "He is your prime minister. If another war

---

[*] Gur was the chief of staff.

breaks out and the IDF falls apart, you'll get the blame." His eyes fixed on the road, Ariel drove quickly and said nothing. For the moment, the proposal remained secret. If Sharon refused, the Labour Party—and even Rabin himself—would make the affair public to denounce him.

In Jerusalem, Ariel dropped me off at the Moment Café (which 27 years later was the target of a deadly attack), at the corner of the street where the prime minister had his residence. I waited for about an hour. "I've accepted the job," he muttered on his return. "I start tomorrow morning." The outrage was universal. From left to right, members of the Knesset were furious that a Likud general had been chosen for a key post in a Labour government.

Sharon chose Rafi Eitan* (not to be confused with the chief of staff Rafael "Raful" Eitan)—a distinguished Mossad officer with whom Rabin had served in the Palmach, the shock troops of the Haganah—as his assistant. Only a handful of us knew of Eitan's exploits as the head of the small team responsible for the capture of Adolf Eichmann in Buenos Aires in May 1960. I also introduced Ariel to the operational officer closest to Eitan, Zvi Malchin, who had physically captured the Nazi in Garibaldi Street.

Unfortunately, there were too many disagreements between Sharon and the left, particularly concerning the new situation in Lebanon. The Palestinians were massacring the Christian community there, and in order to stop the bloodbath, the American secretary of state, Henry Kissinger, recommended Syrian intervention, presenting the Syrians as a stabilizing force. Against the advice of Sharon, who was convinced that Israelis had everything to lose in the long term, Peres and Rabin rallied behind Kissinger's project. In addition, they secretly received Bashir Gemayel, the head of the Lebanese Christians, in Tel Aviv and agreed to furnish him with arms and military trainers.

Today we know the disastrous consequences both for Lebanese sovereignty and for the civilian population of the Syrian intervention in Lebanon and of Israel's support of the Phalangists. The Syrian

---

* Rafi Eitan is also the founder of the pensioners' party that had a spectacular impact on the March 2006 elections.

troops did not withdraw from Lebanon until 2005, after the assassination of Prime Minister Rafik Hariri.

In February 1976, less than a year after taking up his post, Sharon walked out, along with Rafi Eitan. "I'm sorry, Yitzhak," he told Rabin, "but you haven't managed to impose your views on Shimon Peres." That afternoon I joined Lily and Ariel in Ibn Gabirol Street, Tel Aviv. Arik seemed relieved: "Yitzhak accepted my resignation. He seemed disturbed but understanding. His usual stale cheese sandwiches were on the table. He gave me his pen and suggested I write the official press release announcing my departure and the reasons for it." Sharon was silent a moment. "The bald eagle!" he exclaimed. "When I think that I met Ben-Gurion in the same office, at the same table, 20 years ago. What a contrast." Ariel then returned to his tractor, to his fields of wheat, cotton and watermelons, and to the restoration of Sycamore Farm.

One evening I explained to Sharon that the people wanted a radical change, even a revolution, and that if he became chief of staff, he could at least reform the army. "You could ask to be reintegrated for that task," I told him.

"The government would never accept. And anyway, I've had enough of military life."

"So you will never be a revolutionary. It's a shame, because Israel sorely needs it. You prefer to bury yourself in your farm and ignore the fact that you are distancing yourself from the center of action in Tel Aviv and Jerusalem."

"Perhaps you'd like to see me living in a tent, like Gadhafi?"

This contemptuous reply was enough for me; I never approached the subject again.

The Negev farm was Sharon's pride and joy, and he immediately decided to turn it into a profitable business, finance his own development and rapidly pay off his debts. This pastoral interlude did not last long, however. Three years after its creation, Likud was disintegrating. The members of the party had different sensibilities, and they had trouble finding the common direction that Sharon wanted. He resigned from Likud to form a new organization, Shlomtzion, meaning "peace of Zion," the Hebrew name of Salome Alexandra, who reigned over Judea around 76 B.C. and who distinguished herself by effectively protecting her kingdom's borders. Sharon believed himself capable of pursuing the political revolution of 1973, and he believed that his party would make a strong showing in the anticipated 1977 elections.

Shalom Rosenfeld, my editor at *Ma'ariv*, refused to devote even the briefest of articles to Sharon. "Tell your pal he should go back to his farm," he declared over lunch one day. "That's where his place is; he has no business in politics." *Ma'ariv* was betting on two of Rosenfeld's personal friends: Shimon Peres and Levi Eshkol's former military adviser, the celebrated archaeologist Yigal Yadin, who had just created the Dash Party.

It is difficult to get people to talk about you when the biggest national daily newspaper is ignoring you. Sharon, however, charged up and down the country like the devil gone wild. Lily, who accompanied him on all these trips, made him wash his hands and face after he emerged from the crowds and ensured that he always had a fresh change of clothes. She even gave a television interview. Since my newspaper ignored his candidacy, I decided to help my friend by paying for an electoral advertisement in *Ma'ariv* that cost me $1,000.

In the end, Shlomtzion won two seats in the Knesset, one for Sharon and the other for his running mate Yitshak Yitshaki. It was a checkmate, but only relatively. The poll was historic: on May 17, 1977, the Labour Party was finally defeated by Likud, the party that Sharon had created.

Immediately afterward, Sharon proposed a merger to Menachem Begin. Shlomtzion should merge with Likud and form a single party. Deaf to his party's protests, the new prime minister accepted Sharon's offer and even considered naming him minister of national security, having given the defense portfolio to Ezer Weizman. "Out of the question!" politicians and journalists screamed in unison; unless Begin wanted to turn the country into a police state, Sharon must not be placed at the head of this key ministry, which was responsible for internal intelligence and for the fight against terrorism.

Since this post was out of reach, Sharon asked Begin to assign him the post of agriculture minister. Agriculture was close to his heart, and Israel's technological progress in agriculture had gained international recognition.

"You are minister of tomatoes," mocked Ezer Weizman. "And that's all you deserve."

Since Ezer was a friend, I warned him: "Don't argue with him. If you don't support each other now, they'll hang you side by side!"

"Say hello to the *vizir albandora*" ("minister of tomatoes" in Arabic), he retorted, "and tell him to march in step!"

On July 15 the government was sworn in before the Knesset. Ariel was officially named agriculture minister, watched by his mother Vera and by Lily. As well as agriculture, Begin gave Sharon membership in the exclusive security cabinet and made him head of the ministerial committee that dealt with Jewish settlements. In that capacity Sharon oversaw the creation of *yishuvim* (settlements) in Judea-Samaria, around Jerusalem, in Galilee and in the Negev, as well as the reinforcement of localities in the Gaza Strip. The battlefield "tank Sharon" gave way to "bulldozer Sharon," builder of settlements. A map of Israel was on display in his office, where he marked the strategic sites to occupy, the hills to inhabit and the valleys to defend.

This strategy had the wholehearted backing of the two women in his life. Arik's mother, widowed since 1956, still lived in the Kfar Malal moshav. At night she would put a rifle under her bed, just in case. In the daytime she worked the land and continued to do so until she was past 80, to her son's great pride. She harvested avocados, loaded them into her four-by-four and delivered them in person. During the weekend she drove in her four-by-four to Sycamore Farm. She was enormously proud of her son's property. "Look how neat it is," she said to me one day, pointing to the cotton field, which was in flower. "It's very important, you know, for a field to be neat. Fortunately, Arik knows that."

Vera sported a white mane of hair, cropped short, and her high cheekbones revealed her Russian origins. Gilad and Omri, her grandchildren, would tease her gently by saying that the Schneeroff family line doubtless contained Tartar blood; the town of Mohilev, in Belarus, had indeed experienced several pogroms.

Not loquacious by nature, Vera rarely got involved in her son's affairs, but she unreservedly supported the settlement projects in Judea-Samaria. When her strength declined, at the age of 88, Ariel stayed at her bedside until her last breath.

✡

Finally in power after 30 years in opposition, the right dreamed of a new map of Israel, and Begin knew how to galvanize the masses with his pioneering speeches. But Likud did not know how to make this map happen. For Sharon, however—a child of Kfar Malal—it wasn't complicated: irrigation systems needed to be set up, roads marked out and houses built. The division of labor was as follows: Begin would speak about the need to increase Israeli settlements, "in the manner of Elon Moreh," while Sharon would be the contractor.

Sharon turned to a new generation of pioneers from Gush Emunim who were no longer inspired by Marx's *Capital* but were instead inspired by the Bible; these disciples of the great Zionist Rabbi Abraham Isaac HaCohen Kook were recruited from the Bnei Akiva—the youth movement founded on the Torah—rather than from the secular, socialist Hashomer Hatzair. Ariel shared their love of the land of Israel and the certainty that they were the legitimate owners of the land of their ancestors. But this idealism did not encroach upon Sharon's pragmatism, and the mysticism of the settlers left him indifferent. "I am not the Messiah's donkey," he would exclaim when he felt used by the most impassioned among them, referring to the animal on which the Messiah of the Jews is supposed to enter Jerusalem, on the day of his coming.

I discerned in that complaint the echo of a profound conviction: Ariel didn't believe that his role was messianic; he believed that his role involved politics and security, and because of this belief he remained open to necessary compromises. From 1977 to 1981 he established more than 60 settlements in Judea-Samaria. Then, in the course of his various later posts—defense, industry and commerce, infrastructure, housing—he reinforced these settlements and increased their number, until they reached 150. Sharon fought against the whole world to strengthen the Jewish presence in the West Bank and the Gaza Strip, and he did not appreciate it when, years later, those in charge of the settlements preferred Benjamin Netanyahu over him as the right-wing candidate for prime minister.

As the *yishuvim* sprang up all over the country, Lily and Ariel were putting the finishing touches on Sycamore Farm. Lily planted roses everywhere, and Arik planted a young vine that they hoped would reach their bedroom window on the second floor. Saddles hung in the hall, which the three men of the house—Ariel, Gilad and Omri—used to ride the stable horses. Sycamore Farm became their fortress. The relative isolation of the farm deprived the Sharon clan of the daily visits of friends, but it also gave them a welcome respite. Sharon was continually attacked because of the settlements and his firmness toward Arabs. In the calm of the household that Lily created, Arik talked about his military past to their sons and explained to them the vital importance of the Jewish towns that had been created in the country from the second half of the nineteenth century and that had determined the state's borders. The boys were curious about the attacks to which their father was subjected in the press. If Ariel replied patiently, without bitterness, Lily didn't hesitate to insult the journalists who criticized her husband. She forgave nothing.

Almost 50, Ariel Sharon was already portly, and his wife urged him to lose weight. The Tel Aviv tailor had warned her that his client had gone from large to extra large in the blink of an eye. Attentive to her husband's wardrobe, she sometimes also occupied herself with mine, as if I were part of her family. As another sign of friendship, when Sharon's uncle, Joseph, died, she gave me a good portion of the rare editions in his library. Despite these affectionate gestures, however, Lily did not intend to share Ariel, with me or with anyone else. "We're not competing," she assured me one day. "We shouldn't fight over Ariel's affection, because we both love him." I was astonished. I had never suspected that my closeness to her husband weighed so much on her. I thought of her numerous calls to Sharon during the Yom Kippur war, which made the soldiers smile. "Does she want to come and join us in the tanks?" they asked.

✡

Strengthened by his success at the agriculture ministry, Sharon consolidated his place in the Begin government, and all of Jerusalem began to make their way to Sycamore Farm. The couple's hospitality was famous. The Sharons' property also became the venue for secret meetings, such as with the head of the French intelligence service and with American diplomats. Guests at the farm included the American secretary of defense, Caspar Weinberger, Egyptian minister Kamal Hassan Ali, music conductor Zubin Mehta and the violin virtuoso Isaac Stern. And the journalists were not to be outdone—

they, too, wanted to interview Sharon: Abe Rosenthal, editor of the *New York Times*, Sidney Zion of the *New York Daily News* and the Italian journalist Oriana Fallaci. I particularly remember the visit of the press magnate Rupert Murdoch, who arrived in Israel in his private plane accompanied by half a dozen journalists from the *Times* of London and the *New York Post*. After the traditional tour of the farm by the owner, Sharon took the distinguished assembly for a flight over the settlements of Judea-Samaria.

1981

DESTROYING OSIRAK

As minister of agriculture in Menachem Begin's government, you played a key role in a decision that unnerved the United States: the bombing of the nuclear reactor near Baghdad. How did you do it?

As a member of the ministerial defense committee, what we call today the restricted cabinet, I was persuaded of the seriousness of the danger and was among those who recommended the destruction of that Iraqi atomic reactor. I want to be cautious, and so I say that I was among those who urged the aerial bombardment of the reactor; I might have been the first to put forward the idea, but it is possible that others did so before me. We debated the matter for months, and those discussions remained secret for a long time.

How often did you write to Begin on this subject?

Numerous times. Time and again I reminded him of the risk posed by Arab countries' nuclear capacity. I didn't hold the view at all—formulated, I believe, by Shimon Peres—that if both sides possessed atomic weapons, it would act as a mutual deterrent. I believed that we shouldn't count too much on the sense of discrimination of the Arab countries that possessed atomic weapons, and should count even less on their leaders' wisdom or self-restraint. America and the Soviet Union seemed to me more responsible in this area, even though the balance of terror between those two powers had always seemed dangerous. We were already on permanent alert, after dozens of years of daily security problems; with a nuclear umbrella at their disposal, the Arabs would be able to extend the scope of their "limited" anti-Israeli operations, and Israel would perhaps refrain from responding, for fear of a nuclear attack.

Weren't you afraid that news of the project would leak out before its execution?
As the preparations progressed, there were, of course, leaks. The Labour
Party also began putting its oar in. If the operation was revealed, it would
put the pilots' lives in danger and thus risk being canceled. But I can
speak only of the influence that I certainly had on the government's decision. It was in June 1981, on the eve of Shauvot.* When we heard that
our planes had just returned safe to Israeli air space after having destroyed Saddam Hussein's nuclear reactor, the ministers who were gathered in Begin's apartment in Jerusalem erupted into cries of joy. As we
were taking our leave, Begin came up and embraced me; he thanked me
and said that my position had weighed greatly in his decision.

Was it one of the most important decisions made by an Israeli government?
In my opinion, yes, it was one of the most daring decisions an Israeli
government had ever made, comparable to the ones Ben-Gurion
made, for example. And Begin accompanied our action with explana-
tions about the protection of Jewish lives and the duty of safeguarding
our security. In fact, it would be good if the members of Menachem
Begin's family or those who revere his memory published his speeches
on our history, the security of the Jewish people and our duty to ensure the protection of Jews. We could have educated generations of
young people with such a collection of essays. It's a shame that some
of those close to him prefer instead to present him as a man who allowed himself to be influenced.

*In May 1981 you went to Cairo to see Anwar el-Sadat, the Egyptian presi-
dent, to organize a summit meeting between him and Begin at Sharm el-
Sheikh. Several days later, the Osirak nuclear reactor was bombed. Sadat
accused Israel of having set a trap for him.*
The problem was that the Baghdad reactor was nearing the operational stage of producing fissionable material. The matter was urgent.
However, Begin and Sadat also had to meet.

*What is more, according to the Labour Party, Sadat was disappointed with
Begin and no longer considered him a sincere partner in the peace process.*
At that time, while the peace process was clearly underway, the Israeli
left was weakening the government by demanding that it accelerate

---

*   The "Festival of Weeks" or Pentecost, celebrating the Torah.

the process and give even more concessions. Since the resignation of Defense Minister Ezer Weizman, the relationship with Egypt consisted mainly of contact between the two agriculture ministers, Dr. Daoud and me. During my tête-à-tête with Sadat on May 19, 1981, when I told him of Begin's desire to meet him, he immediately responded in the affirmative. We then came up against a great dilemma. If we bombed the Baghdad reactor straightaway, the summit meeting obviously would not take place. On the other hand, the reactor's destruction just after the meeting would seem to imply that there had been an understanding between the two men, and this would do enormous damage to Sadat, which we did not want. The approach to follow therefore seemed clear. First, the meeting should take place. Second, the attack on the reactor should occur once sufficient time had elapsed after the meeting.

Who, other than Begin and you, knew of this?
No one.

Did the idea of arranging the meeting and the bombing come from you?
In April 1981, in my capacity as member of the security cabinet, I had prevented an air raid against the land-air missile batteries that the Syrians had just placed in Lebanon, judging that it would be better not to draw attention to ourselves before the bombing of the Iraqi reactor.* And here was Sadat wanting to delay the meeting that he had accepted in principle. The operation could be launched only on a Sunday, which was the day that the French technicians working on the Iraqi base had leave, and the reactor was about to enter its "critical" stage. At the same time, the approaching elections in Israel made the Begin-Sadat meeting urgent.

Ultimately, the famous meeting did indeed take place at Sharm el-Sheikh. But because of the laws governing electoral campaigns in Israel, our reporters were allowed to photograph only Sadat. We could hear Begin's voice on the television but could not see him! When we were finally gathered around a table for lunch in Sharm el-Sheikh, Kamal Hassan Ali, the Egyptian foreign affairs minister and deputy prime minister, suddenly told me that he had personally made sure that the date of the

---

* These missile batteries were finally destroyed in June 1982.

summit was as close to the Israeli elections as possible. Which was extremely embarrassing. It was Thursday, June 4, 1981, and the bombing of the reactor had been scheduled for the following Sunday. The bombing took place as scheduled.

Shortly afterward, I went to Egypt again to explain to Kamal Hassan Ali, with whom I got on very well, that we didn't have a choice. We had tried to organize the meeting earlier, to separate the two events, and it was he who had delayed the meeting. The Egyptians wanted the current Israeli government to stay in power. They understood very well—as do the Palestinians today—that a left-wing government would find it more difficult to establish peace; they also did not think the left capable of executing the agreement signed by Begin.

So Sadat wanted Begin to be reelected?
Yes. However, Begin's ascension to power in 1977 had worried Sadat a great deal at first. Romanian president Nicolae Ceausescu even told me, when I went there in 1982, that Sadat was very worried that Dayan, Weizman and I were all in the government. It was not Sadat who took the first steps toward peace, it was Begin. From his very first cabinet meeting, Begin had announced that he would strive to meet Arab leaders to try to achieve peace. In terms of historical truth, it is unjust to give all credit of the initiative to Sadat, despite the respect he deserves. It was Begin who had set the process in motion by going to Romania for talks with Ceausescu. I said to Kamal Hassan Ali, "Put yourself in my place; what could I do? Tell you we were about to bomb the Osirak reactor? I obviously couldn't." "It caused us great difficulties," he replied, before asking me how our planes had managed to drop all their bombs inside the atomic reactor.

The raid had a tremendous deterrent effect on Egypt and the neighboring states. I am still puzzled by the reaction of certain people in Israel. While a disconcerted Syria had not yet reacted by the following morning, while Jordan still knew nothing about it, while Saudi Arabia was still sleeping and while the Iraqis were silent, a sole organization criticized the operation: the headquarters of the Labour Party, 110 Hayarkon Street, Tel Aviv. And yet it was one of the greatest missions in the history of Israel! On the political level, Sadat won his bet: Likud was victorious in the elections of June 30, 1981, and Menachem Begin prepared to form a new government.

By crossing the Suez Canal in October 1973, at the head of your division, do you think you contributed to Anwar el-Sadat's coming to Jerusalem in 1977?
My division's crossing of the canal over the bridges we constructed—followed, some time later, by other IDF forces—as well as the development of the Israeli offensive in depth, all led the Egyptians to realize that they had to find a way other than war to settle the problem of Israel's existence. Sadat came to the conclusion that he would not succeed in destroying us by military means. That is why, in my opinion, the crossing of the canal represents the critical phase of the Yom Kippur war. If the Egyptians—who suffered very few losses—had managed to get across, we perhaps would not have ended up with the meeting at Sharm el-Sheikh. I think the effectiveness of our counteroffensive persuaded Sadat to reconsider Egyptian policy. Despite a surprise attack, a combined Egypto-Syrian offensive and the support of reinforcements from Iraq, Jordan and Saudi Arabia, the Egyptians lost. Unable to dictate terms to Israel by force, the Egyptians resigned themselves to negotiation. If they had won, they would have accepted nothing.

You spoke about this with the Egyptian generals after the peace agreement was signed?
I had the opportunity to meet several senior Egyptian officers. They are not as willing to establish friendly relations, even false or forced ones, as certain Israeli officers are; our desire to be liked by everyone, to be accepted by everyone, to reveal everything and demonstrate our sincerity pushed some of our officers into the arms of their foreign counterparts. The Egyptian army doesn't suffer from this peculiarity.

That is really how some of our officers behaved with their Arab counterparts?
With Arabs, Americans and foreigners in general. Egyptian officers don't cross certain limits. It's therefore no good trying to find hidden answers in what they might have said to me.

In May 1981 you were with Sadat to arrange the meeting of Sharm el-Sheikh. The two men who had braved the Suez Canal in 1973 found themselves face to face. He crossed and surprised you, you crossed and surprised him. There was that moment when, having established the bridgehead on the other side, we overheard Sadat's order to his army on the radio: "You must destroy Sharon's division, liquidate Sharon."
I didn't hear it.

But yes, remember . . . and immediately after that order, hundreds of artillery pieces opened fire.

Yes, 160-mm cannon shots and a wave of air raids. From 7 A.M. on October 17 they continued for several days.

During that 1981 meeting with Sadat, he never mentioned the war, the crossing of the canal?

President Anwar el-Sadat mentioned it in 1977 when he landed at Ben-Gurion airport. Welcoming him at the foot of the airplane, Menachem Begin announced, "They are all here; they're waiting for you." And Sadat asked, "Sharon, too?" When he got to me, he shook my hand, and said, "I tried to capture you when you were on the other side of the canal." "Mr. President," I replied, "you can now capture a friend." Sadat had foresight. The meetings with him usually concerned the future and very rarely the past.

What did you talk about in May 1981?

Agriculture and the development of new agricultural regions in Egypt. He said to the agriculture ministry representatives who were attending the meeting, "We have earth, we have water, we have Sharon: go to work." Then he clapped his hands. A young officer immediately opened the door and the president simply said, "The map." Several minutes later, Sadat and I were on our knees with a map of Egypt spread on the carpet; he showed me the regions he wanted to make fertile and asked if I would fly over them in his private plane to give him my opinion as an agriculturist. I accepted without hesitation. I recommended the exploitation of the desert regions of the country, based on Israel's experience. I told him that when I was a child my parents were envious of farmers in regions with black, dense soil, but that modern techniques made it possible to obtain excellent harvests in sandy regions, with rigorous control of irrigation and fertilization.

This meeting gave rise to a special and secret project. Two months earlier, Dr. Daoud had asked me if it was possible to install an irrigation system quickly in an agricultural plot. I replied that it was, without asking any questions. The small team of experts that I had put together flew to Egypt the next day, to Mit-el-Kum, Sadat's native village. They spent a day on his farm, where the *chadouf** was operated

---

*   Rudimentary machine that draws water, used in Egypt since antiquity.

by a buffalo turning around a well. On their return to Israel, the experts asked me if they could obtain the necessary materials in Egypt. "Egypt has everything you need," I told them, "but I'm not sure if you will find it; take what you need from here."

In less than 48 hours, two trucks loaded with material left Israel in the direction of El Arish, where Egyptian vehicles were waiting for them. Everything was eventually completed, while the experts crossed the Suez Canal on a motorboat. It took them barely ten days to install an ultramodern irrigation system. They had also quickly prepared a new patch of land designed for viticulture; the vine-planting season was just ending. Mrs. Sadat came to the farm and expressed her admiration. We left a specialist there to make sure that everything functioned well, and the rest of the team came back to Israel. Sadat was astonished by the speed of the operation. Soon afterward, when he was showing Egyptian journalists around the farm, he said to them, "You see all this modern equipment? The Israelis installed it in a few days." This was how he began cooperation with the Israelis. All this preceded the meeting where, kneeling in front of a map, he showed me the areas he wanted to develop near the Sudanese border and in the western desert.

The following morning, Sadat's plane was waiting for me. After having flown over the southwest, we set off for the south and the Sudanese border, where I saw the famous red earth. The pilots introduced themselves; they had taken part in the great air offensive of October 18, 1973, against my division. One of them had had to eject himself from his plane after it was hit. I was sitting between them, a map spread over my knees, giving instructions: "Higher, higher still, go around again so that I can see better."

Were they the pilots who had attacked on the afternoon of October 18, when Moshe Dayan was in our advance headquarters, on the western bank of the canal?
Probably. And now I was collaborating with the very same combat pilots who had tried to destroy our bridgehead on the Egyptian bank, helping them find new arable land in the desert to produce food. I said to myself that nothing could express peace better.

If Sadat had not been assassinated by Muslim fanatics in October 1981, do you think our relations with Egypt would have developed differently?
Sadat was above all an Egyptian patriot who acted for the good of his country, and I respected him for that. He wanted to call on Israeli aid

to facilitate important technological progress, particularly in terms of agricultural development in arid and semiarid areas. In my view, his force of character, political wisdom and real desire to improve his people's lot could have led to greater cooperation with Israel. That, in turn, likely would have inspired a great number of Egyptians to improve relations with Israel. A better awareness of our common interests could have stimulated the peace process. He and I often discussed the possibilities for Egypt, with its excellent agriculturists, and Israel, which possessed innovative agricultural technologies as well as experts, to conquer the potential markets of the Persian Gulf states—Saudi Arabia and all the big food importers. I thought that such a positive cooperation could lead to peace with other states in the region and weave a web of mutual benefit so that even in times of tension it would be in our two countries' best interests to maintain peace. This cooperation would have had better chances to develop if Sadat had not been killed.

In any event, even if Sadat subscribed to these projects of regional development, his primary concern was his country. And so, in regard to possible Israeli investments in Egyptian agriculture, he never failed to point out that he agreed to sharing knowledge but would never agree to sharing ownership with Israel of even the smallest parcel of Egyptian land. The land of Egypt was sacred in his eyes.

He said that he would not give up even a grain of sand to Israel.
Absolutely. I remember, during the very tough negotiations on Taba, Sadat stuffing his pipe and saying slowly, "The land of Egypt is sacred," and I remember the jealousy that I felt—a profound jealousy.

Because that attitude doesn't exist in Israel?
Because instead of expressing a natural love for Eretz Israel, we have a certain contempt toward everything that could be considered sacred. Shortly after he came to power, Menachem Begin went on an official visit to the United States. Before getting on an El Al plane, he inspected the guard of honor at Ben-Gurion airport, decked out with flags for the occasion, and shook hands with the ministers and friends who had come to see him off; when he got to the blue and white flag, he stopped and bowed slightly. The television cameras filmed it all. During the news bulletin that day, I felt that the tone of the reporter describing the scene betrayed a note of mockery. But when President Sadat came to attend the restoration of the Saint Catherine monastery

to Egyptian hands and bowed before the Egyptian flag that officers had solemnly brought him, and then kissed it, the voice of the Israeli reporter covering the ceremony on the radio was almost shaking with emotion! Where did we get this habit of deriding everything sacred in our four-thousand-year-old history—the flag, our national anthem and even our land?

Going back to the bombing of Osirak, do you think that now, in 1998, such an intervention would still be feasible?
Good question. For several years we have been receiving more American aid, demonstrations of friendship on the part of the American administration and their support in times of difficulty. But at the same time, a certain dependence on our powerful friend has arisen. Could we say that today, in 1998, Israel could decide, as Begin did, to bomb a nuclear reactor? In my view, no. Could Israel now give help to the Kurds, to the Yeminis, to the Ethiopians against Somali tribes or the Sudanese rebels? I don't think so. I'm not saying that Israel wouldn't be capable of it, but I wonder if today, given the mentality of its leaders, Israel could make a categorical decision and stick to it. Morally we are a lot weaker than when Israel consisted of only one and a half million inhabitants. Could we still act without consulting the United States? The slightest proposition from our leaders immediately causes questions along the lines of, What would be the position of the American president and secretary of state? What would the Europeans think? Could they impose economic sanctions on us as they did in the past? It is as if we are gradually losing the power to make independent decisions. On the other hand, all countries are now interdependent.

That was already the case before.
No country in the world has ever acted totally independently, but our latitude has gradually decreased. And that erosion affects all the areas linked to our long-term existence. Washington declares its solemn commitment to Israel—in all sincerity. But when Iraq invaded Kuwait in 1991, the United States took five months to decide on military intervention. Israel wouldn't tolerate Arab domination for five days! Besides, no one can predict the future of the greatest world power. The interest it now has in the Middle East will perhaps diminish. We don't know how things will evolve. Caution is therefore necessary. It is unthinkable that a passing whim based on personal or political concerns

should put us in danger one day. Dealing with national affairs therefore demands a long-term vision, profound reflection and the deployment of the best brains. Israel must strive to win back, as much as possible, its independence. As for our dependence on the United States, we have gone too far.

✡

The Osirak operation had personal repercussions for me. I left *Ma'ariv* after I'd written an article charging that the chief of the Mossad had opposed the bombing for blatantly political reasons, knowing that a successful mission would help Menachem Begin at the polls. After the article appeared, the prime minister—who wanted me to remain with the paper—called and asked me to retract. But I refused to deny the truth, even to save my career.

Concerning Osirak, let us give the last word to Anwar el-Sadat. Shortly after the announcement of the air raid on Saddam Hussein's nuclear center, the wiretapping services caught part of a curious conversation between the Egyptian president and King Hussein of Jordan. "The son of a bitch!" exclaimed Sadat, speaking of Begin. History does not say, however, whether Begin should have taken that expletive as an insult or as a compliment. After all, neither Sadat nor King Hussein held the Iraqi dictator dear.

1981

"SHARON HAS DESTROYED YAMIT"

In 1977 the first real peace negotiations between Israel and an Arab state—Egypt—began. President Anwar el-Sadat made an unprecedented official visit to Jerusalem in November. Less than a year later, Sadat and Menachem Begin started the historic talks of Camp David (September 5–17, 1978), organized by President Jimmy Carter, which resulted in the peace treaty of March 26, 1979. This joint initiative earned Begin and Sadat the Nobel Peace Prize in 1978.

When the Israeli army finally evacuated the Sinai in April 1981, the question arose of what was to become of the villages in the region. Should they be left to the Egyptians or, following a scorched-earth policy, should they be destroyed?

Was it your fault, as it is claimed, that Menachem Begin agreed to the destruction of Yamit?
Everyone accuses me of that, not only on the left. But what do they reproach me for, in reality? For upholding the peace treaty with Egypt and the retreat to the international border? Did they want us to stay in the Sinai? Would they have preferred us to give the Egyptians an entire town on the border with Israel? All the settlements far from the border were restored intact to Egypt, under the framework of the Israeli-Egyptian agreements: Ophira (Sharm el-Sheikh), A-Tur, Ras Soudar, Neviot, Di-Zahav (Dahab) and the whole area between Neviot and Sharm el-Sheikh. The walls of the houses were even repainted and the windows repaired.

By Israel?
Absolutely. We made sure that the military base of Rephidim was in good condition. So why make an exception for Yamit? Why destroy

that place in particular? There was a fundamental reason behind that decision. Cairo planned to install 100,000 people in and around Yamit. I raised this problem with Begin in January 1982, and there was a government debate. At the time Israel thought, correctly, that the arrival of a fairly large Egyptian population near a border that was still unstable would lead to their infiltrating Israeli territory in search of jobs. That situation risked straining the peace we had just signed; Israel could not allow these clandestine entries—not to mention the problem of the Gaza Strip. So the government preferred to hand over all the Israeli settlements in Sinai intact with the exception of the town of Yamit. I have studied in their entirety the transcriptions of the discussions of the council of ministers on this subject. It was a long debate in which every question was asked. If Yamit had to be destroyed, what should be done with the ruins? Leave them or dispose of them? Some ministers suggested covering them with sand. Yitzhak Shamir proposed burying the whole town. The most interesting thing about the affair is that, to this day, none of those ministers has dared to take the responsibility for the fate of Yamit.

A decision made by the Begin government?
Yes.

And on Begin's authority?
Yes.

And since then people say, "Arik Sharon destroyed Yamit."
The behavior of those ministers should have aroused my suspicion. On the basis of other difficult periods, I should have realized that they would be on my side in meaningless public ceremonies but not in my public national battles.

Who are "they"?
My colleagues in government. Yes, I should have understood that when there was the slightest difficulty or simply when they were faced with the possibility of unpopularity, they would rush to hide behind me. But even if I had understood that, I still would not have acted any differently. My shoulders are fairly broad. But in 1978 I should have seen the warning signs of their tendency to unload their responsibility onto me.

During 1977, Moshe Dayan hoped to keep hold of part of the Sinai and all the towns in the area of Yamit and east of a line running between El Arish and Sharm el-Sheik, under legislation that gave Egypt sovereignty over the territory and Israel responsibility for its security. It was likely that as soon as Israel retreated, thousands of bedouin in Sinai would flock to the area of Rafiah to be near the possibility of employment in Israel. The bedouin would engulf the area; they would steal from Jews, who would want to defend themselves; the Egyptian police or army would intervene, and we would have an explosive situation on our hands. To avoid this risk, the Dayan plan allowed us to ensure a continued territorial presence in the area of Yamit.

I was asked to work on the issue, and I submitted my project to the council of ministers on January 3, 1978, after I consulted Dayan at his home in Tsahala. The plan leaked out, and the press got hold of it and started talking about "sham localities." Our idea was to install a maximum presence in the unoccupied areas, whether it was a reservoir, buildings, enclosed land, terraced farming or farmland, and install a sort of wall to protect the aerodrome of Eitam built in north Sinai, beyond the border. The leak must have been because of the large number of organizations participating in the execution of the plan and not because of a deliberate desire to sabotage the plan. In any event, there was a general outcry against the "sham localities," and the government in turn was upset.

Someone whom I will not name played a particularly active role in this media assault. Occupying a high function in the government secretariat, he was subsequently accused of having sold secret information to a German newspaper. Out of respect for this man's father, an eminent personality in the Herut movement, Begin did not denounce him but merely removed him from his post. But this individual orchestrated an intensive disinformation campaign about me in the press, accusing me of having concocted the plan alone, with the aim of harming the negotiations with Egypt. However, when I submitted the plan to the government for the first time—and this figures plainly in the report of January 3, 1978—I had advised that the Egyptians be warned of the plan and that our intentions be explained to them. The ministers voted in favor of the plan on January 3 and renewed that decision two days later.

For a long time I didn't react to the avalanche of articles and declarations on the subject. But after years of silence I decided once and for all to put an end to the affair; I went on television and read out the government's decision. Things calmed down for a time, before raging again once my explanation had been forgotten. The members of the government at the time have never broken their silence on the subject.

JUNE 1982
THE LEBANESE WAR

After leaving *Ma'ariv*, I went to work for the *New York Post*. A short time later, Ariel, who had just been named defense minister, invited me to the farm for another beautiful Shabbat meal prepared by Lily. But the mood was not festive: He told me we might soon be going to war in Lebanon to destroy Yasser Arafat's kingdom of terror. "I'd like you to join me as media adviser," he said. I told my friend, "I prefer to keep my freedom as a journalist, but I'll help you as much as I can." To this, Sharon replied: "It will not be possible, because we're dealing with state secrets and you would have to be bound by very strict regulations." So I said yes and became Ariel's spokesman and liaison with the international press.

In June 1982, I accompanied Sharon to Romania. It was the first visit that an Israeli defense minister had made to a Communist country. President Ceausescu had demanded that the meeting be kept secret. A plane chartered by the Israeli army touched down on June 3, in Bucharest, for a four-day visit. The following day a coded telegram from Menachem Begin alerted us to a special cabinet meeting called in response to an attack the previous evening: Palestinian terrorists had seriously wounded the Israeli ambassador in London, Shlomo Argov. Sharon immediately wrote a coded telegram to Begin: "Add my vote to every decision taken." In his room at the Hotel Sinaia in Bucharest, General Abraham Tamir, Sharon's adviser charged with national security, declared, "We are heading toward a war in Lebanon."

Prime Minister Begin and his defense minister had long been worried about the activities of the Palestine Liberation Organization (PLO) in Lebanon. Under the aegis of Yasser Arafat, the PLO had constructed, from its headquarters in west Beirut, a veritable terrorist state that threatened Israel and carried out deadly operations all over the world. Since the 1970s the PLO had been responsible for numerous hijackings and hostage-takings, including the massacre of Israeli athletes at the Munich Olympic games in 1972, the assassination of the children of Maalot, the murder of western diplomats in Khartoum and the hijacking of a bus on its way to Tel Aviv in 1978 that left 46 people dead. The PLO charter also demanded the destruction of the state of Israel. Like most Israelis, Begin and Sharon considered Arafat public enemy number one and remained convinced of the need to wage a war to destroy the PLO infrastructure in Lebanon.

Sharon didn't hide his position on this matter. His willingness to declare his intentions in the clear light of day took me by surprise more than once. In May 1982, when we were both in the United States, Sharon had explained the distribution of PLO bases to General Alexander Haig, President Reagan's secretary of state, in great detail and aided by a map of Lebanon. "If Arafat continues his terrorist attacks," Sharon added, "Israel will blow up the Lebanese training camps, regardless of Syrian antiaircraft missile sites in east Lebanon." And Sharon had repeated his plans, still supported by his beloved maps, to the editors of the *Wall Street Journal* and the *New York Post*. "I don't want to take the American administration or American public opinion by surprise," Sharon told me. "I want to prepare them for the possibility of action against the PLO in Lebanon."

Sharon neither asked for nor received an American go-ahead for a preemptive strike in Lebanon. Begin and he hoped that the public warnings published in the press would dissuade the Palestinians from carrying out attacks—but the PLO had struck again in June by shooting the Israeli ambassador to London in the head.

If Sharon had been able to, he would have returned to Jerusalem on the spot. But his departure would have alerted the Romanians and with them the whole Communist bloc, and it also would mean canceling a vital meeting with his Romanian counterpart. Just before this meeting, Sharon received the last military reports indicating heightened tension on Israel's northern border. Our government had bombed PLO bases in Lebanon; in reprisal, Arafat had again attacked Israeli settlements in the north of the country.

Over a working lunch with the Romanian defense minister (who wore a uniform, like his officers), Sharon talked, as though nothing were amiss, of a possible aeronautical cooperation. He proposed an agreement whereby Israel would offer its assistance to Romania if the Romanians would supply Israel with the new Soviet T–62 tank. Silence fell on the luxurious room. It seemed to me that the huge chandelier was trembling with tension. Everyone knew why Sharon wanted this model of Soviet tank: the Soviet Union had already sold it to Syria, and Israel wanted to discover its secrets.

After a brief moment of reflection, the Romanian minister replied, "General Sharon, why do you come here looking for this tank? You can get one from your Syrian neighbors." The gathering burst out laughing, without really knowing how to take this response. As a matter of fact, three days later during the Israeli attack on Lebanon, IDF tanks took on Syrian armored vehicles during the battle of Sultan Yaacob. The Syrians abandoned a T–62 tank, and—after trying unsuccessfully to tow it away—the Israelis dismantled it and took away the essential parts to analyze.

After this lunch in Bucharest, Sharon cut his stay short and returned to Israel. Begin had called his cabinet meeting for that evening, after Shabbat. In the Boeing that was taking us home, Tamir declared, "In a week's time we'll be in Jounieh, in Lebanon." Sharon pretended that he hadn't heard. Before a crucial decision, on the eve of war, he would envelop himself in silence, trying to envisage every possible scenario.

A week later we were flying over Jounieh in a helicopter, toward the headquarters of the Christian Phalangists. For six days the IDF forces had been marching toward Beirut from different directions. Several hundred tanks were attacking the PLO bases situated on the road leading to the Lebanese capital. At Jounieh, Sharon was warmly received by the Christian Phalangist leader Bashir Gemayel, who soon thereafter was elected president of Lebanon. The table was groaning under the weight of salads, hummus and skewers of lamb. The IDF chief of staff, Raful Eitan, and representatives from Mossad were also present. Sharon spoke: "Several members of our government have asked me why you don't go to war. I went to the streets of Beirut. The cafés were full of people, and crowds were lining up for the movies."

Gemayel sidestepped the question and merely asked when the IDF forces would reach the Lebanese president's palace at Baabda, near Beirut. Sharon examined the regional map that Gemayel was holding out to him. He noticed a route that did not appear on Israeli military maps: "Are you sure that this road exists?"

"Certain! But Syrian or Palestinian soldiers might be patrolling it," Bashir Gemayel replied. He then asked Sharon to sign the map, as a souvenir. Gemayel told me that he had had a secret meeting in Israel with Prime Minister Yitzhak Rabin and his defense minister, Shimon Peres, in 1976. They had both agreed to the training, and arming, of Phalangists in Israel. Rabin and Peres had also dispatched members of the IDF and Mossad to Lebanon. Begin and Sharon had inherited these privileged links with the Phalangists and continued the tradition of helping the local Christian community. "We transported wounded Maronites to hospitals in our helicopters when neither France nor the Vatican lifted a finger," Sharon told me.

Since 1976, the IDF had successfully organized Christian soldiers into a disciplined military force. The Phalangists didn't take part in combat, however, while Israel suffered many deaths. Bashir Gemayal had dodged the problem, and Sharon had not insisted; Sharon had a war to wage.

On Sunday, after his visit to Jounieh, Sharon realized that IDF forces were slowly advancing, and he flew in a helicopter toward Damour. We arrived in the afternoon at the headquarters of General Amos Yaron. His forces were progressing along the length of the coast, careful not to touch civilians—a difficult task because Palestinian terrorists used the Lebanese population as a human shield. Sharon then decided to go to the Lebanese presidential palace in Baabda, which was held by Christian militia, following the route he had discovered on Bashir Gemayal's map.

We mounted four troop-transport trucks, after I had forced Sharon to put on a helmet borrowed from a soldier at the Damur headquarters. The intelligence officer had told us that the journey would take 45 minutes, but a long and perilous expedition in enemy territory awaited us, passing over cols at a vertiginous height. Ariel said to me, map in hand, "I knew that the Lebanese mountains were high, but I didn't realize how high."

We were driving in total darkness, and Sharon's bodyguards remained on high alert. The intelligence officer who had been wrong about the duration of the journey, and who was also decidedly clumsy, fired a bullet by mistake just as we were driving past a Syrian post. Luckily the Syrians did not identify us.

Arriving at Baabda a good five hours later, I said jokingly to Sharon, "We are living a historic moment: it is the first time that a defense minister has occupied the presidential palace of another country."

The first week of the Lebanese war was almost the last for us. Shortly after midnight, during the night of June 8, we had just taken off from Jerusalem when the engine of our helicopter started making a strange sound. Sharon didn't flinch. Rafi Eitan, Begin's antiterrorist adviser, shouted to me, "Can you hear it?" I could. But if even Rafi had heard it, despite the headphones that covered his ears, it must have been a terrific noise, for he had lost some of his hearing during the war of independence.

The pilot made an emergency landing at a nearby aerodrome. Once safely on the ground, he stood up, white as a sheet.

"What happened?" I asked.

"In another 17 seconds, we would have crashed," he exclaimed.

Sharon got out without saying a word and hurried to find a telephone in the aerodrome. He called the official residence of the prime minister, Menachem Begin, who had not yet gone to bed. I heard Sharon talking in the complicit manner used by men who share a secret. Sharon wanted the planned attack against 19 batteries of Syrian antiaircraft missiles posted in Lebanon to be put back on the agenda at the next cabinet meeting. The previous evening, Begin had failed to convince his government of the need to destroy the missiles. Certain ministers feared that such an intervention would lead to an escalation of tension with Syria and even to a direct confrontation. Begin and Sharon thought otherwise. In April 1981, when the missiles had been installed in Lebanon, the two men had already envisaged a military operation. President Ronald Reagan had dispatched the diplomat Philip Habib to Damascus to convince the Syrians to repatriate the missile batteries. When Habib failed, he came to Jerusalem to appease Sharon and Begin. This time, both were categorical: action was required without further delay.

Another factor had spared the Syrian missiles for a while: the choice made by the Israeli government to give top priority to the destruction of the nuclear installations of Osirak. International opinion would have reacted badly to news of two Israeli raids, one after the other. But a year had elapsed since the day when Israeli F–16s had destroyed Saddam Hussein's nuclear center. The time had come to act. Begin promised Sharon that he would bring up the question of the Syrian missiles at the cabinet meeting the following day. This matter settled, Sharon hung up and boarded another helicopter to reach the Lebanese front-line headquarters, sheltered in a small grove. Raful Eitan, the commander of the front General Amir Drori, the head of military intelligence Yehoshua Saguy and the heads of various commands were present. Faithful to his habit of explaining why the government opposed one particular maneuver and authorized another, Sharon outlined Begin's position on the Syrian missiles. He emphasized that forces had to advance toward the Beirut-Damascus road to cut the principal Lebanese-Syrian axis.

The following day, June 9, found us returning to Jerusalem at 11 A.M. to persuade ministers to attack the aerial batteries. Sharon brought with him the deputy head of the air force, General Amos Amir, who was to direct the air offensives on the northern front. Amos was a calm, cheerful man, a fighter pilot himself; he still wore a gray-green aviator's jacket, letting the neckline of a white T-shirt show. Sharon advised him to zip up his jacket at once, as a mark of respect to the government, most of whom, with Begin at the head, always wore a suit and tie.

The debate was long and bitter. Amos demonstrated how the batteries could be destroyed in several minutes, while minimizing the risks for the Israeli army and nipping the Syrian reaction in the bud, but almost every minister wanted to express reservations. These reservations were motivated only by political considerations: if they opposed the attack, no one could blame them if the attack failed. Amos Amir told the cabinet that time was short and that this was the ideal moment for an attack. Finally, after several tempestuous outcries, the government gave its assent.

When Amos and Ariel emerged from the room, satisfied, I heard Amos say to him, "I felt like you wanted to punch them—with good reason."

Sharon roared with laughter and replied, "You can unzip your jacket now."

We then went before the Knesset's defense and foreign affairs committee, to which Sharon had to give a report, as stipulated by Israeli law. It was half an hour past noon. Sharon feared that some members of the committee (particularly from the left and the Labour Party) would not refrain from divulging secret information, even if it was critical to national security, in order to harm the prime minister and the defense minister—even if it would increase the number of victims on both sides or cause the mission to fail.

During that meeting on June 9, 1982, three days after the start of the conflict, the members of the Knesset asked questions, and Sharon wrote them down, one after the other. One question was, Will Israel attack Syria's anti-aircraft missile batteries? If yes, when? Sharon replied that he would deal with that question later. I could discern jealousy in the eyes of some Knesset members as they listened to this leader who with great confidence explained the IDF's advance on Beirut—not only members on the left, like Yossi Sarid, but also members of Likud. They all feared, as the media confirmed after the meeting, that a victory in Lebanon would mean that the defense minister would succeed Begin as head of the government.

Sharon happily replied to the questions, as if he had all the time in the world. A little after 2 P.M., his military secretary brought him a note. "It's a dispatch from the air force," Sharon announced. "I'm sure you will be delighted to learn that all the missile batteries have been crushed. Syrian planes tried to stop us, but more than 80 of them were destroyed. All our planes have returned safe to their bases."

Judging from the wild consternation of some Israeli Knesset members, one would have thought that the Knesset itself had been bombed. Few were those who, like Yitzhak Rabin, got up to shake Sharon's hand and congratulate him effusively, even though, more than a personal victory for Arik, this mission was a victory for the entire state of Israel.

In the following weeks the IDF continued advancing toward the gates of Beirut. The siege of the PLO's "capital" began on June 25, 1982. Menachem Begin had ordered Mossad to liquidate Arafat—which would have led to the collapse of the PLO and resolved the issue—but the secret services hadn't followed the order. This did not stop Sharon from questioning the representatives of Mossad: "What is happening about the prime minister's order on Yasser Arafat?"

"We are working on it," the representatives replied. "It's in hand." A truly evasive reply that reflected overwhelming incompetence.

Since the aerial bombing of its offices in west Beirut, the PLO had circulated press releases, relayed in Israel by Sharon's rivals, claiming that the IDF had caused the exodus of hundreds of thousands of Palestinian refugees in south Beirut and killed innocent people. The criticism spread, not only to Paris, which openly supported the PLO and its leader, but also to the United States. Sharon showed me the intelligence service's confidential reports revealing how Arafat was rallying his Jewish friends in the Israeli and American left, so that they would organize demonstrations in Tel Aviv against the siege of Beirut. "There are Jews among us who are the enemy of their own people, even when Israel is in danger!" Sharon cried. "They are prepared to fly to the rescue of the greatest enemy that the Jewish people have known since the end of World War II, Yasser Arafat."

Mossad had not carried out Begin's order. As was subsequently confirmed, Mossad wasn't prepared for war, even though it had encouraged Begin and Sharon to intervene in Lebanon and had guaranteed them the help of its Phalangist protégés.

A supporter of action rather than of confrontation between departments, Sharon preferred to negotiate with the Americans to obtain the expulsion of Arafat and his lieutenants from Beirut. Mossad representatives reported on this negotiation, unique of its kind, between the Israeli defense minister and the American emissaries Philip Habib and Morris Draper. The diplomats' aides also took notes—and it is on these that I rely, in the name of history and the future. For the day will come when these files will be made public and bear witness to the audacity, guts and force of conviction shown by the defense minister of the small state of Israel in persuading the United States superpower that the only way to stop Beirut from being the capital of terrorism was to expel Arafat and his 10,000 minions.

Sharon had asked ambassador Habib to relay the following message to Arafat, through the intermediary of the Lebanese government: "He can get out of Beirut in three ways: on a bus for Damascus, on a boat or in a coffin." To win time, Arafat did everything to prolong the war. Commentators in Israel and throughout the world announced that the PLO "would never leave Beirut," and certain IDF officers expressed a similar opinion during meetings with

Sharon. After listening to the pessimists' arguments, Sharon pounded the table with his fist and said, "He will leave!" To put pressure on Arafat, Sharon occasionally ordered the electricity or running water in west Beirut to be cut.

We were sitting with ambassador Habib on the veranda of a villa in Yarza, a district in the Beirut heights where we were staying. It was night and we could see the exchange of fire, like a rainfall of shooting stars, between the IDF and the terrorists in west Beirut, while in the distance we heard the rumbling of bombing. The American diplomat threatened to deploy the 6th Fleet in the sea off Lebanon. "Don't make that mistake," Sharon protested. "You will create a buffer zone around the PLO, and Arafat will stay in west Beirut, which he has turned into the capital of local, regional and international terrorism."

Palestinian propaganda had functioned so well that Philip Habib swept aside these objections and posed an ultimatum: "In the name of President Ronald Reagan, I declare that you should withdraw ten kilometers from the Beirut-Damascus road, because we intend to bring in the 6th Fleet."

I had passed Sharon a note while Habib was declaring that the United States effectively wanted the Israeli siege to end, even if Arafat and his crew stayed in Beirut. I wrote, "Don't forget to speak in the name of Menachem Begin."

Sharon's turn came. "In the name of Prime Minister Menachem Begin," he said, "I declare that we will not withdraw until Arafat is gone." That same evening Ariel gave the order to the IDF forces to occupy the helicopter landing zones (of which there was a limited number) to prevent the equipment of the American 6th Fleet from landing; this order angered the Reagan administration, as I subsequently witnessed during several meetings with representatives of the American embassy in Israel.

At my request, Sharon agreed to speak to the international press to set the record straight, for the IDF was being accused of bombing foreign embassies in Beirut. He went to the television studios at Herzliya and, in one hour, gave live interviews to ABC, NBC, CBS and CNN. I had brought with me aerial photographs that I had procured from the intelligence services, showing the position of Palestinian mortars, which they had deliberately placed next to foreign embassies.

Sharon gave few interviews to the Israeli press, which was for the most part hostile to him; indeed, several journalists seemed even to bear a pathological resentment toward him. As for me, having given up my career to help my friend with media relations, I gave written authorization to every request from the Israeli media to report on the ground with the armed forces. We had nothing to hide. Despite that, some of my colleagues nursed a blind animosity toward Sharon and continued to weaken our country's position by demanding Sharon's removal from power, even if that meant that the conflict would reach a stalemate. I had to refuse requests for accreditation when, for example, Shin Bet, the internal security service, warned us that some well-known French reporter had links with a Syrian terrorist organization or that some renowned Israeli correspondent was working on behalf of the CIA.

✡

For Ariel, it was clear that if the siege of Beirut continued much longer, Israel would lose. That is why, during his secret meetings with Bashir Gemayal and his men at Sycamore Farm, as well as in discussions with Israeli commanders in Lebanon, Sharon made it clear that the IDF would have to be prepared to break through into west Beirut and to the bunkers of Yasser Arafat and his acolytes. Sharon hoped that his plans would leak out, creating a psychological pressure that would prevent us from actually having to force entry into the city.

In July 1982, at the height of the Beirut siege, a meeting was held at the farm. Bashir Gemayal, who had flown in on an Israeli military helicopter, Raful Eitan and Mossad officers examined maps in the dining room, discussing tactics for seizing the town and what to do with Arafat and his terrorists. The conversation continued until late into the night, while Lily busied herself at the stove. When she went to bed, Raful took over in the kitchen. Heading straight for the fridge, he concocted a cocktail of his own invention: two-thirds lager and one-third vodka. "Excellent for the health!" he told me, seeing my astonishment.

The rumor of an imminent Israeli intervention in west Beirut spread to such an extent that propagandists of the left succeeded in convincing parachute brigade reservists to delay joining their units. In the same spirit, Sharon ordered, with Begin's endorsement, that the aerial bombing of PLO targets be intensified. Meanwhile, President Ronald Reagan telephoned the Israeli prime minister and forced him to promise that he would put an end to the bombing.

Arik told me, "I was at the Knesset, in Begin's office, when the call from the White House came through. It was strange how Begin, who was suffering from kidney pain after a fall, shot up from his seat and held himself upright on his cane throughout the conversation. And how at every sentence pronounced by the American head of state, our proud and valiant leader responded with a forceful, 'Yes, Mr. President.' I was appalled. When he hung up, Begin told me that the president said that he had seen the photograph of a Palestinian girl whose arms had been blown off in west Beirut and that he found this sort of image unbearable." We learned later that the photo was a deliberate fraud: the youngster—a boy, not a girl—still had both limbs intact; he'd suffered a broken arm, which not only wasn't the result of the IDF's bombing, but had been inflicted before the Lebanese war.

Reagan's telephone call proved unnecessary. The night of August 12, 1982, following the intensified bombing, Arafat declared that he was ready to leave Beirut aboard a boat with 10,000 of his followers. The siege was going to end, and with it the spilling of blood.

So Sharon passed to the final stage of negotiations on Arafat's expulsion: where and when? We met Philip Habib again on the Beirut veranda, and the conversation was much more cordial. The international press, reporting that Arafat and his henchmen were preparing to leave Beirut, used the term "exodus," a choice that was far from accidental; it evoked the biblical episode of the Jews' departure from Egypt to escape the pharaoh, his warriors, chariots and armies. The chief of military intelligence Yehoshua Saguy and I had heard Habib speak about the evacuation of PLO "combatants" from Beirut; Sharon rejected the term and insisted that they be called "terrorists."

While the two men spoke, I talked in a low voice to General Saguy, just loud enough for Sharon to hear our words. I asked Saguy the English term for a word, and he said, "expel." "No question of calling that an exodus or even an evacuation, then," I declared. A few minutes later, Sharon told me in Hebrew, "Put that down in writing." Even while engaged in diplomatic tussling, Ariel kept his ears open and his senses alert. Perhaps it was his suspicious temperament or his political troubles that made him pay attention to what was being said behind his back.

Then Sharon addressed Habib, whose aide was transcribing the conversation, as was the Mossad representative: "We are talking about the expulsion of Arafat and his terrorists—not an evacuation, nor an exodus. Evacuation depends on someone's willingness, but here we want to force them to leave Beirut. It is a matter of expelling Arafat and his terrorists—and not his 'combatants,'" he hammered home.

Through the intermediary of the Saudi royal family, and at a cost of some several million dollars, the United States chose Tunis to receive the exiled Arafat, entrusting him to the care of President Habib Bourguiba. During an interview with a German newspaper, a close supporter of the head of the PLO declared, "Next time, we will be exiled to Fiji! We are ready to go to any country."

On August 30, 1982, Sharon and I went up to the roof of a tall building not far from the port of Beirut to watch through binoculars as the terrorist leader boarded a ship. French and American soldiers were overseeing the operation. Elite Israeli marksmen were aiming at Yasser Arafat's head, with its famous kaffiyeh; he got onto the ship without incident. Sharon ordered the marksmen not to shoot; Mossad had failed to liquidate Arafat, and Begin had promised the American administration that no attempt would be made on his life during the expulsion.

When Yasser Arafat and 10,000 of his men were expelled from Beirut, people talked about "Sharon's great project." They say that you knew that the Palestinians would rush toward Jordan and overturn the Hashemite regime. Another myth! No one has ever found a single line on this subject in all the official reports—simply because nothing of the sort existed.

All the same, Arafat and his 10,000 men were expelled from Beirut.
And 5,000 additional men, so 15,000 in total. Terrorists and Syrians among them.

What happened after the expulsion?
We knew that Yasser Arafat had left 2,500 armed men behind him in Beirut. We found enormous quantities of weapons and even a helicopter.

✡

Arafat was still alive, but he was no longer in our neighborhood, and that was reason to celebrate. On September 1, 1982, Sharon and Habib organized a festive dinner in Beirut for the U.N. representatives and the foreign armies that had taken part in Arafat's expulsion.

Before the Knesset, Begin gave a speech full of enthusiastic praise for his defense minister, who then spoke himself, outlining his optimistic desire for a "triangle of peace." In Sharon's view, after Egypt, the time had come for peace with Lebanon. Leaving the room, Yitzhak Rabin told me, "That was the speech of a prime minister." No one at the time imagined that Ariel would wait another 19 years to take the reins of government.

✡

During a trip to Washington, Ariel Sharon had lunch at the Pentagon with several American generals and admirals who were clearly impressed by the IDF's exploits. They wanted a report on the progress of the war after Arafat's expulsion, and Sharon told them that several thousand terrorists remained in Beirut and that the Lebanese army needed to be sent in to disarm them. Secretary Weinberger, however, had given us a rather icy welcome. "See how hostile he is to Israel," Ariel had whispered to me during the meal. "It's you they find particularly hard to swallow," I replied.

For Sharon, Arafat's exile to Tunis was only a temporary solution. Sharon had not been able to liquidate Arafat before his departure, but he was waiting for the opportunity to do so, as demonstrated by his reaction when he learned on September 6, 1982, that Arafat had just left the Tunisian capital with the intention of visiting several Arab countries. We received the news on a small air base in northern Israel with Caspar Weinberger and his delegation. We were giving him a demonstration of the latest feats of our automatic planes, which were now capable of identifying potential targets. This news implied an unhoped-for opportunity to reach Sharon's sworn enemy.

"I think the time has come to obey Menachem Begin's order," Sharon said to Raful Eitan. Afterward, in private, he said to me, "After that, I will be able to go back to my farm for good."

1982

SHARON'S BLACK SEPTEMBER

The first time I heard about the assassination of Palestinians in the districts of Sabra and Shatilla in Beirut was on September 18, 1982. It was a Saturday that coincided with the first day of Rosh Hashanah, the Jewish New Year 5743. International press agencies called me, the media advisor to Defense Minister Sharon, to find out our reaction to the massacre of Palestinian civilians. At first I feared that the reports were a new wave of propaganda; during the war in Lebanon, numerous articles had "reported" killings allegedly carried out by the IDF. But this time I was able to confirm the news quickly and had to interrupt the defense minister's New Year's holiday.

A tragedy had already broken the spirit of optimism that had followed Arafat's expulsion from Lebanon. On Tuesday afternoon we learned that the Lebanese president, Bashir Gemayal, elected on August 23, had been seriously wounded by a bomb in Beirut. Mossad did not have precise information on the circumstances of the attack, but everything indicated that Gemayel had probably died, despite the denials of the Christian Phalangists.

In the Middle East the death of a statesman plunges his followers into such disarray that it takes time for them to acknowledge it, as was seen with the assassination of the Egyptian president Anwar el-Sadat in October 1981, the death of Yasser Arafat in 2004 and the murder of Rafik Hariri in 2005. We learned shortly afterward that a Lebanese man, following orders from Damascus, had detonated from a distance a bomb placed near Gemayel's office.

On Wednesday, Ariel and I went to Lebanon to present our condolences to the president's family and to talk to IDF officers. Sharon feared that the terrorists who continued to operate in west Beirut would take advantage of the blow dealt to the Christian Maronites and launch a deadly offensive. Sharon thus ordered the Israeli forces to advance on the western suburbs of the capital. There had already been hundreds of losses on the Israeli side, and to prevent more, Raful Eitan argued that the Christian Phalangists should take up arms. Back in Jerusalem that evening, Sharon repeated Eitan's request during a meeting that continued late into the night. Sharon's and Begin's dream of restoring Lebanese national sovereignty and of making peaceful ties with their neighbor was broken. The international community had to prevent, at all cost, the terrorist factions from destroying the fragile equilibrium that Israel had established in Lebanon.

✡

Following Jewish tradition, on Friday, September 17, the eve of the New Year, I accompanied Lily, Arik and their two sons to the tombs of Margalit and Gur, where we stood in silence for some time. Ariel did not stay long at the cemetery; a helicopter was waiting to take him to Jerusalem so that he could meet the Israeli minister of foreign affairs, Itzhak Shamir, and the American envoy to Lebanon, Morris Draper, before the festivities began. "If we do not liquidate these organizations now, they will start up again and strike us, as well as you, for years to come," Sharon fired at Draper. He spoke loudly—he did not restrain his anger. Draper did not bat an eyelid.

Sharon hurried back to Sycamore Farm to celebrate Rosh Hashanah with his family. I called him the following day to apprise him of the tumult that had swept through the international press agencies. Should we respond to their claims concerning Sabra and Shatilla? "The IDF didn't even enter those camps," he replied.

The following day, a Sunday, the second day of Rosh Hashanah, the gates of hell opened beneath our feet. The radio announced that militants on the left were demonstrating in front of the prime minister's residence in Jerusalem, brandishing slogans that read "Begin is a murderer!" and "Sharon is a murderer!" The talk was of thousands of people massacred by a bloodthirsty Israeli army.

The official report of the Lebanese Red Cross testified later that around 700 Palestinian civilians had been killed by the Phalangist militia. But the truth mattered little; photographs distributed around the world were enough to rouse international outrage. At noon I telephoned Sharon and suggested that he immediately propose, in his capacity as defense minister, a parliamentary commission of inquiry to determine the extent of Israeli responsibility in the massacres of Sabra and Shatilla. He repeated that the IDF was not involved in the affair but that he would speak about it to the chief of staff.

Returning to Caesarea, where I was to dine with my old friend Yeshayahu Ben Porat, a journalist at the daily *Yediot Aharonot* with whom I had written half a dozen books on Israel, I noticed the posters that lined the road: "Begin is an assassin!" "Sharon is an assassin!" The left had already condemned Sharon and Begin without any form of trial. At Caeserea, Ben Porat and I bumped into an IDF general who had commanded a thousand tanks during the war. "What happened?" I asked. He waved away our questions with his hand. "Perhaps an Israeli corporal made a mistake. But really, how is it our problem if Lebanese Christians attack Palestinians?"

Back home, I telephoned Sharon and told him of the posters I had seen. "Will there be a commission of inquiry?" I insisted.

"I talked about it to Raful, and he is opposed to it. In his view it would undermine the IDF's honor."

"Well, they'll demand your head then. They are going to try to put the blame on you."

Ariel interrupted me: "Give me a break a little and let me enjoy the celebration. I've already given the necessary orders."

Several hours later the media of the entire world were chanting the names of Sabra and Shatilla. I called Sharon again: "Ariel, I beg you, set up a press conference immediately! The mobilization against you is taking on crazy proportions!"

"You're getting on my nerves, damn it! What do you want?"

"I want to warn you that you are in the middle of a storm."

"The chief of staff has left for Lebanon. It's his job to refute the lies to journalists."

"No, Ariel, that's not enough. They're going to serve you up to the press. You are Begin's right-hand man. Your opponents want you to fall, and Begin with you."

At that, Sharon raised his voice as he never had with me and yelled into the phone: "You're really being a pain! The chief of staff will respond. And if you think that they're aiming at the party, go and bother

Begin, not me. Why should I be the only one called into question? We have a prime minister, don't we? So let him take care of it!"

That said, my old friend hung up on me.

DECEMBER 1982–
JANUARY 1983
SHARON BESIEGED

"**W**hy do you always give me only bad news, never good?" Over the years Sharon has asked me that question several times, usually with a note of reproach in his voice, as if I wanted to ruin his good mood. It is true that he is a born optimist, even when the situation seems desperate, which explains his tenacity in combat.

"I'm warning you of the worst scenarios so that you can prepare yourself for them. If things go well, so much the better," I would then reply.

Sharon never held it against me. "My friend Uri always foresees events," he explained to those colleagues who criticized our friendship. "Some happen sooner and some later, but they always happen. During the Yom Kippur war, for example. And he has even foreseen something excellent," he concluded, smiling. He was alluding to the fact that, unlike them, I was sure that Sharon would become prime minister.

However, in the winter of 1982–1983, I had only bad news for Sharon. A commission of inquiry had been appointed on the Sabra and Shatilla massacres, chaired by Judge Kahan, president of the supreme court. "You must be prepared to testify," I said to Sharon one afternoon at the end of 1982, in his office at the ministry of defense. He stared at me in silence. He didn't want to believe it; he knew that he, the IDF and Israel were not linked to the acts of violence committed by the Phalangists.

As Sharon's communications adviser, not only had I read everything the media reported in Israel and in the rest of the world, I had also seen the diplomatic telegrams and the intelligence service reports. All held Sharon responsible for the massacres of Sabra and Shatilla, and the White House was demanding his head. Informed by its envoys in Beirut, the American administration knew that Sharon was not responsible for the tragedy in any way, but it wanted to take advantage of the situation and remove Sharon from power. From this confidential correspondence I also discovered that not only Israeli journalists, but also opposition figures and civil servants, were telling American and Egyptian diplomats what they needed to do to overthrow the Begin-Sharon government. For Sharon's political rivals, principally Shimon Peres, head of the Labour Party, and for the left in general, Sabra and Shatilla was a godsend; they expected that Sharon would finally be disgraced. As for Sharon's Likud colleagues, their personal ambitions led them to support their former opponents on the left.

The guillotine was about to fall, and Sharon knew it. An assiduous reader of telegrams, he often showed me one or the other that reported how, during a meeting with the representative of an Arab or other country, an Israeli had indicated the best way to put pressure on Begin or Sharon. "It's strange," he said. "Israelis boast about the excellence of our secret service but are hardly discreet in handing out information to our enemies."

I discovered that the highest-ranking military officers, with Raful Eitan at their head, feared the conclusions of the Kahan commission and were meeting to decide whether to put all the blame on the minister of defense. My friend, Division General Dan Shomron, who later became chief of staff, made a special visit to my office to announce that Raful was gathering every piece of paper that might be used against Sharon. I immediately phoned Ariel at Begin's residence. I discovered later that the chief of staff was listening in on the defense minister's protected telephone line—the one that I had used to warn Sharon. Raful called me to his office. I remember that he was playing with his watch as he declared, "There are people who want to ruin us, Sharon and me." The leaders of Mossad, who had sponsored the Phalangists and whose representatives had been at their side for years in Jounieh, kept a low profile.

In addition to his usual work, Sharon had to prepare his defense. He wanted to engage a legal bigwig, but the best lawyers had already been hired by Mossad leaders, the chief of staff and the other generals. For want of anyone better, Ariel made do with a reservist recruited by the defense ministry, whose name I will withhold. For the preparatory meetings that Sharon held in his office, we formed a team consisting of Sharon's military secretary Oded Shamir and the military historian Benjamin Amidror, as well as the mediocre defender recruited by the military. All the officers, Mossad delegates and senior civil servants, who once wanted to get as close as possible to Sharon, now treated him as though he had the plague. I heard generals conforming their testimonies so as to protect themselves from any accusation.

Sharon's days in power were numbered, and his political rivals were circling him like sharks. Day after day, articles accused him of the massacres of Sabra and Shatilla and of unleashing the Lebanese war; they detailed the IDF's losses, "forgetting" that Sharon had anni- hilated the PLO's terrorist structures in Lebanon and expelled Arafat and his supporters. Sharon protested in vain—not least to the com- mission of inquiry—saying, "Neither Israel nor I was implicated in this massacre."

One day Sharon called me around six in the morning so that I could give him a review of the press. After five minutes he interrupted me: "Enough of this foolishness!" And he decided, with his character- istic optimism, what he was going to do that very day. First, he thought of withdrawing progressively from the region of Beirut; Israel would keep reduced forces in the sensitive points of south Lebanon, to prevent the north of the country from being targeted again by ter- rorist forces.

I often reminded Sharon that the commission of inquiry wanted his head and that he should not expect a fair hearing: "Political lies will dictate the commission's conclusions." Israeli delegates appeased American delegates by saying, "Be patient; Sharon will soon be shown the door." Prime Minister Begin did not get involved; he had weak- ened physically and psychologically since the death of his beloved wife Aliza.

I advised Sharon to take measures to avoid being lynched: arrest the Phalangist leaders, and call for their imprisonment and trial in Is- rael before a civil or military court for their direct responsibility in the massacres. I mentioned this idea to him several times, but Sharon re- mained adamant: "We're not going to arrest our allies, even if they have betrayed us with their criminal acts. We are a state founded on law. It is for the Lebanese people to judge these assassins."

Sharon then went abroad to meet the heads of state with whom Israel hoped to develop relations. In December 1982 we left for Honduras, which was asking us for military help. In political terms, the visit was a success, but Sharon flared up when local journalists asked him, "What was your responsibility for the massacres of Sabra and Shatilla?" "No Israeli is or was responsible!" he shot back.

Back at our hotel in Tegucigalpa, the capital, accompanied by the head of the Israeli air force, David Ivri, Sharon had still not calmed down: "Look at the damage this lie that our politicians and journalists are perpetrating has done Israel; even in the Central American jungle we are blamed for Sabra and Chatila!"

I repeated my suggestion again in New York, at the home of Sharon's cousin Maya, during the lighting of the Hanukkah* candles: "Arrest the Phalangist commanders during their next visit to Israel. That would be an unexpected act that would enable you to stop this infernal ruckus." He did not reply.

On our return to Israel, Benjamin Amidror, the great military historian of Israel, warned Sharon that his line of defense was poor and that the commission would declare him guilty. But Sharon was a man of habit. The moment he had engaged the services of a lawyer, even if he was bad, or an adviser, even if he was terrible, he would not remove him from his post. And if things went wrong, Sharon would repeat, "Blame me, not them." This willingness to take the blame for the failures of his entourage was one of his character traits that I was never able to understand.

✡

Not everyone, however, turned their back on Sharon. On Saturday, January 1, 1983, at midday, I went to collect the actress Elizabeth Taylor from the Tel Aviv Hilton to accompany her to Ariel and Lily

---

* Festival of Light that commemorates the victory of the Maccabims over the Hellenistic dynasty of the Seleucides in the second century before the Christian era.

Sharon's house. She was wearing a white fur hat, and her beauty still bore witness to her magnificent past. She wanted to express her support for Sharon; she held him in high esteem and understood only too well the demonization to which he had been subjected by the international media for several months. "I know from experience the unlikely stories the papers can invent," she told me. Indeed, one had lost count of the articles in the gossip magazines about her problems with alcohol.

At the time, we appreciated every sign of friendship for Sharon, and the kind gesture of an actress idolized by millions of fans was more than welcome. However, the bad luck that hovered over Sharon seemed to extend to everyone who wished him well. While Elizabeth Taylor was riding in a limousine toward Sycamore Farm, her car suddenly braked on a waterlogged section of the road. It was a particularly stormy winter day; broken branches and puddles were strewn across the route. I was following her in a second car; my driver did not have time to brake, and our car ran into the back of the star's Mercedes. Our car was totaled, and I was aching all over, but what about Liz Taylor? I quickly waded across to open the rear door of the limousine. I found the actress in a state of shock and complaining of pain in her ankles and chest. We stopped a passing car that drove us, wounded and in pain, to our destination. Our worried hosts immediately called a doctor.

Elizabeth Taylor behaved as though nothing had happened, but Lily sat her down in a comfortable armchair and covered her with a blanket. Despite the accident, the star kept smiling her dazzling smile and continued to talk in her soft and delicate voice. The meeting with the Sharons gave her visible pleasure, and she seemed to forget the accident. She congratulated Ariel on his action in Lebanon and said she was sure that it would result in a better future for Israel and Lebanon. What is more, she intended to go to Beirut and say as much to the Lebanese!

Dr. Boleslav Goldman arrived; he was a friend of the Sharons, and at that time he was director of the Sheba hospital near Tel Aviv. He listened to Liz Taylor's chest, examined her ankles and neck, and decided that she didn't need to go to the hospital. This was the same Dr. Goldman, who, on December 18, 2005, was urgently called and who ordered Sharon's security guards to take Sharon immediately to the Hadassah Ein Kerem hospital in Jerusalem.

✡

In January 1983 we were en route to Zaire in an air force Boeing. Sharon as defense minister had succeeded in making peace between Israel and several African states that had broken off relations with Israel after the Yom Kippur war; President Mobutu Sese Seko, who had bought arms from us, had invited an Israeli task force to come and train his presidential guard. It was an opportunity for Lily and Arik, and of course for me, to get out of the political and media quagmire in Israel. Shimon Peres, the deputy defense minister, had forged the first links with Mobutu in 1963 and had invited him to Israel. The Zairian general admired Sharon and had sent him several messages of encouragement through their mutual friend Meir Meyuhas: "If they strip you of your post, it will be the beginning of Israel's decline."

Wherever he went in Zaire, Sharon was received with honors, particularly in the rich mining region of Lubumbashi. However, a group of Israeli journalists who had joined us would not give up and continued at every opportunity to press him with questions about Sabra and Shatilla.

On one occasion, journalists were buying souvenirs, and Meir Meyuhas helped me buy two magnificent "talking" parrots with grey feathers and red tails. I obtained a veterinary certificate stating that they carried no diseases. On our return to Israel, at 3 A.M., the parrots' cage was mistakenly loaded with Sharon's baggage and was sent to Sycamore Farm. Less than 48 hours later, before I had had time to retrieve them, I was overwhelmed with phone calls from colleagues: "How could you smuggle in parrots without putting them in quarantine? It's against the law!" I warned Ariel that the press wanted to pin another crime on us; this time, the traffic of exotic birds. "Yes, they are just as ready to bring down parrots," he joked. I sent someone to fetch my birds at once, to save him from this futile controversy. Nevertheless I was pursued by the courts for "trafficking parrots," so I duly placed the birds in quarantine as the law required and paid a fine of around a hundred dollars. Wonderful headlines were in prospect for an anti-Sharon campaign: "Sharon's adviser accused of trafficking

African parrots." One of the parrots, Lippo, kept me company for 12 years.

✡

It seemed to me that Sharon concentrated on his activities in Zaire to escape from the fact that he soon would be relieved of them. Two weeks after his return to Israel, he left again for Zaire, this time on a secret mission. Mobutu had proposed a meeting with Hissene Habre, the president of Chad, who sought a connection with our country against the Libyan dictator Mouammar Gadhafi. A fractured kneecap prevented me from accompanying Sharon, but he later recounted the trip to me blow by blow.

In Zaire, Sharon and Mobutu flew to the palace that Mobutu had built in Badolita. Sharon explained to the Mossad representative, who was acting as an interpreter, that Mobutu had kept this meeting under cover by saying that it was actually an encounter between two delegations, one from Mali and the other from Canada. "Tell him we are members of the delegation from Mali!" Sharon joked.

The "Canadian representative" arrived—Hissene Habre, the Chadian leader. He said that his poorly equipped soldiers had succeeded in defeating Gadhafi's units, even though they were armed by the Soviets. "We need antiaircraft weapons," Habre told Sharon. "We are helpless against Gadhafi's Migs." "You'll have them," Sharon promised. Sharon was thereby respecting Israel's traditional political line of supporting the weak against dictators. Israel had helped the Kurds against Saddam Hussein, had supported the Yemen monarchy against the Egyptian legions sent there by Nasser, and had helped the Christian Maronites of Lebanon against Syria and the PLO, which, together, had massacred them.

"I was talking to a revolutionary African leader who looked like he had come straight from the jungle brandishing a large knife," Sharon told me later. "And if he was ready to fight Gadhafi, Israel's sworn enemy who had sent planes to fight us on the Suez Canal in 1973, Israel was ready to help him." One of Sharon's last orders as defense minister was to send a battery of antiaircraft cannons to Chad. His opponents in the Begin government had persuaded the prime minister to adopt the resolutions of the Kahan commission and to force Sharon to resign.

In fact, before Sharon left for Africa, I had enlightened my friend on this subject. I had it on authority that the commission was preparing to publish its conclusions within the week and that the responsibility for the massacres would fall on him, while Mossad, sponsor of the Phalangists, would emerge cleaner than clean. The famous lawyer Amnon Goldenberg had already scheduled a dinner with the head of Mossad to celebrate their victory. Sharon found it difficult to believe.

FEBRUARY 8, 1983
THE KAHAN COMMISSION
DELIVERS ITS REPORT

On the top floor of the Hilton, overlooking the Old City of Jerusalem, Ariel was tense. It was Wednesday, February 8, 1983, publication date of the Kahan commission report, which condemned the best defense minister that Israel had ever known. Sharon had just returned from a meeting with Prime Minister Begin. "They want to pin all the responsibility on me," he said angrily.

The previous evening he had asked Begin to tell him the report's findings, but the prime minister had refused to do so before the official publication. That morning Sharon's lawyer had therefore given Sharon the report's conclusions over the telephone, and Arik heard this fatal paragraph: "The Kahan commission recommends that Sharon be removed from his functions as minister of defense, for it judges him indirectly responsible for the massacre of Sabra and Chatila. He should have foreseen the possibility of such a massacre and taken the necessary measures to prevent it; he did not do so." As I had predicted, the Mossad figures who had supported the Phalangists were declared innocent. No "indirect responsibility" was attributed to them. Sharon's first reaction was, "I shall resign at once in protest against the injustice done to me!"

Sharon then flew by helicopter to see Begin. I had asked Oded Shamir, Sharon's military secretary, to give Sharon a hastily written note before the meeting: "I advise you not to resign. I know that you are the victim of a great injustice. The day will come when the people of Israel will know that. And even if you resign and go into political exile, the day will come when the Israeli people will see you as a savior and ask you to lead them. If you stay in the government as a minister without portfolio, you will shorten your political exile."

In Sharon's room at the Hilton, where I met him with his lawyer and Oded Shamir, Sharon thanked me for my note and added that he had reminded Begin that the law gave the prime minister the ability to reject, in whole or in part, the conclusions of the official commission of inquiry. But Begin's distant manner made it clear that he would not do so. The relationship between these two men whose mutual trust and collaboration had resulted in the creation of the settlements, the bombing of Osirak and the expulsion Arafat went up in smoke because of a report written in a disdainful tone that revealed the man who wrote it: the supreme court judge Aharon Barak.

The following day I accompanied Sharon to Jerusalem again, where a government meeting was to debate the Kahan report. I did not want to leave him to face this trial alone. Despite his apparent calm, Lily and I knew that he was raging inside. The Israeli and international media were exultant at the prospect of seeing the minister of defense ruined. Hundreds of demonstrators thronged around the entrance to Sycamore Farm brandishing the usual signs, "Begin is a murderer" and "Sharon is a murderer," and covering the neighborhood in graffiti. The body-guards used a little-used country road to drive us to the fateful meeting.

In Jerusalem, the atmosphere in front of the prime minister's office was different: thousands of people were chanting, "Arik, King of Israel." Dan Meridor, the cabinet secretary, hurriedly ordered the windows to be closed. "The atmosphere was like a court-martial," Ariel told me when he came out. Begin, who was presiding over the meeting, Moshe Nissim, the justice minister, and Dan Meridor made sure that a majority accepted the report's conclusions.

The following day, Friday, Sharon attended a legal conference that had long been arranged. With his customary frankness, he did not hesitate to criticize the report's findings. It was on this occasion that Sharon uttered the statement that was to become his leitmotif: "The conclusions of the Kahan commission have created a profound injustice, not only by branding me with the mark of Cain but also by condemning the state of Israel and the whole of the Jewish people."

But Sharon was preaching in the wilderness. The politicians and journalists had finally triumphed, not over our Arab enemies but over Sharon. It mattered little to them if the massacres of Sabra and Shatilla became a weapon to slander the Jews as a whole, not just Arik. Begin did stutter some words, however, in support of his minister: "Goyim kill other goyim, and it is Jews who carry the can."

On the day that Sharon said his farewells to the ministry of defense and, his head held high, inspected the guard of honor, reporters from the *New York Times* and Israeli television approached me to ask my opinion. My response was direct: "Those who do not want Sharon as minister of defense will one day have him as prime minister."

Sharon phoned me late in the night, furious: "Why did you say that on television?"

"Because that is what I believe."

"All right, but why say it? Don't you think I have enough problems?"

The following morning, I understood his anger: one of the biggest Israeli dailies told its readers, twisting my words, that Sharon would do everything to overturn Begin and take his place. When I saw Sharon again, however, after he had taken up his post as minister without portfolio, he apologized for having shouted at me. He showed me hundreds of encouraging letters from Israeli citizens, sometimes quoting my statement. My response to the press became a famous saying in Israel, used even by those who mocked Sharon.

✡

On February 27, 1983, Sharon celebrated his fifty-fifth birthday. Lily had decked the house with flowers and invited all his friends. Even if he didn't let it show, Sharon lacked energy. His political future looked gloomy indeed. The talented graphic designer Reuven Adler, our mutual friend, said to me in private, "I also want to see him back in power, but I don't know how he can reenter the political arena." "There will be a war, and the people will call on him," I replied. Reuven Adler stared at me as if I had lost my mind. After that, every time I said that Sharon would one day be prime minister, Reuven would make a hand gesture indicating that he feared for my mental health, but he also invariably added, "I hope so!" However, when Sharon was elected prime minister in 2001, six months after Arafat launched the second Intifada, Reuven boasted that it was all thanks to the slogan that he had created: "Peace and Security." One forgives friends for simplifying the truth, which I published in *Ma'ariv*: "Arafat's war made Sharon Prime Minister."

✡

Later I tackled the subject of Sabra and Shatilla with Sharon in the more formal framework of an interview.

Let's talk now of the Sabra and Shatilla affair.
That was a defamatory accusation. You know that as well as I do, you who worked at my side during that war and attended all my cabinet meetings in Jerusalem and in Lebanon.

They abandoned you in 1978 and then again after the problem with Lebanon.
Yes, but not at the beginning. So long as it looked like we could gain a rapid victory in Lebanon, members of the government put their shoulders to the wheel and encouraged me, even telling me that it wasn't necessary to consult or inform them about my every act. On the other hand, alarm bells started ringing at the first "difficulties"— the prolonged siege of Beirut and the demonstrations in Tel Aviv, which Yasser Arafat called the "Palestinians' last hope."

Which demonstrations?
Those of the Labour Party and the left, demanding that I be brought to justice. On September 22, 1982, during a stormy session in the Knesset in which I tried to explain my actions in Lebanon, I notably read out reports from the intelligence services.

To what degree do you think today that you could have prevented the Phalangists' massacre of the Palestinians?
Not a single soldier, not a single officer, nor a single Israeli politician was involved in that tragedy. What is more, throughout the war, and well before Sabra and Shatilla, we had constantly heard the same reproach, not least from the mouth of Victor Shem-Tov, the general secretary of Mapam,* before the foreign affairs and security committee: "How can we justify the fact that our men are being killed while the Lebanese are not taking part in the war?" Begin held this against Bashir Gemayel. It seems that Begin criticized him harshly during a last, rather strained, meeting shortly before Bashir's assassination. In fact, Lebanese Christians neither participated in the war nor made the slightest positive statement in our favor. Even if we hadn't undertaken the war on their account, their attitude puzzled the Israelis.

---

*   United workers' party with a Marxist-Zionist bent.

Do you think that you suffered an injustice at the hands of the Kahan commission of inquiry?
A grave injustice. In principle, every individual, even if accused of an abominable crime, can appeal a judgment in the supreme court. With a commission of inquiry, the judgment is a fait accompli. The commission publishes its report and then washes its hands of the affair. As soon as its work is done, it ceases to exist and no recourse is possible.

You brought a charge of defamation against Time *magazine after it published an article stating that you had encouraged Lebanese Christians to massacre the Palestinians. You devoted many months to this trial; do you regret it?*
Absolutely not. On the contrary. I realized afterward how hard it was to fight against that powerful media empire. The trial began in summer; the leaves of the trees outside the court turned brown and fell. Winter snow began to fall. I remember a pregnant journalist who was following the debates. Week after week we watched her pregnancy develop; she gave birth shortly after the case ended.

✡

On February 14, 1983, the day that Arik left his post as defense minister, *Time* published an article entitled "The Verdict: Guilty," based on information from the magazine's correspondent in Israel, David Halevy. Among other things, Halevy stated that Sharon had encouraged the Phalangists to take revenge on the Palestinians during the condolence visit that Sharon had made to Bashir Gemayel's family the day after the assassination. If the journalist was to be believed, this detail was stated in the secret Appendix B of the Kahan commission report. I was in a good position to know that his statement was a web of lies, since I was present, along with a good half dozen IDF, Mossad and Shin Bet officers, during that famous visit to Lebanon.

Sharon demanded an official retraction. When *Time* did not deign to respond, he resolved to pursue a case of defamation. I then received a phone call from a well-known New York Jewish lawyer from the Anti-Defamation League (an organization created by the American B'nai B'rith to combat anti-Semitism), Arnold Foster. Soon after, we were in the Manhattan office of Milton Gould, of the law firm of Shea and Gould, one of the most respected attorneys in North America.

Gould immediately declared that, as a Jew, he considered defending Sharon a mitzvah (a religious duty or charitable act). Arnold Foster took on the role of raising the funds to cover the costs of the case.

We crossed the Atlantic many times for the trial until the judgment came in January 1985, in Sharon's favor, 23 months after his complaint had been filed. Judge Abraham Sofaer split the verdict into three segments—so that while the jury did not find that *Time* had acted with malice, it did rule that the magazine's article was both false and defamatory. And in an unprecedented act, the jurors read aloud in court a statement in which they declared that "certain *Time* employees, particularly correspondent David Halevy, acted negligently and carelessly." For Arik this was the tremendous moral victory he had sought. For him it was never about money; indeed, to finance the lawsuit he had sold the house in Zahala where he, Margalit and Gur had lived together.

How was the trial conducted?
On three fronts: legal, public relations and financial—because my defense was extremely expensive. In terms of public relations, it seemed obvious to me that over and beyond my own case, this was an opportunity to clarify Israel's positions, and I repeatedly did so with the leading journalists who were covering the trial. Curiously, there, too, I found myself alone, without any support from our ambassador to the United States or our consulate in New York. Worse still, Israeli journalists who didn't thrash me in their articles were reprimanded, particularly by Shimon Peres. Strangely enough, his attitude toward me changed when he became prime minister.

Israel undoubtedly lost an opportunity to restore its image, given the interest that the American public had in the trial. Unfortunately, our country is always deficient in the area of communication. Even if I was the complainant in this defamation trial, the case extended far beyond the personal: the state of Israel had been called into question because, according to *Time*, I had encouraged the massacres of Sabra and Chatila in my capacity as minister of defense. The government did not even pay for my security costs, so I obtained permission to finance my bodyguards' wages by giving lectures at universities and other institutions, which were generously remunerated. My difficulties eased somewhat when Peres took over as head of the national unity government, in rotation with Shamir.

Perhaps because you had helped Peres form this government in August 1984?
I don't think so, even though the idea of forming a national unity government in rotation came from me. Peres and I had similar views in
many respects.

*But why was Peres as prime minister more inclined to help you than your
Likud colleagues were?*
I think it's connected with biased interests—according to which an in-
dividual can be sacrificed in the name of a supposed national interest.

Was this typical of Shamir but not Peres?
Not Peres in fact, no. From that point of view, he was a good person.
Not that I agree with everything he did. Our relationship went back
to the time when I led the 101st Paratrooper Battalion and he was the
head of services at the ministry of defense. Peres did not act out of
personal interest but out of a sense of duty. Under orders from Shin
Bet, I was not authorized to travel without bodyguards, and yet that
cost was not covered by Peres's predecessor. I also remember the help
that I received from Arnold Forster, a great defender of the Jewish
cause in the United States and throughout the world. I initially
brought my action against *Time* in Tel Aviv, and it was he who urged
me to appeal to American justice. He telephoned me on his own initiative, telling me that the case was so important for the Jewish people
and the state of Israel that it must take place where it would have international repercussions.

In New York?
Yes, in *Time*'s backyard.

When the jury declared that the editors of Time *had lied and had defamed
you, what were your thoughts?*
That I was in the right. I wanted it to be clear that *Time* had lied in
stating that I had initiated or encouraged the massacre. One often asks
oneself, after an event, how one dared launch into certain undertak-
ings. At the time, the trial seemed vital to me, despite the difficult
fight that lay ahead, and I didn't hesitate for a single moment.

1983–1984
ARIEL, DON'T RESIGN!

When Sharon left the ministry of defense, I dissuaded him three times from resigning from a government in which he was now nothing more than minister without portfolio. In his autobiography, *Warrior*, published in 1988, Sharon quoted only one of those instances, from the summer of 1983. That year Sharon attended government meetings but was frustrated by his lack of real influence. He spent a lot of time working the fields and playing chess with his younger son, Gilad; his older son, Omri, was now in the army. Sharon told me in as many words that he intended to resign from the government to devote himself entirely to agriculture, a way of life that he valued.

One afternoon when I felt that his lassitude threatened to overwhelm him, I invited myself to the farm. Lily and I listened to him hold forth, over a plate of roast mutton and salad, on his grievances with the government—he had no real function, but he was still held responsible for Begin's confused policies, though he increasingly disagreed with Begin. "I don't want to be the scapegoat any longer. I've made up my mind: I'm going to resign."

I tried in vain to dissuade him. Lily, on her part, supported Arik as she always did—obviously she would be happy to have him at home more often. After enjoying her homemade cake, we went out onto the lawn. "Earlier," he told me, "I was on my tractor, flattening large clumps of earth, and I found myself stammering, almost out loud, as though I were addressing Begin: 'You, too, Menachem, you've let me down.'" Sharon's voice was full of anger and sadness. "Yes, Menachem has let me down. We both decided to go to war, together, and with authorization from the government. He knows that I had nothing to do with Sabra and Shatilla, but he has betrayed me for his own, and his government's, political benefit."

"That's true, but to resign would still be a mistake. I understand your anger, but I know and feel that the majority of Jews are on your side and believe that you are the victim of an injustice. Your dismissal, under the pretext of Sabra and Shatilla, is proof of the country's general deterioration. As a journalist, I already knew that the army was weaker, but it was only when I was working beside you at the ministry of defense that I saw the extent of the damage. Our Arab enemies are delighted that you have been removed from power, and they are not alone: people are so delighted by your downfall that they're drinking a toast to the event with vodka in Moscow and with whisky in Washington. This situation may well lead to problems for Israel and to armed attacks. If you stay on your farm, in two years' time the Jews who believe in you might say, 'You're peacefully looking after your vineyard while Jews are being assassinated or are fighting for their lives.' How will you respond? That the Kahan commission and Begin wronged you, that you were upset and angry and that you want to be left alone? Or will you say to them, 'I'm coming!' Obviously you will run to help. But you will have to start again from zero, whereas now you belong to the government and have maintained your influence."

As Sharon acknowledges in *Warrior*, "If my friend Uri Dan had not dissuaded me, I would have resigned that evening." I don't know how I succeeded in changing his mind. Perhaps it was by suggesting that he should find Begin and tell him everything he said about him while driving his tractor beneath the burning Negev sun.

The crucial meeting with Begin was arranged for the following day. Entering the room, Ariel found Begin murmuring, "What a tragedy, what a tragedy." He had just been told that another Israeli soldier had been killed in Lebanon. Sharon lost no time in getting to the point: "Menachem, a leader's role is to make decisions, and good ones, not to cry and complain." Begin knew that since Sharon had been stripped of his functions, he had criticized the prime minister's policy in Lebanon, but he can hardly have expected that Sharon would tackle the subject straight on. "But that's not why I asked to see you," Ariel continued. "I wanted to tell you that the day I said farewell to the ministry of defense, when I was inspecting the guard, I suddenly thought of my father, at work in our orange groves at Kfar Malal, when I told him that I was going to join the Haganah. He put down his tools to congratulate me and then said, 'Never hand a Jew over to foreigners.' That was exactly why I chose Haganah, not Palmach, which had handed your Irgun* men over to the British. But you, Menachem, you gave me away!"

When Sharon recounted this meeting, his voice was still full of anger: "I looked him straight in the eyes. He was pale. He had nothing to say." A month and a half later, on August 29, 1983, Menachem Begin surprised his government by announcing his retirement from politics. "I can't take it any more," was all he said.

Thus the struggle began between Likud ministers Yitzhak Shamir and David Levy to succeed him. For the first time since his dismissal, Sharon regained some political influence; his support helped Shamir win the election. (When Sharon left the defense ministry, I returned to journalism, resuming my position as the *New York Post*'s correspondent in Israel.) When Shamir had asked for his support, Arik asked me whether I thought Shamir would bring him out of hibernation. I replied, "No. He's an ingrate." Nonetheless, since Ariel thought Shamir was the best candidate, he supported him without considering his personal interests.

The following winter, again Sharon started thinking about leaving the government and getting out of politics altogether to live a peaceful life among his sheep on his land in northern Negev. This time he told me of his plans in Paris, on a gray, rainy day. We were returning from the United States, and our flight included a stopover in the French capital. We had first gone to Texas, invited by the Jewish community in Corpus Christi. Sharon had agreed to give a lecture, on condition that the trip include a visit to the biggest farm in America, the King Ranch, and to a cattle farm in San Antonio. I can still see him strolling about the prairie, amid cows and calves, clearly in seventh heaven and filling his lungs with the smell of manure as though it were the scent of some luxurious perfume.

The Israeli ambassador to France, Ovadia Sofer, welcomed us on our arrival at Charles de Gaulle airport. He told Sharon that he had arranged several meetings with Jewish leaders and French personalities. Sharon politely refused; he would rather see Paris. And so it was that we were ambling around the city on a winter's day, surrounded by Israeli and French security agents—extra protection was required for

---

* National armed organization, more radical than Haganah.

the man whom the French, European, American and even Israeli media called the "butcher of Sabra and Shatilla." Despite the biting cold, all three of us walked along the river and through the second-hand booksellers of the Left Bank, where we discovered old postcards of Eretz Israel dating from the eighteenth and nineteenth centuries. The postcards showed the division of the sacred land into the 12 tribes of Israel. Sharon said angrily, "These old postcards show the biblical names of Judea and Samaria, and back home those idiots talk about the West Bank!"

After our walk, we warmed ourselves with a cup of hot chocolate at the Deux Magots. "Look at the passersby," he said to me, "and the Parisians, so elegant underneath their umbrellas. And those beautiful bare trees. Even the waiter is chic, with his black jacket and a bottle opener hanging around his neck!" Then he saw the sign of Brasserie Lipp, on the other side of the Boulevard Saint Germain: "Is that a good restaurant?"

"Are you joking? It's one of the most famous restaurants in Paris! They do a legendary choucroute."

"Reserve a table for tonight. We'll go there with Lily," he declared.

Sharon loved good restaurants. On the other hand, he thought little of cafés, and I had to use all my ingenuity to convince him that day to sit down with Lily in the Deux Magots. When I quizzed him on the origin of this aversion, he replied that when you worked the land from sunrise to sunset, you had no desire to waste time sitting in a café. And then he dropped the bomb: "I can't bear this shameful position of minister without portfolio any more. I'm going to resign as soon as we get back to Israel. There's nothing left for me in government. I'd rather look after my farm, drive my tractor, enjoy life."

"Yes, you don't have a portfolio, but you have a suitcase! I understand your resentment toward the government. Shamir and all the Likud ministers are pushing you out and the media are thrashing you, but the majority of the Jews, both in Israel and in the rest of the world, are on your side. Pack your bags and take advantage of the opportunity you're being given to express yourself in the United States, France and Britain; you only have to choose where you want to go."

"I know, but I feel like I'm wasting my time. I can do great things on the farm. And I can't bear contempt and mockery any more."

"What weapons do your enemies have? Ariel, you have the blessing—or the curse—of playing an active role in the destiny of the Jewish people. And you are resigning? You are going to look after your sheep and your cows? For how long? You're only 55, and your mother lived for more than 80 years. What will you do in the year 2000?" Sensing that he was wavering, I continued: "You should do battle both to clear your name of false accusations and to become, when the time comes, prime minister."

"Stop saying that!" Nevertheless, he let me continue.

"Tell your rivals, and those who hate you, that you have a political program from now to 2000. Then speak about your priorities for Israel. That way you'll stop them from burying you politically. They're scared of your shadow—that's why they keep saying you're finished."

Sharon remained silent.

"Uri is right," Lily declared.

They returned to Jerusalem while I stayed a little longer in Paris. Before my departure, Sharon called me to suggest that I buy the *Times* of London. On the front page there was an interview with minister Sharon, who announced, "I will stay in politics until 2000."

JANUARY 1991
SCUD RAIN OVER ISRAEL

"It's fantastic to see so much rain!" Sharon exclaimed on the other end of the telephone. This was the farmer of the Negev desert and the resident of a semiarid country speaking. He feared years of drought, rejoiced when it rained—even late—and knew the importance of controlling the groundwater table. Since coming on to the political scene, Sharon had also devised enormous projects to desalinate brackish water, to the benefit of Palestinians and Jordanians—who all needed water as much as the Israelis did.

That rainy night in January 1991, however, when Sharon called me from his farm, he was less concerned with water than with fire. Once the United States and its allies sent their troops to attack Kuwait and drive back the Iraqi invader, Saddam Hussein had unleashed a deluge of ground-to-ground Scud missiles, virtually all of them aimed at the residential districts of Tel Aviv and its surroundings. The wailing of sirens sent inhabitants, wearing gas masks, hurrying into airtight shelters; it was feared that Saddam would equip his missiles with chemical or biological warheads. For the first time in the history of their country, Israelis were the target of bombing in the very heart of their land. Traumatized, tens of thousands of citizens fled to wait until the war was over—to Jerusalem, Eilat, the Negev, Galilee or, in the case of the most privileged, to foreign ski resorts. "Our house is full of refugees," Ariel explained. "Friends of my sons, some of our friends. It's ridiculous!"

As a member of the Shamir government's security cabinet, Sharon was angered by the inaction imposed on our forces to please the powerful American ally. "It's an attack on our power of dissuasion," he thundered. "Every day the cabinet discusses how we should respond, and every day they decide not to make a decision!"

One evening when I took Sharon to inspect the damage wrought by a Scud missile at Ramat Gan, one of the locals took him to task: "Why don't you do something?" Sharon retorted, "You should ask the prime minister that question." The soothing declarations of Yitzhak Shamir, his defense minister Moshe Arens and the army leaders gave the impression that a response was imminent; in reality, we were paralyzed because the Americans had persuaded our prime minister to let them destroy the missiles. Yet it was our cities that were being attacked, and the only solution the United States gave us was their ground-to-air Patriot missiles, which were supposed to intercept Scuds before they fell. But the collisions of missiles and countermissiles caused even more damage.

Meanwhile, Palestinians in the West Bank were dancing for joy on the roofs of their houses and were chanting, "Long live Saddam! Hit Tel Aviv!" while their leader Yasser Arafat went to Baghdad to demonstrate his support for Saddam Hussein. As for the survivors of the Shoah and their descendants, they were wearing gas masks in their Jewish state. During this first Gulf war, President George Bush and his secretary of state James Baker had put us in grave danger by forbidding us to respond, so as not to alienate the Arab countries that were against Iraq. "And we are the ones who will pay the price of that uncertain alliance," Sharon commented.

At the end of Operation Desert Storm, Arik rejoiced that the Americans had stopped their offensive before taking Baghdad and that they had left Saddam Hussein in power. "Otherwise Israel would have paid an even greater price—if they had caused the fall of an Arab leader, the United States would have tried to win back approval from the Arab world by demanding that Israel make large concessions to the Palestinians," he said.

History gave the son of the victor of the first Gulf war, President George W. Bush, the role of overthrowing the Iraqi dictator in 2003. This time Prime Minister Sharon took precautions and promised discreet but concrete assistance to the American forces, in return for the assurance that no Iraqi missile or plane would threaten Israeli soil.

1993–1994
ARAFAT RETURNS

In 1982, the IDF had successfully expelled Arafat and his 10,000 supporters from Beirut. But in August 1993 we received some astonishing news: Prime Minister and Defense Minister Yitzhak Rabin was preparing to sign the Oslo Accords, which would authorize the PLO leader to return to Eretz Israel. The following September 13, the agreement was ratified at the White House by Rabin and Peres, Rabin's minister of foreign affairs, under the aegis of Bill Clinton.

Sharon was clearly worried by this situation, which he thought would usher in a new wave of terrorism. The events that followed Yasser Arafat's arrival in Gaza in July 1994 and the creation of the Palestinian Authority confirmed his prediction. I saw just how worried he was during the traditional gathering of Pessach, which I spent with him and his family. Omri and Gilad, as well as officers from their respective units, were present. It is customary during this evening of the Passover Seder to read the Haggadah, the account of the Hebrews' enslavement and their passage out of Egypt. That night, Sharon added his own analogy: "The modern pharaoh is called Arafat. May ten plagues befall him." And he poured out the four ritual glasses of wine for each guest.

During the meal we deplored at length the inertia of the public, which wanted, against all odds, to believe in the illusory peace of Rabin and Peres. To my mind there was only one way of rousing people's consciousness: taking inspiration from Mahatma Gandhi and organizing peaceful resistance to the Oslo Accords. "Perhaps you could start a hunger strike?" I suggested. "Are you joking?" Ariel replied. "Everyone will think it's only an attempt to lose weight!" This would not be the last of the idea, however.

Sharon kept his composure even when he thought that Yitzhak Rabin was going to give Palestinians vital territories in the West Bank—the town of Maaleh Adoumim, for example. "I'll go and see Yitzhak and explain the numerous problems that would cause," he announced.

"Wouldn't it be better to let him get embroiled with Arafat so that his government will fall?" I asked.

"It's not just about him; this concerns all of us. It's a question of responsibility. It's my duty to warn him if I think his policies are dangerous, and I intend to do so, believe me."

Nothing transpired from these meetings between the two men. Since the time when they served side by side in the army, Yitzhak Rabin had had confidence in just one man in matters of security: his companion in arms Ariel Sharon. From 1993, Rabin told friends that if it had been conceivable at the time, he would have included Sharon in his government; in other words, if Sharon had been the leader of Likud, Rabin would have formed a government of national unity with him. But Likud was then in the hands of a garrulous young leader who was an expert at exploiting the media: Benjamin Netanyahu.

Rabin did not always simply accept his old friend's criticisms. Having visited one of the Jewish areas in the Gaza Strip to look into the numerous suicide bombings carried out against Israeli soldiers, Sharon didn't beat around the bush in describing the situation: "I told him that he had to build a new road to separate the traffic of the Gush Katif residents from the Palestinians. Yitzhak told me to mind my own business." Nevertheless, the following day Rabin went to the area and ordered Sharon's advice to be carried out.

You met with Yitzhak Rabin shortly before the signing of the Oslo Accords. What did you say to him?
That in principle I wasn't opposed to an agreement with the Palestinians, but that in my mind an agreement with Arafat would be a historic error of colossal proportions. That is what I thought then, and I still think so now. Unlike some of my colleagues, however, who thought that their rabid diatribes would force the head of the government to go against his word, I believed that it would be very difficult for Rabin not to execute an agreement that he had signed himself. But—and all

my efforts went in this direction during my meetings with him—I thought it possible to introduce changes to minimize the risks that our country was running.

Geographical changes?
Geographical and philosophical.

Did he listen to you at times?
Yes. I'm not saying that I had a decisive influence over him, but I think that at times he followed my advice.

In August 1995, however, you—who normally avoid ostentatious acts—went on a hunger strike in front of the prime minister's office in Jerusalem.
That's right. I wanted to bring public attention to the disastrous proportions that the agreement was taking on. Of course, one can express oneself in the Knesset, but words were not enough anymore; a powerful gesture was needed. Unfortunately, the hunger strike had less impact on opinion than I had hoped. With better organization and the involvement of the international press, the hunger strike probably would have attracted more attention.

How long did you fast?
Eight days. Lily regularly brought me water, but that's all.

Didn't Rabin invite you to his office or send you a message, given your long friendship and the help that you had so often given him?
I think I helped him.

You think?
I'm joking! Of course I helped him. But, so far as I remember, he didn't send me any kind of message during my hunger strike.

Do you remember your last meeting with him, before his assassination?
Not precisely. There was a whole series of meetings on military and security matters. Incidentally, Rabin always listened to me very carefully.

Particularly when the attacks increased?
He consulted me, as if we didn't belong to opposing parties. We discussed everything: political questions, the Middle East, problems

linked to Iran and Iraq. Our meetings also dealt with the future demarcation of the territories and with what buffer zones should be
maintained.

Was Rabin worried in the end about the future impact of the Oslo Accords?
He was anxious about the accords from the beginning. Before he went
to Washington to shake Arafat's hand on September 13, 1993, he told
me that handing over Jericho was unnecessary. That Israel could no
longer act in certain territories worried him as well. If he accepted the
idea of a Palestinian state in Gaza, he would have happily, as he said to
me, "let things drag on another 20 years in Judea-Samaria." I always
insisted on one point during our meetings: the need for a national
consensus. A peace process demands concessions; because of that, it is
almost always as painful as a war. Rabin understood that. There had to
be national unity or, at least, as great a consensus as possible, otherwise we would witness a schism in Israeli society, which would impede
the implementation of the peace process.

   I deeply regret Rabin's death. Relations between us were friendly,
or, rather, we had a mutual esteem. I think that had he survived the attack, an agreement would have released the tension. I don't say that he
was assassinated because of the disagreement between the political
parties; no party is linked to the assassination. But to resolve tensions,
you have to make bold decisions. Yitzhak Rabin hesitated, perhaps for
fear of losing power, as in 1977, or for fear of not managing to create a
large enough consensus. But sometimes you can't do everything.

*After Rabin's death, there you were helping his successor as prime minister,
Benjamin Netanyahu, to implement the Oslo Accords, despite the lack of a
national consensus.*
I never stop saying that you need to find common ground. But when
one camp thinks that it can topple the government at any moment, and
the other finds it difficult to govern with partners, you have to dare to
take sides, and Rabin didn't have the courage. He couldn't bear the
thought of being held hostage by Meretz,* and yet he also refused to be
imprisoned by Likud. There was no solution to such a dilemma. Responsibility for Rabin's death has been pinned on the Israeli right, but

---

* A small secular party on the extreme left.

neither Likud nor the nationalist camp had the slightest connection
with it. In terms of provocation and of incitement, we followed the bad
example of our opponents. Although most have fortunately been removed, the writings still remain on the walls of Jerusalem and Tel Aviv,
and along the roads leading to my farm in the Negev: "Sharon is a
murderer," "Begin is a murderer," "Begin is a war criminal" and
"Sharon is a war criminal." If Rabin had formed a coalition, everyone
would have had to make concessions, and we would have been forced
to find a common ground and make progress.

You don't regret having helped Netanyahu to win the elections against Peres?
No.

TERRORISM AND WAR

THE SAME BATTLE

A riel Sharon and I discussed the issue of terrorism during a formal interview conducted in 1998, the fiftieth anniversary of the creation of the state of Israel. At the time, many leaders underestimated the danger of terrorism. Not Sharon. Even the most unrelenting of his critics recognized his foresight on the subject. He responded to this murderous violence instantly and mercilessly, and he was the first to identify terrorism as a strategic threat as serious as "classic" conflict—if not more so.

For dozens of years you have insisted on the need to fight terrorism. Why?
Some people have tried to draw a line between issues of individual security, connected to terrorism, and the general security threats that Israel faces from Arab countries. This distinction has always seemed artificial to me, while many still see terrorism as a small local problem, an annoyance more than a truly serious problem—despite the human losses involved. Terrorism is a constant in the Middle East. Even before the creation of the state of Israel, Arabs killed Jews during the riots of 1920 to 1929 and 1936 to 1939, not to mention all the terrorist actions that have been committed over 120 years. The Shoah itself is linked to Arab terrorism of the 1930s since it encouraged the British government, then masters of the country, to publish the White Paper of 1939 that limited the number of Jewish immigrants to Palestine to 75,000 people over five years. Those were precisely the years that saw the horror of Nazism. There is no doubt that without that White Paper hundreds of thousands, even millions, of European Jews could have been saved. At the time when Jews could still escape, the doors of Eretz Israel were closed to them!

How can history have been rewritten to such an extent that terrorism officially appears for the first time only in 1967? The murders committed by Palestinian Arabs under the British Mandate, and the ones committed after the creation of the state of Israel in 1948, have been since euphemistically rechristened "infiltrations by Arab refugees." This trend is not accidental; it is deliberate and is aimed at associating Arab terrorism with the "wrong" that we have done Palestinians, who present themselves as victims—our victims—and this automatically justifies their terrorist attacks since 1967. Rubbish.

Let us also not forget that the first war in Israel's history—provoked by the aggression of Egyptian, Jordanian, Syrian, Lebanese and Iraqi armies just after our declaration of independence—was the result of terrorist acts directed against the Yishuv ever since the United Nations approved the plan to divide Palestine into two states. And so from November 1947 to May 1948, when the war of independence began, the country faced five months of barricades on major roads and bloody confrontations with the Arab inhabitants of Palestine.

At the beginning of the 1950s, the state of Israel tried to protect itself against Arab terrorism by appealing to the United Nations, but its pleas were in vain. Confined within the "Green Line,"* Israel was separated from Judea-Samaria by a 309-kilometer border in uneven, practically indefensible land. Our country was therefore forced to employ a policy of reprisal. The situation quickly became unsustainable on both sides: Israel could not live under terrorist threat, and the Arabs could not tolerate our reprisal operations. Thirty years later, Operation Peace in Galilee[†] was also a response to the PLO's terrorist activities. Far from being a localized phenomenon, Middle Eastern terrorism has global repercussions. It is a vital problem that risks provoking lasting conflicts.

Like the suicide attacks that we are witnessing today?
One can never predict the consequences of a terrorist act. Some cause 1 death, others 5, 50 or even 300 or 400 deaths; everything depends on the target. Where there are heavy losses, Israel must respond with

---

    *   The armistice lines of 1949.
    †   Israeli name for the war in Lebanon (1982).

force; Arab countries then react in turn, and the tension escalates. Terrorism hijacks the peace process, particularly agreements that have already been signed; if Israel is forced to resort to reprisals, our treaties with Egypt and Jordan are undermined. Israel could also find itself confronting serious problems: What if Syria provides missiles to terrorists in Lebanon, Nablus or Ramallah? What if, in an escalating situation, Egypt decides to send additional forces into the Sinai, in contravention of the peace treaty? These might seem apparently minor, even insignificant, incidents, but a terrorist act can create a serious dilemma. To those who claim that "we must live with terrorism" or that "terrorism will always exist," I reply that things are not so simple. So long as there is terrorism, there cannot be peace in the region.

The Arabs claim that we, too, are terrorists. An Israeli television channel broadcast a film called Biladi, Biladi,* *which claims that Palestinian terrorism is a response to Israeli terrorism.*
That supposedly objective stance is in fact pure and simple propaganda. If ever our situation gets worse—and I hope that it does not—the makers of that film, which distorts the facts and questions the historic right of our people to their native land, will know that they are among those principally responsible for our suffering.

For more than 50 years you have fought terrorism with reprisal operations. In 1971, in the Gaza Strip, you eliminated terrorism within a couple of months and for a duration of 15 years; in August 1982 you expelled Arafat and his hooligans from Beirut. How do you explain your meetings with Abu Mazen and Abu Ala?† They figured among the leaders of the PLO and were lieutenants of Arafat. Have you also given in to fear of terrorism?
I have neither folded before terrorism nor changed my mind one iota in regard to this plague. However, it seemed imperative to me that we explain our position to the Palestinian Arabs, with whom we must live. I decided to meet these men when I understood that after so many years of negotiation since the signing of the Oslo Accords, Israelis of both the left and the right still cherished their illusions; ei-

---

* "My country, my country" in Arabic.
† War names of Mahmoud Abbas (president of the Palestinian Authority) and Ahmed Qorei (his former prime minister).

ther from naïveté or to protect various interests, they never offered the Palestinians the foundation of a serious settlement. I always refused to meet Arafat for a precise reason: because he personally ordered the assassination of civilians—Jewish and Israeli women, children and old people, as well as Israeli citizens of other faiths such as the Druzes and the bedouin who serve in the Israeli army. That does not prevent me from thinking that it is vital for the Palestinians to know our point of view. We have to define what is possible and also—above all—what is not. Either we decide that we don't want an agreement or we play the game and, as I think we should, make a sincere effort. That involves above all setting things out clearly and trying to understand the other's point of view. The Palestinian leaders that I have met are neither the "righteous among nations" nor choirboys. Their ideology and their actions have caused much suffering, but, despite their not very respectable past, they have not personally ordered bloody attacks. This is my criterion. Are these meetings likely to weaken our position? I acknowledge that they undoubtedly will. If I reveal that I am willing to talk to them, some people could conclude that anyone can negotiate with anyone. I weighed up the pros and the cons before organizing these meetings, and I think that I have made the right decision.

What was the attitude of our government leaders toward Palestinian terrorism? Yitzhak Rabin, for example.
He was clearly against terrorism. But he was among those who believed, mistakenly in my view, that one had to distinguish between national defense and the question of terrorism. I am convinced that since the 1950s these aspects of our survival have been indivisible.

In 1985 you criticized the government's reaction to the massacre of 20 Jews by Palestinians in an Istanbul synagogue. Then came the Intifada. Rabin, who was minister of defense at the time, did not agree with the measures that you were calling for, and the issue that divided you resurfaced.
Rabin committed a fundamental mistake.

Did you tell him?
Repeatedly.

He didn't want to listen to you, or he didn't understand?
Rabin wasn't infallible. He made mistakes, like everyone, and he was wrong on this point. He wasn't the only one not to realize the true nature of the first Intifada in 1987. At the time Shamir also said to him, "It's a passing wave—a little wave of violence."

Was Shamir head of the government in 1987?
Yes. Neither he nor Rabin took the incident seriously, despite the warnings of the security service against a policy of waiting and withdrawing.

Warnings that were issued several months before the start of the Intifada?
Yes. Prime Minister Shamir and Defense Minister Rabin underestimated the importance of the problem. I told them that we were facing a new situation, but they replied, "No, it's only a passing fever." Shamir was prepared to go all the way in terms of measures against terrorism; the problem was that a coalition government is based on cooperation between individuals. The bigger your personal prestige, the greater the credibility assigned to your views; a coalition works differently. In short, the government of the time did not take the threat seriously.

Was Menachem Begin more rigorous in the fight against terrorism?
Shamir was as resolute as Begin on the need to fight terrorism. One must not forget that since the Yom Kippur war Israel slowly lost the independence—in a relative but real way—that even a small country can enjoy.

In what sense?
Regarding the United States, for example. On the one hand, the links between the two nations have strengthened. We have come a long way from the 1960s when President Kennedy refused to receive Ben-Gurion in Washington, despite his stature as a leader, but would agree only to meet him in New York. On the other hand, some of our government leaders have made Israel excessively dependent on our powerful ally.

(right) *The famous 101 unit.*

(below) *1948. The war of independence. Sharon serving in the Haganah, the Jewish defense army.*

(below) *March 1955. David Ben-Gurion inspects the paratroopers of the 890th battalion; Sharon is on his left. Only the right-hand side of the photo was published: at the time, the very existence of this unit and the identity of its leader, Ariel Sharon, were kept secret.*

(left) *The best officers of the 890th battalion, who distinguished themselves during the reprisal raids of the 1950s. Top left is Meir Har-Tzion, Sharon's brother-in-arms.*

(right) *On October 31, 1956, we fell into an ambush on the Mitla Pass.*

(left) 1956. *Ariel and Margalit, his first wife, pregnant with their son Gur.*

(left) June 1967. *Sharon in the Sinai desert after the victorious Six Day War.*

(right) *With Gur, his eldest son, who died at the age of 11.*

(above) *October 1973. The Yom Kippur war.*

(left) *October 17, 1973. Sharon is wounded.*

October 17, 1973, 1600 hours: *"Moses returning to Egypt." Moshe Dayan and Ariel Sharon disembark on the western bank of the Suez Canal.*

WANTED

(right) *Caricature that appeared in* Ma'ariv.

(below left) *Ariel Sharon and me on the bank of the Suez.*

(below right) *The general resting.*

(above) *Lily, Vera, Ariel, Gilad, and Omri Sharon on the occasion of Gilad's bar-mitzvah.*

(right) *1978. The creation of the Elon-Moreh settlement in the West Bank.*

(below) *May 19, 1981. Ariel Sharon, minister of agriculture, and Anwar el-Sadat in the presidential palace of Cairo. This is the only existing photo of the meeting.*

(left) *June 1981. The whole Israeli government in a plane with Menahem Begin and Anwar el-Sadat, after the meeting at Sharm el-Sheikh.*

(right) *1982. Sharon and me in front of the Beaufort castle, citadel of the crusades in southern Lebanon during "Operation Peace in Galilee."*

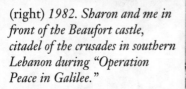

(left) *June 1982. Yitzhak Rabin asks Sharon to help him intensify the siege of West Beirut. Two friends united in the aim of defending Israel.*

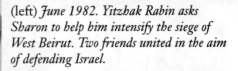

(right) *1982. Sharon negotiating with the American diplomats Philip Habib and Morris Draper, in the company of General Abrasha Tamir, in the villa on the heights of Beirut.*

(above) *August 30, 1982. Arafat expelled from Beirut, in the sights of the IDF's elite marksmen. Prime Minister Menahem Begin had promised Ronald Reagan that he would not try to assassinate the PLO leader.*

(left) *Beirut, September 1982. Dinner with Philip Habib to celebrate Arafat's expulsion, in the company of all the international "mediators."*

With Bashir Gemayel, shortly before his assassination.

January 1, 1983. Liz Taylor, with Ariel, Lily, and Dr. Boleslav Goldman.

(above) *Official trip to Zaire: "Tell them we are the Malian delegation!"*

(right) *"Operation Desert Storm," which began on January 17, 1991.*

(left) *Sharon made this declaration to me on October 10, 1998. It was a promise he kept.*

(above) *Audience with Pope John-Paul II in the Vatican.*

(right) *February 6, 2001, 2202 hours: Ariel Sharon has just learned that he has been elected prime minister.*

(below) *Blair House, Washington: I interview Sharon after his meeting with George W. Bush.*

(below) *March 10, 2001. My "collector's" menu sticking out of Sharon's pocket as he introduces me to the President of the United States.*

URI DAN **KIPPUR**

(above) *I waited 30 years before making public the photos I took during the Yom Kippur war.*

(left) *Born in a moshav, Ariel Sharon thought of himself above all as a farmer.*

(below) *September 2005. Exclusive interview in the office of the prime minister.*

(right) *A moment of contemplation before the grave of his second wife, Lily, who rests on the Hill of Anenomes on Sycamore Farm.*

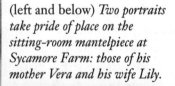

(left and below) *Two portraits take pride of place on the sitting-room mantelpiece at Sycamore Farm: those of his mother Vera and his wife Lily.*

OCTOBER 1998
THE WYE PLANTATION AGREEMENT

"I will never shake Arafat's hand," Arik told me in October 1998, the day he became minister of foreign affairs. I thought that this statement—although hardly surprising to those who knew him—would interest the *New York Post*, for which I was the Israel correspondent. The following day it was on the paper's front page, above a photo of Sharon.

Two years after he was elected, Benjamin Netanyahu finally acknowledged that Sharon was the best person to handle Israeli diplomacy. From the moment that he took office, the new minister of foreign affairs was subjected to strong pressures from the Americans to agree to a further withdrawal from the West Bank, while Arafat continued to orchestrate attacks against Israel. President Clinton organized a summit meeting at the Wye Plantation, near Washington, D.C., with Arafat and Netanyahu, who wanted Sharon to accompany him. It was bound to be a difficult negotiation.

I was also in Washington to cover the event. My cell phone rang while I was dining at McCormick & Schmick's, an excellent seafood restaurant. It was Sharon. He had just emerged from a reception and recounted, in an amused tone, the first contact between the summit participants: "Clinton, Secretary of State Madeleine Albright, CIA Director George Tenet, Netanyahu and I were already in the dining room when Arafat and his delegation entered. Arafat shook hands with the Americans, and then with Netanyahu. When he reached me, I looked away and ignored the hand he was holding out. He hesitated a moment, his hand stretched out, and then I saw him from the corner of my eye execute a military salute." Arik said this in confidence, and he knew that he didn't have to remind me not to quote him.

Sharon added that during the conversation, while everyone was advancing their pawns, he had declared that if there were peace, Israel planned to construct a railway between the Gaza Strip and the West Bank. Arafat leaped up and exclaimed that he was a trained engineer, and that he had been involved in a similar project in Kuwait. He had said the same thing when Sharon had spoken of the plan for a large port in Gaza. Addressing Clinton, Sharon had then specified, "I will know that peace has come the day that I can order a John Deere tractor from the United States and have it sent to Ariel Sharon, Sycamore Farm, via the port of Gaza. That would be possible, however, only if the Palestinians stop assassinating the Jews and inciting hatred against them."

During the nine days of the Wye Plantation summit, Sharon evaded all the ruses to make him shake Arafat's hand. An Arab member of the Knesset, one of Arafat's advisers, spread the rumor that the handshake had occurred, and, in spite of all the denials, the Israeli press instantly concluded that Sharon had followed in the footsteps of Rabin, Peres and Netanyahu.

At the time, Bill Clinton and Madeleine Albright were pushing for new Israeli withdrawals from the West Bank, withdrawals of around 11 to 13 percent. Sharon's presence helped Netanyahu resist this pressure and insist on a withdrawal carried out in sections of 2 or 3 percent, according to a prearranged timetable and accompanied by mutual concessions: seizure of the illegal weapons held by Hamas and other terrorist organizations, cessation of incitement and so on. The principle of territorial concessions was therefore enshrined. Sharon declared himself ready to accept such concessions, but only on condition that the Palestinians respect the rule of reciprocity—while doubting that Yasser Arafat would honor the terms.

During the Wye summit, Clinton also promised to announce the release of Jonathan Pollard, so as to allow Netanyahu to explain the territorial concessions. In fact, Pollard was the main bargaining chip of the summit. This U.S. Navy intelligence service analyst had noticed that information that should have been given to the Israeli government under a bilateral agreement with the United States was not in fact being transmitted. He decided, on his own initiative, to put himself at Israel's service. When the FBI uncovered his secret activities in 1985, Pollard requested asylum at the Israeli embassy in Washington, but he was refused. He was sentenced to life in prison without parole for having passed secret information to an allied state. Since then, the issue of Pollard's release had arisen in every Israeli election campaign. In 1995, Yitzhak Rabin was the first to talk about opening negotiations for Pollard's release, but his efforts were in vain.

Sixteen hours before the official signing of the Wye Plantation agreement at the White House, George Tenet threatened to resign if Clinton carried out his promise to release Pollard. Netanyahu then consulted the members of his delegation to decide whether they should sign the agreement. Sharon was against it, since Clinton could no longer honor his word, but he was in the minority.

The next day, a Friday afternoon, the cream of the American administration was at the White House. Clinton's public relations advisers wanted to label the event a "historic turnaround in relations between Israel and the Palestinians." Whereas the Oslo Accords were content with Arafat's fine words in exchange for territorial concessions, the Wye Plantation agreement outlined Arafat's commitments precisely. King Hussein of Jordan left the Mayo Clinic, where he had been undergoing treatment for cancer, and, frail and white, came to validate the Israeli-Palestinian agreement with his presence.

Now these commitments had to be put into practice. Sharon managed to persuade the organizers of the Wye Plantation summit to address the issue of the Palestinian leader's incitement, which was visible throughout the press, on children's television programs, in movies and elsewhere. For Israel, this was the heart of the problem: all means should be used to eradicate anti-Israeli sentiment among the Palestinian population. Bill Clinton and Madeleine Albright, who had notably discovered the existence of army training camps for Palestinian children in Gaza, lent their support. Thus the creation of a tripartite American, Israeli and Palestinian commission charged with studying the issue figured in the final text of the Wye agreement.

On December 1, 1998, I received a call from Sharon, who was telephoning from an airport. "Uri, I want you to lead the Israeli delegation on the commission."

"But how can I fit that in with my full-time job as a journalist?"

"Figure it out, do what you have to do, but I want you to look after the commission." He added, "I'm waiting for the governor of Texas, George W. Bush. I've decided to take him on a helicopter ride over Judea-Samaria to explain the link between the settlements and Israel's security." Even Sharon, with his fertile imagination, could not foresee the implications that this meeting would have in years to come.

For the moment, the Democratic administration tried to implement the Wye Plantation agreement, in particular the Israeli withdrawal from the West Bank. Bill Clinton came to Jerusalem in person. In a historic first, he also went to the Gaza Strip. On December 15, Ariel, the political correspondent of the state radio station Kol Israel and I were all watching the live television broadcast of the landing of the *Marine One* helicopter at Gaza airport, where the American head of state was received with great pomp by the president of the Palestinian Authority and his entourage. It was planned that Arafat would announce on this occasion the removal of the clause in the Palestinian charter calling for Israel's destruction. But Arafat's words were, as usual, ambiguous, and the charter was not amended. From his armchair Sharon commented that Clinton was doing all he could to assist the negotiations between Israel and Palestine but that "Arafat is still Arafat." We knew from a CIA report that Arafat had done absolutely nothing as yet to confiscate illegal weapons held by Hamas, Islamic Jihad and other armed groups.

The American president engineered another meeting between Netanyahu and Arafat in the industrial zone of Erez, at the border of the Gaza Strip. Sharon was also present and gave Bill Clinton an inventory of the Palestinian arms that Arafat was supposed to collect— thousands of weapons and explosives that the Palestinians used less than two years later when the second Intifada got underway. Again Arafat, the master of doublespeak, promised to respect his side of the Wye agreement. "If he collects the weapons, he will get new territory; if he doesn't, he will get nothing," declared Netanyahu and Sharon in unison.

A gala dinner, with hundreds of guests, at the Hilton in Jerusalem concluded the U.S. president's visit. Everyone wanted to be optimistic, including Sharon and his wife. I joined them to listen to the speeches of Netanyahu and Clinton. Lily indicated to me with her eyes a guest sitting at their table, and I recognized Aharon Barak, president of the Israeli supreme court, who in 1982 was one of the three members of the Kahan commission of inquiry and who, according to Arik, played a determining role in the decision to remove his defense portfolio. I whispered in Lily's ear: "Barak didn't want Sharon as minister of defense; now he's got him as minister of foreign affairs."

FEBRUARY 1999
LILY IS ILL

One fine afternoon in February, Arik called and asked me to meet him at once. The anxiety in his voice alarmed me. I was in the middle of a meeting with an old paratrooper colleague but excused myself and rushed to Tel Aviv, to the ministry of national infrastructure, which Sharon was heading along with the department of foreign affairs. His devoted secretary Sarah smiled at me sadly before she announced me. Sitting at his desk, wearing a dark suit, Sharon had never looked so lonely. Without pausing to offer me my customary drink—black coffee and a glass of soda water—he leaned forward and said in a subdued voice, "Lily has cancer."

Stunned, I sat down.

"She wasn't feeling well recently," he went on. "We went to the hospital this morning. The doctors diagnosed lung cancer and advised her to undergo more tests in New York. We're leaving this evening. Thank you for coming." There was nothing to add. Ariel simply wanted to share his pain with a friend who had supported him in the most tragic moments of his private life—Margalit's and Gur's deaths, and now Lily's illness.

Lily was Ariel Sharon's secret weapon. She had taken on the extraordinary challenge of raising children in a normal, affectionate family atmosphere with a husband who was continually in the middle of a storm, first military and then public and then political. She had built a fortress to protect her family from the hatred of the crowds demonstrating in front of their property touting banners that read, "Begin is a murderer" and "Sharon is a murderer." Lily and Arik gave each other strength. Their story was one of biblical dimensions: two people determined to face life together through all its troubles.

✡

In January 1999, along with other journalists, I covered Ariel's trips to Moscow and Paris. Our ambassador in France, Eliahu Ben Elissar, informed Sharon that the reception scheduled at the town hall had been canceled by order of the French government. The government offered Sharon, who was the Israeli foreign affairs minister, only an official meeting at the Quai d'Orsay with his counterpart Hubert Védrine—indicating that the government was reluctant to receive Sharon. Taking this as an affront to his dignity and to the state of Israel, Ariel told me that he was going to cancel his visit. I advised him against that; it was exactly the reaction that the French hoped for. Instead of falling into the trap, Sharon should meet Hubert Védrine and explain to him just how counterproductive France's pro-Arab and pro-Palestinian stance was.

Emerging from the Quai d'Orsay, Sharon told me that he had firmly denounced France's hypocritical policy toward Israel, ever since General de Gaulle's embargo ordered in 1967, before the Six Day War: "I reminded Védrine that instead of giving us the 50 Mirages that cost 50 million dollars, the French government sold them to Libya, and in 1973, Gadhafi gave them to Egypt as his modest contribution to the Yom Kippur war." But Sharon did more than just settle old scores. He also spoke about the possibilities of a balanced French policy that promoted agreement among Israelis, Palestinians and Jordanians. For example, by participating in Sharon's great desalination project, France would contribute to cooperation between Israelis and Arabs in a region where the scarcity of drinking water risked causing serious conflict.

In Moscow, Sharon received a much warmer welcome; post-Soviet Russia wanted to strengthen its relations with Israel. The Israeli delegation stayed in the President Hotel, reserved for the Kremlin's official guests, and Sharon attended the traditional Bolshoi ballet in a box reserved for VIPs. Lily was in seventh heaven.

One of the guests that Sharon met at the gala dinner given in his honor was a young, elegant man with an inscrutable face. His name was Vladimir Putin, a former high-ranking KGB officer. Meir Dagan, Netanyahu's antiterrorist adviser, was sitting next to Sharon. It was around this table that the man who would be elected president of the

Russian Federation in less than two years and the man who would lead the government of Israel in three years had their first conversation. At the time, they spoke of developing cooperation in the fight against Islamic terrorism. Moscow was worried about the subversive action of terrorists in the Muslim ex-Soviet republics. Putin explained that Arab terrorists were passing through Jordan to infiltrate Chechnya, where the rebels were helped by a still little known Islamist group called al-Qaeda, directed by a certain Bin Laden. Dagan, who spoke Russian, told me that Sharon had promised Putin that he would pass on the information gathered by the Israeli secret service to Russia.

That constituted an extraordinary change in the relationship between the two countries. For 25 years Arafat had enjoyed unconditional Soviet support; PLO terrorists, trained by the KGB, used weapons that had been supplied by the Kremlin against Israel. And here was Sharon, the PLO's fiercest enemy of all time, playing the role of Russia's special ally in its war against Islamic terrorism. Years later, when President Putin called Prime Minister Sharon to offer his condolences following a suicide attack against Israeli civilians, he said, "You don't need to tell me about Arafat; I know him inside out."

✡

Despite her illness, Lily continued to accompany her husband on his trips abroad. She took the opportunity to visit museums and art galleries. The Sharons were used to keeping their problems away from the public eye, and they did all that they could to lead a normal life. They had also never allowed national affairs to get in the way of their agricultural enterprise. Sycamore Farm flourished despite its difficult beginnings, plagued by droughts and lack of manpower. The two boys also helped out and accompanied their parents in their walks around the property.

I met Ariel and Lily at the Park Lane Hotel in New York at the end of that particularly cold February in 1999; we had breakfast in the hotel's luminous dining room. The results of the tests carried out at the Sloan-Kettering Cancer Center showed that Lily could be treated in Israel. Pale but smiling, Lily refused to talk about her illness and announced that she planned to go to the Metropolitan Museum to see an exhibition. I felt that she wanted above all to calm Arik, who, his eyes misty, was full of attention to her. Arik even accepted with good grace her insistence, once again, that he ate too much and should go on a diet.

I was reminded of another meal, 15 or so years earlier. Arik had just won his defamation trial against *Time* magazine, and we were celebrating that great moral victory, for which we had waited almost two years, with a dinner at his cousin Maya's. During the evening Lily had started singing a popular Israeli song, "The World Is a Narrow Bridge," and Arik had joined in the chorus, "And what counts is not to fear." Ariel Sharon was driven by two motors: his love for Eretz Israel, and his love for his wife and family. Today Lily was his first concern. He wanted above all to support her in her fight against illness.

✡

Sharon told me that Netanyahu hoped to initiate secret negotiations with the Syrian president Hafez el-Assad and had asked Sharon to make contact with foreign mediators in New York. Sharon advised Netanyahu to demand a total peace agreement with Syria in exchange for concessions on the Golan Heights, which would nonetheless allow Israel to keep strategic control of the Hula Valley and Lake Tiberias. Sharon had also warned Netanyahu that he was making a mistake: such an initiative would not diminish American pressure on the question of concessions to the Palestinians, while Yasser Arafat had still not fulfilled the obligations of the Wye Plantation agreement.

For my part, I related to Sharon what happened at the tripartite Israeli, Palestinian and American meetings. Despite the efforts of Dennis Ross and Aaron Miller from the State Department, and the efforts of the Israeli delegation, the Palestinians had not changed: incitement against Israel continued unabated in their media and school textbooks.

We ended our breakfast in New York when Sharon's communications adviser brought him a review of the Israeli press. The headline in the left-wing daily *Haaretz*, his fierce opponent, claimed that Ariel was suspected of having received or given bribes during his visit to Moscow to gain business for Israel; the paper stated that he would be questioned by police on his return from the United States. "Always the same lies," Sharon sighed, putting the pile of clippings to one side.

Lily flared up: "They want your hide!"

Arik tried to calm her: "Don't take it so much to heart, Lily. It's only gossip."

Nonetheless, in Israel the law was waiting resolutely for him. The day of his return, Sharon underwent nine hours of interrogation, during which radio bulletins went out every hour, the media speculating as if Sharon had already been judged and condemned. Emerging from the police station at 9 P.M., Arik called me from the car that was to take him home: "The interrogators barely know what they're talking about. I had to give them a lesson on how countries establish relations and on my mission as minister of foreign affairs to improve relations between Israel and Russia. They seemed more ignorant than hostile. When they decided to suspend the interrogation because of the lateness of the hour, I demanded that they continue, all night if need be, so that we could be done with this business."

These allegations, publicized in *Haaretz* and taken up by other papers, were based on the testimony of a legal adviser from Sharon's ministry, who was piqued that his boss had lost confidence in him. As for the police, some officers had wanted to use a "Sharon affair" to gain a promotion. Eventually the story died down, although Likud had been damaged by it.

The approaching general elections in 1999 saw Netanyahu losing speed and authority. The security services even dared go against his will by refusing to close Orient House, the headquarters of the Palestinian leadership in east Jerusalem. Yaacov "Yasha" Kedmi, head of the section dealing with the former Soviet Union, noisily resigned, making serious accusations about the prime minister, and then joined Ehud Barak, who won the election.

Meanwhile, between treatment sessions at the hospital, Lily supported Arik as best she could, never once complaining. And so she accompanied him to Rome, where he was to carry out his last mission as minister of foreign affairs by having an audience with the pope. Shortly before this important visit, Lily took to her hotel room in great pain. Nevertheless, she was ready at the allotted hour to accompany her husband to the Vatican.

John Paul II warmly welcomed the Israeli delegation. Sharon invited the pope to visit the "Promised Land" and gave him a 300-year-old card of Eretz Israel, entitled *Terra Promessa*. "Terra Sancta," added the pope. "Holy land for everyone, but promised for the Jewish people." He announced his intention of traveling to Jerusalem in a year's time, on the occasion of the beginning of the third millennium of the Christian era. A scoop for a journalist such as myself.

During their long private interview, the pope revealed a particular interest in the peace process. Sharon assured him that if Arafat ended his reign of terror, Israel would surprise the Palestinians by their willingness to reach an agreement. "We want peace," Sharon told the pope; "but we won't give in to terrorism." Then, speaking of the pope's next visit to Israel, Sharon reminded him that the Bible was the best tour guide, since place-names had not changed, from Mount Tabor to Bethlehem and from Jordan to Jerusalem. John Paul II accompanied us to the door of his receiving room and said, as he took leave of us, "Next year in Jerusalem." We ended the day on the beautiful Piazza di Spagna, a moment of enjoyment and optimism culled from the menacing shadow of Lily's cancer.

Five months after Barak's electoral victory over Netanyahu, the state attorney Elyakim Rubinstein published his conclusions on the "corruption" affair. Rubinstein found nothing in the dossier that the police had submitted to him that incriminated Sharon. The damage, however, was done. Sharon's name was tarnished, Likud had fallen, and I ask myself what it cost Ariel and Lily in terms of health.

It was in the midst of this difficult situation that their house burned down in December 1999. Learning of the disaster, I immediately telephoned from the United States. Lily answered from her car, bravely hiding her suffering. She told me that when he told her about the fire, her son Gilad had said that he had two lots of news for her: the bad news being that all her clothes had been destroyed by the fire, and the good news being that she could buy herself a new wardrobe. She concluded humorously, "Now everyone will know that we have a warm house."

Soon, however, it was Lily's illness that took precedence. Ariel knew that his wife's days were numbered. At 2:30 in the morning Arik called me from the hospital: "Lily has just dozed off. I'm going to try to get a few hours' sleep. I want to be beside her when she wakes around six. She's in terrible pain." Even in normal times Sharon would call me in the early hours of the morning. He knew that he would find me awake—not because I suffer from insomnia but because, as the Israeli correspondent for the *New York Post*, I lived on American time.

The nights from January to March 2000 were not normal for Sharon. They were the hardest nights of his life since the deaths of Margalit in 1962 and of their son Gur in 1967. He spent the nights at the Sheba-Tel Hashomer hospital at Lily's bedside, knowing that her death was inevitable and that he was powerless in the face of it. On my visits to the hospital, I found him at Lily's bedside—sometimes passing his hand tenderly over her pain-wracked face and over her hair, sometimes sleeping in his chair. Lily would whisper, "Don't wake him. He's so tired."

Sharon took a room in a hotel next to the hospital. Once Lily fell asleep, with the aid of powerful analgesics, he called me at dawn to go over the events of the previous evening. Despite the deterioration of her health, Lily urged him not to abandon his political role as the leader of Likud and the head of the parliamentary opposition. His workday began once he left his wife's bedside a little after six in the morning. So far as the public was concerned, nothing in his behavior betrayed the tragedy that he lived daily and that would last nearly three months. Even I, his close friend, found it hard to imagine what emotions raged beneath such self-control. I asked Sharon where he got the superhuman strength in order to live in two worlds—his head in political affairs and his heart with Lily. He replied, "If there is a superhuman strength, it's Lily's in her fight against illness. She is an incredibly courageous woman. A fighter."

In March 2000, while I was covering the pope's visit to Jerusalem, I called Lily in her hospital room. She was following the historic trip on television and commented, "The pope kept his promise to come to Jerusalem. I'm sorry that I can't be at Arik's side to welcome him." I didn't know it at the time, but that would be the last I heard Lily's voice. At midnight on Friday, Arik called me and announced flatly, "Lily is dead. We were all gathered around her bed—Omri and Gilad, Inbal, the grandchildren, and the rest of the family. She went calmly and with dignity, as she wanted. There's no point in coming here now. The funeral will be on Sunday on the Hill of Anemones."

The first news bulletins that morning announced Lily's death. The commentators predicted that it would influence Sharon's political future. Lily and Sharon were so closely linked, they said, that Sharon wouldn't have the heart to continue. The media was so keen to bury

Sharon politically that they didn't have the decency to respect his mourning. It made me sick. When the main interviewer of Kol Israel called me live during a broadcast, he was undoubtedly astonished to hear me say, "Lily and Arik were like a tree firmly planted in their Negev farm. A stormy wind has broken one of the main branches of the tree, but the trunk stays solid and will resist the storms to come." A minute later, the strangled voice of Sharon was on the phone: "Thanks, Uri, for what you just said. I'll see you this afternoon at the funeral."

A large crowd surrounded Sycamore Farm's Hill of Anemones: people from every part of Israel, of every social class and every age— everyone who had had the privilege of meeting this exceptional couple. Lily and Arik loved walking on this hill, beyond the prickly pear hedge, especially when the anemones were in flower. There, before a freshly dug grave, Sharon said goodbye in a broken voice to his favorite anemone.

During *shiva*, the week of mourning, the Sharon family received people who came to offer their condolences in a huge tent decorated for the occasion. From Prime Minister Ehud Barak to average citizens, all were welcomed with the same courtesy. Yet as he listened to them, Arik sometimes had an absent air, as though he were elsewhere.

SEPTEMBER 28, 2000
CONTROVERSIAL VISIT
TO THE TEMPLE MOUNT

From a chronological and historical perspective, Ariel Sharon's visit to the Temple Mount preceded his accession to power on February 6, 2001, when, for the first time and against all expectations, he was elected head of the Israeli government. In fact, there is a close link between the visit and the election. Secular, like me, but respectful of Jewish tradition, Sharon nonetheless was careful not to establish any mystical or biblical connection between that controversial visit and his election as prime minister four months later. When he decided to go to the Temple Mount, Sharon's aim was above all to send a message to Prime Minister Ehud Barak, who planned to give Yasser Arafat access to this most sacred of places for the Jewish people.

✡

On Sunday, September 24, 2000, at around 4 P.M., Sharon called me from New York while I was in Jerusalem with a friend of ours, a foremost expert on the Arab world in general and on the Palestinians in particular. Sharon wanted to discuss a project we had already talked about: a visit to the Temple Mount, which would block any thought on Barak's part to make concessions. Sharon's mind was made up: "I'm going to be interviewed on Kol Israel in an hour. Listen and you'll hear me announce my intention to go to the Temple Mount next Thursday, the day after my return to Israel." We rejoiced at the stand he was taking. Hopefully, it would alert the public to the fact that Ehud Barak was about to renounce Israel's absolute sovereignty over the Temple Mount, which had been recovered in 1967 almost two millennia after the Romans had chased us from it.

As the head of Likud, Sharon was then leader of the opposition in the Knesset. The question of the Temple Mount had preoccupied him since the failure of the second Camp David summit the previous July, between Barak and Arafat, under the aegis of Bill Clinton. I had covered the meeting for the *New York Post,* and Sharon had telephoned me from time to time in my hotel in Washington to know how events were unfolding. Sharon was dubious about Barak's proposal to give Arafat sovereignty of the Temple Mount esplanade if Arafat agreed to recognize Israeli sovereignty of the Western Wall and its foundations, where the remains of the Temple were buried. Barak believed that he could put an end to Israeli-Palestinian conflict with this unprecedented concession—although Yasser Arafat, true to form, always had the audacity to claim that there had never been a Jewish sanctuary on the Temple Mount. This didn't wash with Bill Clinton, however, who immediately quoted to Arafat passages of the New Testament that mentioned the Temple of Jerusalem. Barak went one better: "When Jesus roamed the streets of Jerusalem, when he lifted his head he didn't see church bells or minarets but only the Jewish Temple!"

During our telephone conversations, Sharon did not hide his anger: "Barak is making all these proposals to Arafat without having received the backing of the government, and certainly not of the Knesset." To which Barak would have retorted that submitting his proposals to the Knesset was futile without first obtaining Arafat's agreement. Using the same method, which he believed was very shrewd, Barak never confirmed—any more than his government did—what the Israeli media were repeating so enthusiastically: that in giving Arafat control of the Temple Mount, "Barak was moving the peace process toward an agreement with the Palestinians."

One day in August 2000, Sharon invited me to join him at the Jerusalem Hilton (today the David Citadel Hotel) to discuss Barak's maneuvers. We had just attended the funeral of the Israeli ambassador to Paris, Eliahu Ben Elissar, who had died suddenly. Sharon was accompanied by his spokesman, Raanan Gissin. "The problem with Barak," Sharon observed, "is that he continues to negotiate despite the failure of Camp David. Who knows what new concessions he'll agree to in order to make peace with Arafat no matter what. The public doesn't care. People believe that peace is in progress, and they continue to enjoy their summer holidays in peace and quiet."

"You should wake up the public and make sure that this attempt to use the Temple Mount as a bargaining chip fails."

"I'm ready to do it, but how? Give me some ideas." That was Sharon's way of working, to listen to a variety of ideas and then to decide alone which one he would follow and to assume responsibility for it.

I suggested that Sharon hold a weekly press conference in front of the Western Wall, accompanied by Likud members, during which he would denounce Barak's proposals. I was sure that the local and foreign media would pick up the story.

"Note that down," Sharon told Gissin, who was armed with his notebook and pen. When, at the beginning of September, I asked Arik why he hadn't yet done anything in this direction, he replied that he had been too busy. Shortly thereafter he went to New York to meet the foremost leaders of the Jewish community. During a meeting with Syrian Jews, he expressed concern that the foreign press, influenced by Palestinian propaganda, used the Arab term "Haram el-Sharif" for the Temple Mount. Some of those present said that they were prepared to publish entire pages of press releases explaining the importance of this sacred place for Jews.

Sharon remained firmly convinced that our sovereignty over the Temple was the fundamental basis for Israel's sovereignty over Jerusalem. He had headed the ministry of industry and commerce in the mid-1980s, when Arab rioters threw stones at the Jews coming to pray on the Mount. Sharon was the only minister to go there then; he invited me to join him at six o'clock in the morning. I still have the photo of that visit, at dawn on a freezing day. For Sharon, it was not a provocation but a confirmation of Israeli sovereignty over the site. He sought to prevent the Palestinians' attack on Jews praying at the Western Wall. Our visit passed without incident and the stone throwing ceased.

When Sharon went to the Temple Mount on September 28, 2000, it was therefore not a first for him, but this time he was acting as the leader of the parliamentary opposition. The media, who treated him like a political has-been, barely mentioned his declaration of intent. As for Barak, he continued his route and even invited Arafat to dine at his home. Barak thought that he could still prevent an armed conflict, despite secret service intelligence revealing that Arafat had decided in April 2000 to reopen hostilities at the first pretext.

The Palestinians, particularly the Waqf, the religious authority responsible for holy sites, had assured Barak and Shlomo Ben-Ami, his
minister of internal security and foreign affairs, that Sharon's visit
could proceed as scheduled. In fact, Sharon's arrival on the Temple
Mount, under heavy police protection, caused barely any incidents,
aside from the invective of Arab members of the Knesset. But appear-
ances are often deceptive.

The following day, Friday, September 29, 2000, a day of prayer
for Muslims and the eve of the Jewish New Year, Palestinian policemen killed an Israeli border guard who, under the framework of the
creation of mixed units provided in the Oslo Accords, was patrolling
the border in Kalkilya alongside them. Arafat's offensive was underway. To justify this recourse to violence and to rally his people, Arafat
claimed that this action was a response to Sharon's visit to the Temple
Mount; indeed, Arafat called the violence the "al-Aqsa Intifada"—the
name of one of the mosques on the site. Arafat's henchmen immediately began rioting on the Temple Mount and attacked both Jews
praying before the Western Wall and also the Israeli security forces. A
number of Palestinians were killed during these confrontations with
Israeli police.

That Friday, I accompanied Sharon to the Kiryat Shaoul cemetery, where his first wife and their only son were buried, for the annual
commemoration of their deaths. I had joined him at this ceremony for
30 years; this was the first time that it poured with rain. We were
soaked to the skin, but the Kaddish, the prayer for the dead, went on
uninterrupted. Omri, who had been strongly opposed to his father's
last initiative—he even spoke of a "not very intelligent act"—shot
angry looks at me. I suppose he thought that I was the instigator of the
visit to the Temple Mount. The fact is that Ariel Sharon made his decision alone, knowing full well that the international and Israeli media
would believe Arafat's lies—as indeed was the case.

NOVEMBER 2000
SHARON TARGETS THE TOP

At around midnight on November 22, 2000, Sharon called me to ask if I would accompany him to Gush Katif. The Israeli settlements in that area of the Gaza Strip had become the target of Yasser Arafat's terrorists, as well as of those of Arafat's head of security in Gaza, Mohammed Dahlan. Prime Minister and Defense Minister Ehud Barak could not stop the loss of human life. Two days earlier the Palestinians had blown up a school bus in the small town of Kfar Darom. Two people had been killed and nine wounded, including five children. The public was outraged: Tehila Cohen, a girl of eight, lost both legs, her six-year-old sister Orit lost her right leg, and their seven-year-old brother Israel also lost both legs. Ariel Sharon wanted to offer his condolences to the families and give support to the whole community affected by the attack.

We left the house at seven o'clock precisely and got into an armored GMC truck, accompanied by armed bodyguards. Omri Sharon and Uri Shani, who led Likud under Ariel's direction, followed us in another vehicle. Along the way Sharon pointed out buildings, trees and bushes that served as hiding places for Palestinian ambushes. After listening to mothers describing the bus's explosion, he said to me, "You see the courage of the people of Kfar Darom? Do you understand how important it is that they hold out?"

Despite the dire situation, the residents gave Sharon a warm welcome. They hoped that he would soon come to power. When local officials told him, to his great consternation, that the IDF had not razed the Palestinian houses from which the shots were fired, Sharon promised them that he would take up the matter with Barak. That day, more than ever, he was attentive to people's needs, gave them encouragement and advice drawn from his military experience, and renewed his promise to be their spokesman to the authorities. Sharon was proud of these people and their heroism.

At the end of this visit, which would be his last in-depth tour of the Gaza Strip, we had to stop at a military barricade designed to prevent ambushes. Sharon had to wait patiently between the sandbags of this IDF post until the road was made secure. The soldiers who were not on guard were listening to their commander speaking; when this young officer spotted Sharon, he invited him to talk of his experience fighting terrorism. Ariel willingly accepted and spent an hour talking to the conscripts. It was an extraordinary sight: the leader of the opposition, a reserve general with a glorious career, who was held up at a surrounded military position in the middle of the Gaza Strip, boosting the morale of very young soldiers. The press had not caught wind of the event; knowing my colleagues and the way that they supported Barak, I am certain that they would not have missed the opportunity to denounce Sharon for this "political maneuver." But the media had written Sharon off as politically dead, and they barely paid him any attention. Arik, however, was preparing to become Ehud Barak's opponent, both on the national and on the international front.

Two weeks after the trip to Gush Katif, Sharon attended a press breakfast organized in Manhattan by Ken Chandler, the publisher of the *New York Post*. Not content with answering questions or speaking about the state of war, for the first time Sharon set out his ideas on how to resolve the conflict: left-wing governments had made the mistake of thinking that they could come to an overall agreement with the Palestinians, but rather than an "all or nothing" approach, Sharon preferred intermediate solutions—steps toward peace—and advocated an establishment of trust between the two sides. Here was the "hawk," the man of war, advocating dialogue with the Palestinians.

On December 9, 2000, Ehud Barak resigned. A new prime minister would be elected on February 6 of the following year. Sharon, an official candidate, intensified his visits throughout the country. The prime minister would be elected by direct universal suffrage, under the electoral law passed in 1992. A new reform has since reestablished the previous system of proportional representation with one round of voting.

Shortly thereafter, in January, Sharon asked me to leave immediately for Moscow—"tomorrow at the latest, if you can't today." Why this urgency? According to his sources, Arik had not yet managed to get the support of immigrants from the former Soviet Union who had arrived in the 1990s; they represented thousands of votes. He had therefore made contact with Jewish personalities in Moscow who had agreed to campaign on his behalf on the television channels and radio stations that could be picked up in Israel. This created a significant advantage since the limit on airtime allowed each candidate under Israeli law did not apply in Russia. Sharon asked me to provide his Muscovite supporters with complete documentation, including photos, on his activities in the army, agriculture, industry, housing and so on. In 24 hours I got together documents and photos, and then procured a visa and air ticket. Not being a political activist, I refused to let Sharon finance my trip from his electoral campaign funds. I was simply doing a friend a favor and was only too happy to do what I could to help.

In Moscow, Sharon's supporters were resolute. In three days, their messages of support began appearing on television and radio. Arik telephoned me from Netanya, after an electoral meeting with immigrants from Ethiopia. He was bubbling with enthusiasm: "I'm already hearing about television programs from Moscow. Good work!" The ironies of fate. Sharon had spent a good part of his life destroying military equipment supplied to Arab armies by the Kremlin, and here I was in Moscow mobilizing Israeli votes in Sharon's favor, through Russian means of communication.

✡

The director of Sharon's election campaign, Reuven Adler, had distributed immense posters of Sharon throughout the country, with the caption "Peace and Security," while the terrorist offensive unleashed by Arafat in 2000 continued unabated. Crossing the Arab city of Umm el-Fahm, I saw the word "murderer" scribbled on one of these posters that had been torn—no doubt scribbled under the influence of the Labour Party's odious campaign in which the parting prime minister Barak blamed Sharon for the death of a thousand Israelis during the Lebanese war, while Barak's justice minister Yossi Beilin published notices in the Israeli Arab press reminding electors of Sharon's "responsibility" in the massacres of Sabra and Shatilla.

Three weeks before the election, Adler called me and announced, "I'm with Arik and Arthur. You are right—Arik will be prime minister." The American Arthur Finkelstein, a political adviser who had directed Ronald Reagan's campaign in 1980 and Benjamin Netanyahu's in 1996, had chosen to work for Sharon.

"You didn't believe me when I told you in 1983," I replied.

"That's true. Arthur, who read your articles in the *New York Post*, swears that he still doesn't know what you based your prediction on. But now he says that if the polls are to be believed, no other candidate can win." I heard Sharon's voice in the background, and Adler added, "Arik says that he didn't believe it either."

FEBRUARY 6, 2001
ARIEL SHARON, PRIME MINISTER

On the evening of February 6, 2001, a handful of close friends and supporters—Sharon's campaign director Reuven Adler, the Israeli-American businessman Arieh Genger, his friend Cyril Kern, Hollywood film producer Yoram Ben-Ami and I—had come to await the result of the vote with Ariel and his son Omri. We all knew the result in advance; at least, we hoped we did.

At 10 P.M. precisely, the announcement came: "Ariel Sharon is elected prime minister with an impressive majority"—with 62.58 percent of the vote, to be exact. Shouts of joy erupted around Sharon, who remained fixed in his chair, avidly watching the television screen, his expression inscrutable. Finally, after half an hour, he got up to reply to the messages of congratulation that came flooding in over the phone. Then he pointed at me, and said, "Uri was the only one to believe it!" He was silent for a moment and then added in a sad voice, "Shame that Lily isn't here to see this." It was nearly a year since Lily had been laid to rest on the Hill of Anemones on their property. Arik often went to visit her grave and would come back strengthened, more determined than ever to return to the fight. Arik whispered in Reuven's ear, "I'm afraid I'll burst into tears. You know, I think I've changed."

A call came from the White House. When he hung up, Ariel told us, "It was Bush. He said, 'When we met, I wasn't the president and you weren't prime minister. Now we'll be able to work together.'"

The losing candidate, Ehud Barak, also called. Sharon expressed the wish to meet him as soon as possible; he would readily welcome him into his government. But Barak had decided to quit political life.

At 3 A.M., Arik phoned, hiding his emotion under a forced humor: "What do you think? Is there a connection between my visit to the Temple Mount and my winning the election?"

I responded in the same vein: "I'm planning the second volume of the book *The Temple Mount Is in Our Hands*, subtitled, 'The 132 days between Sharon's ascent of the Temple Mount and his ascent to power.'"

Later that morning Sharon called me again: "I went to Lily's grave to try to share this moment with her. Now I'm going to the Wall." Which was still in our hands, at the foot of the Temple Mount.

2001
FIRST IMPRESSIONS,
AND REFLECTIONS
ON PREVIOUS YEARS

What were your feelings the day after your election as prime minister of Israel?

I assumed the post of prime minister reverently, calmly and with all due solemnity. For me, leading the government of the Jewish state also meant taking on responsibility for the entire Jewish people, who contributed to the realization of the magnificent dream that had accompanied us for two thousand years. The citizens of Israel had elected me at a particularly critical time—at the time of the war of attrition launched by Yasser Arafat on September 29, 2000, that continued with incessant waves of violence and terrorist attacks. I promised the citizens of Israel that I would restore security and the peace that they deserved. Another reason why an overwhelming, and unprecedented, majority demonstrated their confidence in me was my long experience of managing critical situations and my reputation as a specialist in missions that others said were impossible.

Is this a new "mission impossible"?

The evening of February 6, I had the feeling that I was taking on the biggest task that I had ever had in the turbulent history of the state of Israel. I foresaw, long before they appeared, the clouds that would darken our sky, and I tried to disperse them, in my various functions in the government and in the opposition, all the while reinforcing our presence in Eretz Israel under conditions that were extremely difficult. But I never lost hope. It's not in my nature.

But some of your critics sometimes say that your political career was chaotic.
Yes, indeed. For example, my resignation as minister of industry and
commerce in 1990, in the second government for national unity led
by Yitzhak Shamir, surprised the public and surprised Shamir himself.
I resigned to protest against the government's policies. As I explained
in my letter to the prime minister:

"It is a question of national principle. Under your mandate,
Palestinian terrorism has proliferated everywhere in Eretz Israel and
has caused numerous deaths of innocent Jews and Arabs. The government's policies have caused recklessness and disorder in the lives
of Jews. I believe that terrorism can be eradicated by other means and
cannot support this strategy. In my view, law and order can be
reestablished in our country in a relatively short time, allowing us to
achieve peace with the Arabs on the basis of our historic right to
Eretz Israel.

"During the mandate of your government, Arab terrorism has allowed crime and violence to reign even on the streets of Jerusalem.
Our capital, the heart of the Jewish people, is once again divided, with
terrorist leaders safely installed in the eastern part of the city—and the
government of Israel resigns itself to this situation. Your political program has put Israel on the road to the establishment of a second state
in Eretz Israel.

"Prime Minister, you say that you want room for tactical maneuver. So far as Jerusalem is concerned, there cannot be maneuvers, or
tactics, or anything else, and when it comes to the security of Jews'
lives, we cannot tolerate any kind of freedom to maneuver. Security is
an immediate concern. The government's power to decide the most
vital issues concerning our security, existence and well-being has been
confiscated. The cabinet has ceased to function. Questions of life and
death are decided by one or two individuals who have seized these
powers, contrary to the most fundamental rules of every democratic
regime worthy of the name."

And I concluded my letter:

"I am not giving up my ministerial post lightly. But there are moments when one must act. There are moments in the life of a country
and of a person when one must wake up, prepare and fight with all
one's strength before disaster strikes. And there is little time left for
Israel and the Jews to turn that corner."

What were the circumstances leading to your resignation?
The wave of Palestinian terrorism—henceforth known as the Intifada—had reached new heights. In addition, Defense Minister Yitzhak Rabin and Foreign Minister Shimon Peres, encouraged by President George Bush senior and his secretary of state James Baker, were ready to open the path to negotiations with the PLO. Journalists, analysts and political activists were once again quick to write my obituary and to announce, sometimes rejoicing, that I had come to the end of the line. Their joy was a little premature.

Shortly after my resignation, the Labour Party toppled the Shamir government and tried to form a government led by Peres, refusing a coalition with Likud. But, from the sidelines, I prevented Peres from putting his plan into practice and ensured that the leadership returned to Shamir, this time without the participation of the Labour Party. And so, four months after I had left the government, Shamir entrusted me with the post of minister of construction and housing and gave me a new mission impossible: to absorb the large wave of immigration that occurred after the collapse of the Soviet Union—half a million new immigrants, who represented a magnificent contribution of talents and energy.

The state of Israel faced a truly daunting task: to provide a roof for hundreds of thousands of new arrivals from the former Soviet Union, and also from Ethiopia. In addition to the difficulties of integration, this massive influx of people created a serious problem: Israelis in precarious financial conditions were forced to leave their accommodations because landlords preferred to rent to the newcomers who were able, thanks to help from the state, to pay a year's rent up front. The day that I took up my post, 2,208 Israeli families had been made homeless, and the number was increasing rapidly. Hundreds of thousands of immigrants were arriving, and sometimes I had to come up with around 300 places to live a day. It was a period of record construction in our history. We built 144,000 new homes and renovated 22,000 others from top to bottom.

Providing the new arrivals with a roof was the first priority, but I also knew, from having observed it since childhood, that only large waves of immigration allowed people to be well distributed in the country. Unfortunately, I held this post for only two years, and then other events intervened.

The Gulf war?

Exactly. When the United States launched Operation Desert Storm against the Iraqi dictator Saddam Hussein, Saddam targeted the civilian population in Israel with his Scud missiles, between January and February 1991. My ministry had to take care of victims and undertake repairs of the damaged housing. Although Shamir agreed to cooperate with the Americans during this first Gulf war by not responding to the Iraqi missiles, Washington refused to guarantee the loans that we needed to absorb the huge wave of immigrants from the former Soviet Union. Yet Shamir, anxious to please the American secretary of state James Baker, even agreed to take part in the Madrid conference initiated by the United States in October 1991 in an attempt to bring peace between Israel and the Arab states and, above all, to persuade Israel to negotiate with the PLO.

Did you agree with this decision to negotiate with the PLO?

I saw it as a threat to our security. During the special cabinet meeting I voted against this step that elevated Yasser Arafat to the rank of an official negotiating partner, when his organization's charter still demanded the destruction of the Jewish state. Once again I found myself in a minority. And so, to minimize the danger, I intensified the settlement efforts, not only in Galilee, where the majority of inhabitants were Jews, but also in Judea-Samaria, the Gaza Strip and the Golan Heights.

I advised Shamir against holding the elections planned for the winter of 1993. Unfortunately, he ignored my warning and brought the election forward to spring 1992. We lost. Yitzhak Rabin, the new prime minister, formed a government composed solely of Labour Party and left-wing members. For me, our failure was without doubt the result of the division in the national camp, a division that threatened Israel's future. All my protestations were in vain.

In the opposition, how much real power did you have?

Carrying on the struggle from the opposition benches was not easy. But I had a secret weapon: the fact that people believed that my sole objective was to become prime minister. It is true that I would have liked to take on the role, but not at any price. When I said that people exaggerated my ambition in that regard, my opponents—and even some of my allies—did not believe me. For me, national interest has always taken precedence over personal interest. If I had reversed my priorities, I might have been elected prime minister much earlier. But I was never prepared to go against my principles, in terms of security or of the Jews' inalienable right to live in Eretz Israel. So, even from my awkward position in the opposition, I struggled with every legitimate means against the Oslo Accords, before Rabin signed it on the White House lawn on September 13, 1993.

Was your concern about the Accords justified?
The incessant series of suicide attacks, the cars that were blown up and other terrorist acts already more than proved that Yasser Arafat had not respected the agreement that he signed with Rabin and Peres. The polarization of Israeli society was so exacerbated that it led to a horrible, criminal act—the assassination of Yitzhak Rabin. An earthquake shook Israel that night. Nothing like it had happened before in our young democracy, the only democratic country in the Middle East. It was in that atmosphere of frequent Palestinian terrorist attacks in the heart of Jerusalem and Tel Aviv that the campaign for the May 1996 elections took place. The candidates were the leader of Likud, Benjamin "Bibi" Netanyahu, and Rabin's successor as head of the Labour Party, Shimon Peres. The election of the prime minister by direct vote, newly introduced in Israel, gave no other choice.

Did you take part in Likud's electoral campaign?
I mobilized all my forces to help Netanyahu, and he emerged the victor on May 17, 1996, by a narrow margin. His majority was, however, sufficient to form a government. The national party was at the helm again—but now Israel had committed to respect the various terms of the Oslo Accords. Likud therefore had no recourse but to introduce amendments to the terms, so as to reduce as much as possible their immensely harmful potential.

What was your role in this?
I was given the portfolio of national infrastructure, a powerful ministry created specially for me by Prime Minister Netanyahu, with the mission of developing all our infrastructures, from traffic to energy

sources, at the dawn of the new millennium. I went to China and Russia to try to establish economic cooperation with the two powers, proving that even a small country such as Israel is capable of contributing to a reciprocal and constructive collaboration. I also initiated projects to ensure future cooperation with Jordan and the Palestinians, reinforcing the peace process by the creation of common economic interests for all parties. The seawater desalination projects that I had set up were awaiting implementation.

How would you assess your ministerial contribution?
It wasn't easy to restore clarity and stability in the shadow of the Oslo Accords. On top of that, Netanyahu did not possess the necessary political experience. I tried to help him as much as I could, particularly when the United States, under the presidency of Bill Clinton, was urging Israel to evacuate certain towns because of the security risk, and was urging us to give up certain sites even though they were an integral part of our history. In cabinet, I voted against ceding Hebron to the Palestinians; this would endanger the Jewish community resettled in the town. The number of deaths among those heroic Jews who have continued to live in Hebron since then has justified my fears. King David spent seven and a half years in Hebron, where he was crowned, and the town is mentioned 1,023 times in the Bible. And that is what we are asked to give up?

You were part of the ministerial committee of national defense?
As a member of that committee, I tried several times to initiate a gradual, measured withdrawal of the IDF from southern Lebanon. I thought that we should end our presence in that area, but we also had to ensure that Hezbollah, the terrorist organization supported by Iran, would not pose a threat if we withdrew to the international border. My attempt failed. Indeed, the IDF did not leave southern Lebanon until May 2000, on the order of Prime Minister and Defense Minister Ehud Barak—and it took place so hastily that it encouraged new aggressive desires in the enemy; Hezbollah redeployed its missiles on our northern border. This withdrawal also led the Palestinians to think that they could chase us from the heart of Eretz Israel with terror and violence—which is what Arafat has tried to do since fall 2000.

Nevertheless I tried during this time to establish a dialogue with the Palestinian Authority. During the summer of 1997, I received one of Arafat's close aides, Abu Mazen, in my home. I even accepted a principle that earned me criticism from own political party: the establishment of a Palestinian state. This was ultimately unavoidable, because we had given Arafat control of the territories of Judea-Samaria and the Gaza Strip. So I showed that I was ready to reach agreement with the Palestinians, in the light of this important fact. I had concentrated most of my efforts on reducing the security risk that the birth of such a state would constitute for Israel. At the same time, as minister for national infrastructure, I strengthened the Jewish settlements in Judea-Samaria and in the Gaza Strip, as I had always done in my previous ministerial roles. Almost 20 years after I changed the map of Israel, I could contemplate with satisfaction the numerous flourishing settlements, as well as Greater Jerusalem and its satellite towns, which I had continually developed, consolidated and enlarged.

What would you be prepared to give up if Palestinian terrorism ceased? Would you recognize a Palestinian state that constituted 50 percent of the territories?
I said 42 percent, not 50 percent. A little flexibility is not out of the question. Palestinians suffer from our roadblocks and from an absence of territorial continuity, and that should be remedied. I'm talking about a long-term nonaggression pact that would outline expectations rather than set fixed dates. We must establish large development projects with the Palestinians that would make us interdependent. I have proposed the creation of a large seawater desalination project, which would be the biggest in the world. We must get into the habit of working together in economic areas, and of building peace.

The Palestinians would not be satisfied with 42 percent.
Because of the Palestinian position, giving up more would not guarantee the end of the conflict. What is the alternative to my gradual plan? Giving up more and more strategic and historic possessions without even achieving peace? We must give only the minimum, to establish a basis, a springboard, for a cooperation designed to bring about mutual confidence in the long term. Let's not forget that Arafat now controls 97 percent of the Palestinian population.

Why not evacuate isolated places, like those in the Gaza Strip?
Let's take Netzarim, which the Palestinian terrorists continually attack. Why do they do that? Because they understand something that certain Israelis do not want to understand. Netzarim was created to allow us to stop Palestinians from unloading tanks and other war equipment in the port of Gaza. Not so long ago we intercepted the *Santorino*, a boat that was making for Gaza with a dangerous arsenal of Katyusha rocket launchers, in violation of the agreements signed by the Palestinian Authority. It is not a coincidence that Netzarim was built next to the port of Gaza. Netzarim had to be created to establish a buffer zone between Gaza and Khan Yunes and to give us access to the sea. Netzarim is therefore vital to our security. Kfar Darom, which is also the target of incessant attacks by the Palestinians and which was created in 1946, allowed us to delay the progress of the Egyptian army toward Tel Aviv in 1948. It was a critical moment, and Kfar Darom played an important role in the defense of the newborn Jewish state. In addition to their strategic importance, Israeli settlements in the Gaza Strip have a Zionist value. Zionism was and is still based on the Jewish peopling of Eretz Israel.

Nevertheless, your political line on the Palestinians has changed.
The peace agreement signed by Rabin in 1994 with King Hussein of Jordan influenced my point of view. Until then I thought that Jordan was the Palestinians' country and that the solution to our conflict with them had to involve this country. Now the peace treaty with the Hashemite kingdom and the Oslo Accords signed with Yasser Arafat have changed the map and, as a result, have changed my own perception of the situation.

What was your relationship with King Hussein?
A relationship of friendship and trust was established between us at our first meeting in his Aqaba palace in fall 1997, when I accompanied Prime Minister Netanyahu. As a farmer, I was interested in sheep-rearing in Jordan, while the king wanted to know how I had crossed the Suez Canal in 1973, an operation that he seemed to know about in great detail. We talked about developing water resources for our two countries, always thirsty for the smallest drop of that precious substance. A warm relationship was forged between us that evening, to

Netanyahu's astonishment. It developed to the degree that when two Israeli Mossad agents were arrested in Amman—after their failed attack on Khaled Mash'al, the leader of Hamas in Jordan who was responsible for terrorist acts in Jerusalem—Netanyahu asked me to go to see King Hussein at once, to resolve the problem. During our nocturnal meeting in his palace, the king agreed to release our men and to restore normal relations between our two countries.

So the prime minister recognized your abilities?
A year later, in October 1998, Netanyahu gave me the portfolio of foreign affairs, in addition to the one for infrastructure. After the brutal lessons of the early part of his mandate, Natanyahu seemed to have realized that he could count on my help more than on anyone else's. And so we went together to the Wye Plantation talks.

What happened on your return to Israel after the talks?
I immediately recommended to the prime minister that he form a government of national unity. Unfortunately, Netanyahu ignored my suggestion and was isolated by members of his own political family. Getting it wrong yet again, some of our traditional allies in the Knesset shortened the government's stay in power and provoked Netanyahu's fall in May 1999. After he lost the election to Ehud Barak, Netanyahu decided to leave politics for a while. Elected as leader of Likud, I accepted Barak's offer to join his government. Barak decided to govern alone, however, which precipitated his demise—which came much earlier than anyone could have imagined.

What was happening within Likud at that time?
Several of my political allies and, of course, my opponents within Likud saw me as an "interim pope." They thought that, at over 70, I would soon be ripe for an old people's home. It also was a particularly dramatic time, made worse by a personal tragedy—my beloved wife Lily's cancer. Even after our house burned down, in December of the same year, and with it all the personal touches that Lily had contributed, she kept encouraging me to go back to the political battle every morning.

With an extreme effort I managed to turn Likud into the main opposition party and fought against the dangerous steps taken by Prime

Minister Barak, who was ready to evacuate the Golan Heights, right up to the bank of Lake Tiberias, and to make important concessions to the Palestinians.

In March 2000, Lily passed away before my eyes. I will never forget that melancholy night of Shabbat. I was now alone and grief-stricken, dealing with the next phase of the battle—without Lily, but not alone; our sons Omri and Gilad were at my side, more loyal than ever in their support.

What was this new phase?
In July 2000, Barak and Arafat took part in the Camp David talks. After the failure of his negotiations with Syria, Barak arrived at Camp David to submit an unprecedented raft of Israeli concessions to Yasser Arafat, which Clinton entreated Arafat to accept. To Clinton's astonishment, as well as Barak's, Arafat rejected the proposals outright. While Barak had hoped to exchange the proposed sacrifices with a declaration from Arafat that the PLO call a halt to its war against Israel, Arafat was already preparing his weapons. At that moment he was ordering his henchmen to prepare an offensive against Israel based on violence and terror, thinking that he could force the Jewish state to accept his demands unconditionally.

What was Barak prepared to give up?
In August–September 2000, I learned from reliable sources—in Jerusalem and in New York—the nature of the concessions offered by Barak, who, even after the failure of the Camp David talks, declared himself ready to discuss an agreement with Arafat. It seemed that a single man, Ehud Barak, planned—without any previous consultation and without obtaining the sanction of the government, the cabinet or the Knesset—to give Arafat almost 97 percent of the West Bank, thereby dismantling about a hundred Israeli settlements. Even more serious, it seems that Barak, once again his own boss, was ready to cede the majority of the Old City of our capital Jerusalem to the PLO, as well as effective control of the Temple Mount, the heart of the Jewish people, our most sacred site, a site that had figured in our dream of a homeland throughout our exile.

Despite my public warnings, both in Israel and abroad, I seemed again to be preaching in the wilderness. The problem was that neither

Barak nor the two or three ministers whom he had let into the secret wanted to acknowledge publicly the concessions that he was envisaging, and even less to admit that he was still holding secret negotiations with Arafat, using the United States as an intermediary. What is more, the Jewish public in Israel and abroad clearly had no idea of the danger that we would run if armed Palestinians were on the ramparts of the Old City, threatening the center of Jerusalem.

Arafat persisted in wanting to consult more than a billion Muslims before agreeing that Israel should keep the Western Wall. Arafat then claimed—as he continued to do for a long time—that the entire Temple Mount had long belonged to Muslims and had never been the site of a Jewish sanctuary. A ridiculous lie, typical of the crude Palestinian propaganda that also seriously undermines the Christian tradition—a lie on a par with the slogan, "Jesus, first Palestinian victim of the Jews," which blithely ignores the glaring contradiction of acknowledging the primacy of the Jewish presence in Jerusalem. Barak had therefore hurtled Israel into a horribly messy situation, from which I tried to extract him. On September 6, 2000, in the hope of calming me, he called me from New York, where he was attending the extraordinary U.N. session in honor of the new millennium. He said that he would give his approach another month, and after that perhaps he would discuss the possibility of forming a government of national unity with me. I replied, "Ehud, I'm ready to help you. If you get out of this trap now, I promise I will never use it against you, but you must get out."

What was the Jewish public opinion of all this?
It was very worrying. Two weeks after this conversation, I went to New York for my usual round of meetings with Jewish leaders and friends of Israel. I realized that the people I was talking to were afflicted with the same apathy that the Israelis had when it came to Barak's generous program. They showed concern—and a certain anxiety—only about a single point: the concessions that Barak was ready to make on Jerusalem, including the Temple Mount. So I decided to act by carrying out the only gesture in my power: to go to the Temple Mount. I announced my plan on Kol Israel, and the government informed the Waqf, the authority that dealt with the mosques established there.

Early in the morning of September 28, 2000, accompanied by several Likud members of the Knesset, we availed ourselves of our sovereign right to visit the Temple Mount. I spoke to the journalists who had come to cover the event and said, "I bring a message of peace. Jews have the inalienable right to come here." But Arab-Israeli members of the Knesset, members of extremist anti-Zionist parties, incited the Palestinians to provoke the police by throwing stones at them—a familiar spectacle, always initiated by the Palestinians. My visit to the Temple would have remained a political gesture—in the framework of my struggle against the concessions that the government was preparing to make—if the Palestinians had not deliberately used it as a pretext to unleash their campaign of violence and terror that was in the works since the Camp David summit.

The following day, at the end of Friday prayers on the Temple Mount, the Palestinians openly clashed with the police and threw stones at the Jews praying at the Western Wall, leading to numerous deaths among the Palestinians and several wounded among the Israeli police. In hindsight, one might say that Yasser Arafat decided that day to launch a war of attrition against Israel that would go on for months. I was obviously aware of the ulterior motives behind the claim that it was my visit to the Temple Mount that led to the start of Palestinian hostilities. The propagandists of the Palestinian Authority called this supposedly spontaneous uprising the al-Aqsa Intifada, thereby inciting the most extremist Arab-Israelis to join forces with them. Unfortunately, some foreign media—particularly in countries such as France, with which I had very strained relations at the time—fell for this lie. The Palestinians also succeeded for a time in spreading the rumor that I had entered the mosques on the Temple Mount. In reality, I had limited my visit to the esplanade and announced in advance that I had no intention of entering places of worship. To Ehud Barak's credit, I must acknowledge that during his meetings with Jacques Chirac in France, with Hosni Mubarak in Egypt and with other heads of state, he fully supported my right to go to the Temple Mount and emphasized that my gesture was in no way designed to undermine Islamic sacred sites, but rather was to protest against his government's policies.

Increasingly insincere, Yasser Arafat demanded that an international commission of inquiry be set up to examine the causes of the violence—probably hoping to make me responsible. Clinton agreed to Arafat's demand and set up, with Barak's permission, a commission chaired by the former U.S. senator George Mitchell. In May 2001,

when I was already prime minister, this commission published its conclusions, which absolved me of any responsibility. While I had no need
for my name to be cleared, I was nonetheless happy to hear Mitchell
declare in an interview on CNN the day that the commission's report
was published: "We have come to the conclusion that Ariel Sharon's
visit to the Temple Mount did not trigger the hostilities."

Barak did everything that he could to persuade Arafat to put an
end to the attacks, while the number of Palestinian victims increased
as Israeli security forces sought to minimize Jewish losses. Since the
beginning of the Palestinian war of attrition, I had been ready to respond to the prime minister's appeal and join his government so that
we could face this war together. Unfortunately, Ehud Barak equivo-
cated. He wanted to please Israeli public opinion, which sensed the
need to unite the country's main political forces, but at the last moment he withdrew his offer, believing that he could reach a peace
agreement with Arafat by himself.

Meanwhile the terrorist attacks had multiplied and had become
more vicious. After getting lost near Ramallah, two Israeli reservists
were savagely lynched in public. At Kfar Darom in the Gaza Strip, a
bomb killed two teachers and mutilated three young children. Suicide
attacks killed people in towns all over Israel. Arafat responded in the
negative to all of Washington's efforts to persuade him to stop the violence, while Barak was negotiating under fire—for the first time in the
history of conflict between the Arabs and the state of Israel. These
bloody events shook Israeli political life. In December 2000, Ehud
Barak suddenly announced his resignation, hoping that he would
achieve a more resounding victory in the coming election if he did not
have to stand against Netanyahu. Netanyahu had retired from the
race after having tried in vain to make his candidacy for prime minister dependent on the legislative elections being held at the same time.

Did you think that you had a strong chance of being elected?
After Netanyahu withdrew, yes. From the beginning I promised to
form a government of national unity to ensure the security of Israeli
citizens and to promote peace. This electoral campaign was one of the
shortest, but also was the most ruthless, in our parliamentary history.
The more the polls predicted a sure victory for me, the more my opponents were willing to use any weapon against me, however unworthy.

Those responsible for Barak's election campaign did not realize that they were also harming their country by having the audacity to claim that "a vote for Barak is a vote for peace, and a vote for Sharon is a vote for war," when the war had been going on for four months.

It was, in fact, the first electoral campaign that took place in the shadow of war. Holding intensive negotiations while the bombs exploded, Ehud Barak tried until the last moment to reach some—or any—kind of agreement with Arafat to save his chances in the election. Bill Clinton and his government put all their weight behind Barak, and the doors of the White House remained open to the Israeli and Palestinian negotiators. Yasser Arafat made a grave mistake in thinking that Israeli society would buckle under violence and give in totally to his demands. Arafat received a clear response on February 6, 2001, at 10 P.M., when it became apparent that the Israelis had chosen me with, as it turned out, more than 62 percent of the vote. I felt no pride and did not celebrate my victory. I was reserved, calm and sad. Sad because my wife was not at my side to witness the confidence that the people had once more placed in me at a time of crisis. I found it difficult to hold back my tears.

I always thought that time would come.
You were the only one to believe it. For me, this election was additional proof that when someone fights tirelessly for just principles, remaining loyal to them even if he has to pay a high price for doing so, he will gain recognition in the end. I formed a government of national unity, first and foremost to bring the people together after a long period of division and fragmentation. This situation was exacerbated after the Oslo Accords: many of those who believed that they would eventually see peace with the Palestinians had lost that confidence since that deadly autumn of 2000. I formed a government with the Labour Party and others, so that we could tackle the country's social and economic problems and enable Israel to enter the twenty-first century on a sure footing. I also formed that government with the purpose of reaching Arab-Israeli citizens who were ready to live peacefully with us in the Jewish state, as well as to ensure a return to law and order. I took on this enormous task while knowing clearly that the Jewish state faced a historic and decisive struggle.

FEBRUARY–
MARCH 2001
CONDOLEEZZA'S LEGS

No sooner had he been elected prime minister than Sharon had to confront his first crisis—and what a crisis! He was accused of having made sexist remarks about Condoleezza Rice, the new national security adviser at the White House. And it was said that she had taken these inappropriate compliments very badly. A major diplomatic incident loomed. When he had heard of Condoleezza Rice's appointment, Sharon had declared himself, according to the Israeli press, "impressed by her beautiful legs." Sensitive to female beauty, Arik had always complimented women freely, even in Lily's presence. But people who wanted to assign an ulterior motive to his statement blew his innocent tribute out of proportion. Israeli journalists in Washington went one better by claiming that "Condoleezza is furious about Sharon's chauvinist comment."

Arik realized that he had to defuse the situation at once. The day after his election, while he was still in his office at the Likud headquarters in Tel Aviv, he asked the Israeli-American businessman Arieh Genger to deal with it. Genger, who later played a crucial role in bringing together Sharon and the Bush administration, immediately called the White House. He explained to Condoleezza Rice that the prime minister regretted the misinterpretation of his words and apologized on Ariel Sharon's behalf if his words had hurt her. The consummate diplomat, Rice replied that incorrect and out-of-context quotations were classic media foibles and that so far as she was concerned, the matter was closed. Sharon heaved a sigh of relief, conscious of the work that lay ahead in establishing a relationship of trust with the new American administration.

Arik and Condoleezza had known each other since mid-August 2000. At the time of their first meeting she belonged to the team of Texas Governor George W. Bush, Republican candidate for the White House. Sharon had taken the opportunity to set out his vision of the situation to his American guest: previous Israeli governments had made the mistake of thinking that the Oslo Accords would lead to peace, but Sharon believed that it was a process in which each new step depended on the success of the previous one. Sharon also emphasized that the settlements in the West Bank and the Gaza Strip formed Israel's first line of defense. An excellent working relationship, reinforced by a warm personal relationship, was established between the prime minister of Israel and the White House adviser. Every time a misunderstanding arose, Rice would bring up "the 2001 crisis" to tease Arieh Genger, asking him if Sharon had been "misquoted or misunderstood?"

A month later, on March 19, 2001, we took off for Washington, where Sharon was to undertake his first official visit as prime minister. I had already accompanied prime ministers to the White House on numerous occasions—Yitzhak Rabin, Benjamin Netanyahu and Ehud Barak—but to cover my friend Ariel's first official trip to the United States was a very special experience for me, especially since he and I recalled only too well how in 1982 the American leaders had sought to topple Defense Minister Sharon by any and all means. Without his saying a word, I suspected that Sharon was preparing a surprise for me.

Sharon was staying at Blair House, the official residence of the president's guests, opposite the White House. We journalists were staying, as was customary, at the Madison Hotel. While dozens of accredited journalists were flocking around Sharon and George W. Bush, Sharon looked for me and then gave me a contented smile, before replying to the questions that were fired at him from all sides. The warmth and friendship between the Israeli and the American were obvious. Once the press conference was over, the crowd made for the exit. That was when I heard someone shouting out my name. I would recognize that voice among thousands of others, but I kept on going, too shocked to turn around. But Sharon called me again: "Uri!"

Two Israeli colleagues brought me to order: "Uri, the prime minister is calling you!"

I turned and joined Ariel Sharon and George W. Bush. My prime minister introduced me to his host, explaining our long ties, and the president asked me about my work for the *New York Post*. Then Sharon said, "Thank you again for dinner, Mr. President."

"But you hardly ate anything!" Bush guffawed.

"You remember that I asked you earlier to sign the menu for a friend who collects them? Well, here is the friend in question!" And Sharon produced the menu, under the president's amused gaze, and gave it to me.

JUNE 1, 2001
SUICIDE BOMB AT
THE DOLPHINARIUM

June 1, 2001, was a perfect summer day that, seemingly, nothing could spoil; I was dining with Ariel Sharon at his farm in the Negev along with his son Gilad and Gilad's wife, Inbal. Their eldest boy Rotem was three, his twin brothers were barely four months old. We were in Sharon's favorite room, the kitchen, illuminated by a large bay window. Rotem was running around us, going over to his grandfather from time to time for hugs. On the radio a commentator was describing the funeral of Feisal Husseini in East Jerusalem. Husseini, a darling of the international news media, was the director of Orient House in East Jerusalem and a member of the PLO's executive committee—"a cunning and dangerous enemy," Sharon commented, as he sprinkled copious amounts of salt onto the chicken and rice dish that Inbal had just served him. "Husseini told the leaders of Palestinian organizations that the Oslo Accords were a Trojan horse that had enabled them to get into Israel and into Jerusalem," Sharon continued, "and from which they would emerge when the time was right to establish the Palestinian state with Jerusalem as its capital!"

Despite this recent elimination of a terrorist leader in the West Bank, Sharon believed that security forces were not yet responding satisfactorily to suicide attacks. During the six years in which his predecessors had promised Israeli citizens that the Oslo Accords would lead to peace, the Israeli war machine had become rather rusty, no longer meeting the criteria of operational efficiency and speed that Sharon had established when he still belonged to the army's upper echelons. Sharon encouraged the IDF and Shin Bet to work more closely together, so as to identify and neutralize the terrorists before they arrived in Israel's big towns.

Over dessert we talked about Sharon's autobiography, *Warrior*. Now that Sharon was prime minister, his American publisher wanted to republish it with a new preface summing up his activities of the last 12 years. Arik asked me to edit it, because "my head and my time are taken up with the war." I did not know then just how much he would need every second of his time to deal with this ruthless conflict.

That night, around midnight, I learned that a suicide attack had taken place in the Dolphinarium, in front of a dance club popular with the young people of Tel Aviv. I hurried to the scene. It was a horrific massacre, with bodies torn to pieces amid pools of blood. There were 21 people dead and more than 100 wounded. The murderer had gone into the middle of a group of teenagers waiting to go into the club—and then he blew himself up. Barely four months before, Israelis had elected Sharon to put an end to the terrorist acts orchestrated by Arafat. This grave attack, committed right in the heart of Tel Aviv, was a challenge.

Drastic and rapid measures were needed. The suggestions made by the leaders of the security and intelligence services, called together the following day, smacked too much of acts of vengeance; Sharon judged that the suggested actions would only harm Israel and its image. He knew only too well that his opponents wanted to see him killing innocent Palestinians indiscriminately; then they would try to hand him over to an international court—in Belgium or The Hague—who would treat him as if he were a war criminal like Slobodan Milosevic.

The minister of foreign affairs, Shimon Peres, called Sharon in the middle of a meeting to urge him to begin negotiations with Arafat. Sharon refused point-blank. The German minister of foreign affairs, Joshka Fischer, was in Israel at the time, and he tried to intervene, promising that Germany, in the name of the European Union, would put pressure on Arafat to stop the violence. For their part, Likud ministers demanded that Arafat be sent back to Tunisia.

On Saturday, June 2, the Dolphinarium massacre was front-page news in the international press. In the departments of state and in the foreign affairs ministries of European countries, it was hoped that Israel's response would not take the form of a widespread military attack. That showed a poor understanding on their part of Ariel Sharon. His objective was Orient House, haunt of Arafat's henchmen and headquarters of the PLO in Jerusalem, where foreign ministers and diplomats made official visits as though it were the Palestinian embassy in Israel. Sharon wanted to occupy it on Saturday evening and to expel its occupants; since this would be a national rather than an international operation, however, it came under the jurisdiction of the police, not the army, and a certain amount of time was needed to assemble the necessary numbers—at least a thousand men. So Sharon had to wait for another opportunity. The lack of response to the tragedy, military or otherwise, surprised the Israeli population.

On the following Sunday evening, 48 hours after the attack, Sharon went to Ichilov hospital to visit the wounded: a blonde teenager with a face lacerated by nails that had been mixed with the explosive charge, a young man with a sad expression who was waiting to know whether he would have to have a leg amputated, and all the others, more or less seriously wounded. Sharon stopped in front of every bed and listened to the wounded in silence, without revealing the enormous suffering that he felt: "In hard times, a leader doesn't whine, he makes decisions and acts."

Journalists were waiting for Sharon in a small room on the ground floor of the hospital. They fired questions at him about how Israel was going to react to this terrible attack. And he, his face pale with restrained emotion, astonished them with his laconic reply: "Restraint is also a strength." With me, he was more open. When Sharon called me in Paris, on Sunday, June 10, 2001, he told me, in a hollow voice, "I've just visited a baby wounded in an attack. I touched his hand, he was in agony. It was horrible." He continued, "The 400,000 are coming."

Sharon was alluding to a fierce discussion we had the previous Friday. He had called from his farm to criticize an article that I had devoted to a child who had been seriously wounded in a Palestinian attack. I retorted, "The 400,000 are coming, this time to ask you what you are doing about terrorism." I was referring to the organizers of the anti-Sharon demonstrations after the massacres of Sabra and Chatila who claimed to have assembled 400,000 participants, or 10 percent of the population of Israel, a massively inflated figure.

✡

On August 10, 2001, Kol Israel interrupted its news bulletin to announce that another suicide attack had just occurred in Jerusalem at the Sbarro restaurant, a popular pizzeria that was always packed at lunchtime.

I drove to Tel Aviv in the company of George Kalogradis, the vice president of Walt Disney World International, and Dror Gabbai, head of services at the ministry of foreign affairs. Sharon wanted to meet Kalogridis and thank him for having organized, in spite of powerful Arab pressure, a successful exhibition on Jerusalem, the capital of Israel, at Epcot Center in Florida. Sharon welcomed us in Ben-Gurion's small office, still unchanged. I suggested postponing the meeting to a better time, but Sharon seemed to have all the time in the world. His secretary came and went, keeping him informed of the increasing death toll. The mayor of Jerusalem, Ehud Olmert, called from the Sbarro restaurant. There were nine casualties already, and among them were several members of the same family. His expression blank, Sharon hung up and said, "We have asked Arafat to call a halt to the wave of suicide bombings, but he ignores us and plays innocent." Shin Bet had known that an attack on Sbarro was being planned. Thanks to an agreement signed with the head of the CIA, George Tenet, the Americans had joined the Israelis in asking Arafat to arrest the terrorist, who had been identified. Arafat claimed that his security service had not been able to find him.

When we left his office an hour later, Sharon knew the final tally of the attack at the Sbarro restaurant: 15 dead and almost 130 wounded. His outward behavior gave away none of his fury. You had to know Sharon well, as I did, to realize that while he was calmly talking to us, his mind was elsewhere, reviewing the various methods of countering terrorism and limiting the damage—because, in spite of Tenet's optimistic forecast, the CIA seemed incapable of stopping these hostile acts. On the contrary, the attacks were increasing.

So the initiative passed to the Israelis. Sharon's response was lightning fast. I was woken up at 4 A.M. by the telephone. It was Arik telling me with a sense of duty fulfilled that he had taken control of Orient House and closed Arafat's offices in Abu Dis, an Arab suburb of East Jerusalem. This was the hardest political blow dealt to Arafat since Sharon's rise to power. Neither Arafat nor his men imagined that Sharon would dare chase them from their offices and seize their records, which turned up a treasure trove of documents, including Arafat's top-secret plans. On examination, the plans revealed Arafat's direct involvement in numerous attacks.

Needless to say, Arafat immediately called on the Europeans, who, as usual, lost no time in condemning Israel. Sharon's own minister of foreign affairs, Shimon Peres, who still dreamed of a partnership with Arafat, tried to persuade Sharon to restore Orient House and the Abu Dis offices to the Palestinians. "That's out of the question," Sharon retorted.

OCTOBER 2001
AFGHANISTAN

The September 11 attacks caused a drastic turnaround in American foreign policy. George W. Bush declared war on terrorism and sent his troops in pursuit of Osama Bin Laden, the head of al-Qaeda, who claimed responsibility for the attacks. Sharon did not think that it would be easy to capture Bin Laden. The Americans believed that Bin Laden was hiding in the region of the Tora Bora caves, in eastern Afghanistan, but the country's irregular terrain gave him an essential asset. I suggested, jokingly, that Sharon propose to Bush that Sharon, with his wealth of experience, lead the hunt for Bin Laden and that, in return, the United States declare Yasser Arafat persona non grata at the negotiating table with Israel. But Sharon wasn't inclined to joke about such a subject: "I've said and repeated to Bush and his envoys that Arafat is our Bin Laden, but they are not willing to acknowledge that."

Paradoxically, Yasser Arafat's status was becoming stronger after the September 11 attacks. It is true that, unlike his predecessor Bill Clinton, Bush had rallied to Sharon's position and refused to invite Arafat to Washington until he put an end to the attacks that Israel had been subject to for more than a year. But the State Department, now led by Colin Powell, was following a complex program designed to ensure that the United States would have the support of the Arab world in the event of a war in Afghanistan. The old concept of the "Arabists" at the State Department, who had their moment of glory under Reagan and Bush senior, was now in vogue again: Israel must make concessions to Arafat, so that Arafat would join the other Arab leaders willing to assist the western coalition against Afghanistan.

Sharon termed this idea "mad," but it immediately received the support of the minister of foreign affairs, Shimon Peres. The resulting headline in the Israeli press was, "Arafat in, Sharon out in the global war against terrorism." That shows the degree to which the Israeli media were still opposed to Sharon and in favor of Peres, the initiator of the Oslo Accords. The U.S. State Department rejoiced. The advocates of this Arabist strategy saw nothing absurd in going to war against the terrorist Bin Laden, while enlisting the terrorist Arafat in their coalition.

For Sharon matters got worse when Washington and Jerusalem became involved in an incessant coming and going of American and Israeli military men, the Israelis imparting to their counterparts the know-how that had been so painfully acquired during Israel's long struggle against terrorism, including methods and special means. But when Bush seemed to be falling into the trap, Sharon held a press conference on Thursday, October 4, 2001, in which, to a packed room in Beit Sokolov, the headquarters of the journalists' association in Tel Aviv, he announced that Israel would not agree to being sacrificed like Czechoslovakia after the Munich agreement of 1938.

On Friday morning the headlines of the Israeli press, immediately reproduced by the American media, accused Sharon of having compared Bush to Chamberlain, the Munich appeaser. Angry reactions poured out of Washington; civil servants were even heard uttering insults against Sharon in the corridors of the State Department. That same afternoon Colin Powell called Sharon to warn him that the United States and its allies were preparing to launch their offensive in Afghanistan within 48 hours. On Sunday, October 7, when the United States and its allies had just launched their offensive, Sharon called me late at night: "Israel is ready for every eventuality and is taking measures to prevent the intensification of terrorism."

Sharon explained that in order to put our security forces on extraordinary alert without attracting attention, he was not following the normal procedure of warning the defense minister, Benjamin Ben Eliezer, a member of the Labour Party. Sharon had spoken directly to those in charge of the fight against terrorism and told them what measures to take. It was feared that, to demonstrate solidarity with the Taliban regime, Palestinian terrorist organizations and the Lebanese Hezbollah would increase their attacks against Jewish targets in Israel and throughout the world. Sharon added that Colin Powell had warned him on Friday afternoon of military intervention in Afghanistan within 48 hours; the American administration was clearly concerned about Israel's security.

So, Sharon in, Arafat out? Not yet—that was still to come.

DECEMBER 2001
CHRISTMAS IN BETHLEHEM

Sharon spent the day of December 1, 2001, at the Park Lane Hotel in New York, which had been transformed into a fortress protected by dozens of American and Israeli security agents. Three months after the al-Qaeda attack against the World Trade Center and the Pentagon, New York—and the rest of America—was still tending its wounds. The attack had unleashed an unprecedented wave of patriotism. In Afghanistan the Americans were hunting for Bin Laden and his men, while the clearing operation was continuing at Ground Zero.

As soon as he arrived in New York on November 30, Ariel visited the ravaged World Trade Center site to express Israel's solidarity with America. He spent a long moment of silence before the ruins and then listened to Mayor Rudolph Giuliani describe the tragedy, with its rescue operation and the heroic actions of New York policemen and firemen. Returning to the hotel, Sharon began preparing for his meeting with George W. Bush—the third meeting that year—which had been planned for Monday, December 3, at the White House. Sharon's aim was to delegitimize Arafat as a negotiating partner because of the war that Arafat had been fomenting for more than a year. "It's as if," Sharon had said to me in the plane taking us to New York, "the president of the United States now agreed to negotiate with Bin Laden. Arafat is our Bin Laden."

Sharon's argument held sway, and unlike his predecessor, Bush did not invite the head of the Palestinian Authority to the White House. The State Department, nonetheless continued to urge Israel to negotiate with Arafat, as it had done during Sharon's visit to Washington the previous July. "Luckily American policy toward us is determined by the White House," Sharon emphasized. "Condoleezza Rice and her team know that I've done everything to put negotiations on the right track. In the beginning, I asked for seven days of complete cessation of terrorism before we could open negotiations. I then renounced that stance in favor of Tenet's plan, which promised a cease-fire. Then the Americans sent us General Zinni to try to introduce a cease-fire in stages. He wasn't any more successful than the others. Arafat thinks that he can destabilize Israel with his war. He is wrong. On Monday, I must persuade Washington to let us fight terrorism our own way, without foreign intervention. In fact, the Americans have explicitly told me that if I created a government of national unity, they would not put pressure on Israel to make concessions to the Palestinians."

When I was critical of the fact that the Labour Party had joined his coalition, he agreed that Peres was his political opponent and that Israeli public opinion identified Peres with the Oslo Accords that had brought Arafat to Gaza and to the gates of Jerusalem. Peres's repeated failures did not prevent him from continuing to meet Arafat in the hope of sweet-talking him. Nevertheless, for Sharon this coalition "was essential to maintaining national unity at a time of war."

At the Park Lane Hotel, far from Jerusalem and the war, Arik prepared for this meeting with Bush. Arik was supported by Arieh Genger, his trusted aide and intermediary with the American president and his advisers. Genger was an Israeli entrepreneur, who had bought Haifa Chemicals as part of his Trans Resources group; he had settled in the United States a long time before and was of great help to Sharon. The friendship between the two men went back to 1973. During the Yom Kippur war, Sharon noticed that his tank commanders needed binoculars, and he had called Genger to ask him to send some urgently. This was immediately taken care of. Since then, Sharon and Genger had grown ever closer.

At the end of 1981, Genger left his business in New York to reorganize Israel's war industry. But a media and political campaign set up by Defense Minister Sharon's enemies stopped Genger from being assigned the task. Genger was criticized for being a *yored*, a negative term indicating an Israeli citizen who "goes down"—that is, emigrates abroad. Sharon would have liked Genger to attend his first official meeting with President George W. Bush in March 2001. Genger was a brilliant negotiator who knew as well as Sharon how useful Genger's knowledge of the mysteries of American political and financial power could be in tough negotiations. In addition, even though Sharon spoke perfect English, in a tussle with Bush and his advisers Sharon sometimes felt lost. At their first summit meeting Bush had made Sharon promise not to make personal attacks on Arafat. Sharon blamed this regrettable commitment on a misunderstanding.

In June 2001, Genger had acted as, in effect, an interpreter for Sharon, who had unfortunately—or fortunately?—lost his voice during his second meeting with President Bush. Genger caused a stir by saying, in front of Vice President Dick Cheney, Condoleezza Rice and Colin Powell, "Mr. President, you got it wrong." Sharon had to conceal the role of this trusted aide in his relations with President Bush from his minister of foreign affairs, Peres, and also from some of his advisers who were prone to "leaks." The White House had demanded absolute secrecy in talks, a condition that was fulfilled until the legal adviser to the Israeli government, Elyakim Rubinstein, pronounced Genger unfit to be an envoy because of his industrial and commercial interests in Israel.

That December 1, 2001, Genger was still able to act from the sidelines and prepare the ground for a productive meeting between Bush and Sharon. Everything was going according to plan when suddenly, at 6 around P.M. in New York and after midnight in Israel, the news came: 11 dead and almost 180 wounded in a double attack in Jerusalem. That Saturday evening, at the end of Shabbat, two human bombs had exploded in a crowded pedestrian street in Jerusalem. Twenty minutes later, while the emergency services were arriving, a car bomb exploded in an adjoining street.

Undoubtedly, Ariel wanted to return to Israel at once. Locked up in his room with his advisers and his military secretary, General Moshe Kaplinsky, Sharon was inundated with news. Interrupting their programs, American television channels broadcast the terrible images live. As a journalist, I was not allowed to participate in the official meeting, but I got a note through to my friend: "You must go back to Jerusalem, though it's inconceivable that your meeting with Bush will be canceled because of a deliberate terrorist attack by Arafat. I am sure the president will understand." Half an hour later Arik called me in my room: the meeting would take place the next day at noon in the White House. The President had agreed to cut short his weekend at Camp David. The following day, a Sunday, we left New York at dawn and went to Washington, where Blair House had been put at Sharon's disposal.

Sharon seemed satisfied when he emerged from the White House. George Bush had been very receptive and was willing to compare Israel's fight against Palestinian terrorism to that of the United States against al-Qaeda. We were about to leave Blair House for the Andrews military aerodrome when my cell phone rang, interrupting our conversation. It was William Safire of the *New York Times*, who wanted to interview Sharon before he left. Initially Arik refused, saying that he had a cold and was tired, but I managed to persuade him and held out my phone. The article in the *New York Times* the following day can be summed up in a few words: "It's us or Arafat—and it will be us!"

On Wednesday, December 12, at about 6 P.M., bus number 189 exploded after two charges hidden went off in a bend in the road just before Emmanuel settlement in the West Bank. Seconds later grenades exploded, and there were bursts of machine-gun fire. The toll was heavy: 11 dead and 27 wounded. Once again Shin Bet had known that an attack was being planned in the West Bank and even knew the identity of some of the assailants. Under the rules laid down by General Zinni, the Palestinian security services were supposed to arrest terrorists making their way to an attack if details about the terrorists were communicated to them in time; the details had been communicated, but once again—as with the suicide bombing at the Sbarro restaurant in Jerusalem—the Palestinian authorities had ignored the warning.

Sharon's patience was at an end. Since Arafat was flouting the agreements made with George Tenet and Anthony Zinni, it was high time to limit his freedom of movement once and for all. Until then, the head of the Palestinian Authority had moved freely between the Gaza Strip and Ramallah in the West Bank and had personally directed the terrorist offensive on both fronts. And so the Mukata'a (Arafat's compound in the West Bank) was sealed off, and remained so almost without interruption until October 2004 when Arafat became unwell and was authorized to leave Ramallah for Paris.

But the coming of Christmas gave Yasser Arafat the opportunity that he wanted to affect public opinion. From the Mukata'a, Arafat defied Ariel Sharon by announcing that he would attend the midnight mass in Bethlehem, even if he had to walk there. Since 1994, Arafat had attended the service held in the Church of the Nativity in order to pose as a protector of this important Christian site. "Arafat will not go to Bethlehem. He isn't Christian. If he wants to pray, let him go to the mosque of Ramallah!" Sharon thundered. Furious, Sharon noted all the routes, even pathways, linking Ramallah and Bethlehem on a map and on aerial photographs, and he ordered the army to erect barricades. I found out that Arafat planned to slip through Sharon's net in a car with diplomatic license plates that belonged to a respectable bishop who was visiting Arafat, and I warned Sharon, who reassured me in an impatient tone, "He will not go!"

The decision to confine Arafat that Christmas Eve of 2001 provoked an outcry: vehement protests from European countries, an emotional appeal from the Vatican, and indignant articles in the international press. One question served as their leitmotif: How could Sharon dare to forbid the president of the Palestinian Authority from celebrating Christmas in Bethlehem? Yasser Arafat was so established in his role as a "partner" in the peace negotiations that even various eminent Israeli figures tried to make Sharon reverse his decision. Some of his advisers accused Sharon of having made the whole Arab world turn against Israel and of having made the fight against terrorism a personal matter. The president of the country, Moshe Katsav, went beyond his purely symbolic role and made it known that he had advised Sharon to allow Arafat to move freely. Katsav even arranged secret meetings in Ramallah with delegates of the Palestinian Authority's legislative council to proclaim a *hudna* with them—a tactical cease-fire generally used by Palestinians to reconstruct their military base before resuming hostilities.

Within the government, Labour ministers did not hide their disapproval. Both the foreign affairs minister Shimon Peres, winner of the Nobel Peace Prize with Rabin and Arafat in December 1994, and the minister of defense Benjamin Ben Eliezer remained convinced that Sharon "doesn't understand Arafat." But the prime minister was firm, and cameras around the world showed the empty chair of the keffiyeh-wearing Arafat in the Church of the Nativity.

JANUARY 2002
A BOATLOAD OF WEAPONS

On January 4, 2002, Sharon received the American envoy, General Anthony Zinni, at Sycamore Farm; Zinni had just returned from the United States, where he had spent the holidays. Zinni planned to meet Arafat on the same day, in a new attempt to put an end to the war he had begun. As was customary in the Sharon household, an Israeli breakfast was served in the dining room that adjoined the kitchen. George W. Bush's envoy explained how he intended to reinstate, under American control, cooperation between Israel and the Palestinian Authority on matters of security. Sharon's military secretary went back and forth between the table and the office, updating the prime minister with notes on the situation.

As Zinni was taking his leave, Sharon asked him to tell Arafat that he should no longer worry about his consignment of weapons on board the cargo ship *Karine A*. "It's in our hands," Sharon said. General Zinni was obviously surprised, and Sharon explained that large quantities of weapons, acquired in Iran by Arafat, had been loaded onto a cargo ship, the *Karine A*, chartered by the Palestinian Authority and headed to the Gaza Strip. An Israeli marine commando team had boarded the ship at sea the previous day, and the ship was expected at any moment in the port of Eilat.

Zinni met Arafat at the Mukata'a a little while later and gave Arafat the bad news. Arafat blanched in astonishment and hurriedly denied that the ship had any connection with the Palestinian Authority. Arafat continued his vigorous denials even after the Israeli government released its official announcement of the seizure of the *Karine A* and its cargo of weapons.

When I saw him later that day, Sharon did not hide his pride at the success of the operation executed by the famous marine commandos, thanks to the excellent work of the intelligence services: "Our men approached the ship in the open sea, far from Israel, surprised the crew, who offered no resistance, and discovered the cases of weapons hidden beneath a pile of toys." Sharon knew that, even if they were warned, the Egyptian authorities would do nothing to intercept the *Karine A* in the Suez Canal: Egypt looked the other way when arms were smuggled in the Sinai. What is more, if the cargo ship had been boarded in its territorial waters, Egypt would have accused Israel of piracy. So the ship had to be intercepted in the Red Sea, before it got to the canal and reached the Mediterranean; otherwise, it would have been too late to prevent the ship from unloading its cargo of weapons. The boarding of the *Karine A* in the Red Sea, hundreds of kilometers from Israel, had to take place in record time if the crew was to be prevented from raising the alarm. Then, to reach Eilat, the boat would cross the Straits of Tiran, which are under Egyptian control. Unfortunately, President Mubarak was spending that weekend at Sharm el-Sheikh, so the number of coastguard ships had been increased for his security. For this reason, before informing General Zinni of the operation, Sharon had waited until he knew that the *Karine A* was sailing in the Gulf of Aqaba.

On the evening of Sunday, January 6, Sharon arrived in Eilat, where he congratulated the members of the commando team and inspected the captured arsenal displayed on the quay: antitank weapons and, most important, a large quantity of long-range rockets capable of reaching towns in the heart of Israel and of threatening Ben-Gurion international airport. In the cold wind that blew over Eilat, the military attachés and members of the diplomatic corps, as well as representatives of foreign media and other guests, could take stock of Yasser Arafat's lost arsenal. The president of the Palestinian Authority was still protesting that he was the victim of an Israeli conspiracy and that he was not involved in the affair. Needless to say, his denials were given voice in the international press and in certain Israeli newspapers. Washington seemed momentarily caught off guard; some important parts of the American media, and even the State Department, were ready to believe Arafat's fable of accusing the Lebanese Hezbollah of being responsible for the cargo of the *Karine A*. George Tenet, who wanted to keep Arafat involved in the peace negotiations and who had not followed the affair as it unfolded—any more than the

CIA had—was so skeptical about Israel's accusations that he refused to see General Yossi Kupperwasser, deputy chief of the IDF's military intelligence. Furious, Sharon appealed to the White House to make Tenet receive the Israeli delegation, which was bringing the CIA irrefutable proof of Arafat's direct involvement.

In January 2002, Arafat made his biggest mistake toward the United States: he sent Bush a secret missive in which he accused Israel of having deliberately staged the whole affair of the *Karine A* to denounce him—a letter that President Bush considered an insult to his intelligence. After this blunder, Arafat was discredited in the eyes of the White House.

MARCH 2002
MASSACRE ON PESACH

As had been his habit for many years, Arik telephoned me on the eve of Pesach in 2002 to wish me and my family happy holidays. Arik added, "I'm going to perform the ritual Seder with our guest Cyril, who's just arrived." The businessman Cyril Kern had been a close friend of Sharon's since the war of 1948, when the young volunteer had come from London to defend the new Jewish state. Sharon particularly loved the Pesach holiday. He asked each of his guests to read in turn from the Haggadah,* and he filled the glasses of ritual wine himself, while looking after the Seder, the meal that commemorated the exodus from Egypt.

I had been invited with my family to visit our friends Sarah and Avner Platek. At about 8 P.M., a phone call from a friend called me from the table: "There has been a terrorist attack on the Park Hotel in Netanya, with many victims." I hurried to my car and drove toward the bomb site. A storm was raging; the gusts of wind and rain seemed like bad omens. On the radio, the presenter delivered his litany: 10, 15, 30 dead . . . A terrorist disguised as a woman had blown himself up in the dining room of the Park Hotel. Around the building, neither the rain nor the cold wind blowing in from the sea could clear the smell of death—traces of explosives and of human flesh. Debris had fallen from the ceiling, and burst water pipes formed great pools red with blood.

Sharon was already en route to the ministry of defense, where he had called in both the chief of staff Shaul Mofaz and the head of Shin

---

* Traditional text, read during the Seder service, that recounts the story of the Israelites' Exodus from Egypt.

Bet, Avi Dichter, as well as their deputies, to work out possible plans for retaliation before submitting them to the security cabinet that was due to meet the following day. Israel had never experienced such a sad Pesach. The trauma was so deep that even the spokesmen of the left called on the government to punish Arafat, the man whom, until that day, they had called a "partner for peace." But how? The heads of the IDF, Shin Bet and Mossad immediately rejected proposals to evacuate Arafat via helicopter to the Arabian desert or, purely and simply, to liquidate him—measures that they believed would provoke grave Palestinian, Arab and international reactions.

For his part, Sharon's hands were tied by his promise to George Bush. As Sharon often said to me, "The relationship of trust between Bush and me rests on the certainty that we will both keep our promises." If Sharon had been able to fulfill his secret dream, the Mukata'a would have been destroyed and Arafat reduced to the status of a homeless person. But Arafat lived in the Mukata'a and was not willing to leave. So by order of the cabinet, before the meeting had even finished, armored vehicles and Israeli bulldozers were already gathering around Ramallah. The tanks took up their position to prevent Arafat's men from going in or out of the Mukata'a while, under the still gaze of television cameras, bulldozers started destroying the administrative buildings around the large building where Arafat had gone underground, sheltered behind sandbags and under the permanent surveillance of special intelligence service units.

APRIL 2002
"MASSACRE" IN JENIN

I flew with Sharon by helicopter to the theater of operations in Jenin, the "capital" of Hamas and Islamic Jihad, and the spawning ground of many suicide bombers, most notably the ones responsible for the Park Hotel massacre in Netanya. Before leaving his office Sharon removed his tie and the jacket of his dark suit and put on a windbreaker. In the helicopter he put on headphones against the noise and to be in contact with the pilot. The counteroffensive that Sharon was directing was in full swing. For the first time since the beginning of the war, the army was charged with taking back control of the territories handed over to the Palestinian Authority. This was also the first Israeli infringement of the Oslo Accords signed by Rabin and Peres, which gave Arafat control, in the West Bank, of Ramallah, Nablus, Jenin, Bethlehem and Beit Jallah. For months shots had routinely been fired from Beit Jallah at the residents of the Gilo district in Jerusalem.

Since he could not neutralize the terrorist infrastructure without the intervention of the IDF, Sharon sent troops to Jenin, Ramallah and Bethlehem to flush out the terrorists, liquidate their leaders and destroy their laboratories for explosives. Chased by Israeli soldiers into Bethlehem, some armed terrorists used the Church of Nativity as a hiding place. The machine of Palestinian disinformation started up, with communiqués to the media and scoops whispered to foreign journalists lounging in the bar of the American Colony Hotel in east Jerusalem: "The Israelis are carrying out a massacre in Jenin. There have already been more than 500 deaths among the civilian population, including women and children." In reality, Israeli soldiers were indeed operating in the Jenin refugee camp—that is, in an inhabited zone—but instead of storming buildings, they went from house to house by digging holes through adjoining walls. This tactic, which sheltered them from gunmen waiting in ambush, also reduced civilian casualties to a minimum. Only when armed men shot at them did the IDF soldiers use armored bulldozers to knock down a house where assailants were hiding. These were not tanks but were armored vehicles that had previously been used in street combats in Jenin.

The final tally was 54 Palestinian casualties—5 of whom were civilians, the rest were terrorists—and 22 Israeli casualties. Despite this, the world had already accepted the false accusation of a "massacre in Jenin," attributed to the "butcher of Sabra and Shatilla." At the United Nations, voices clamored for the creation of a commission of inquiry; Foreign Affairs Minister Peres accepted the idea in principle and declared that it would clarify the misunderstanding. International opinion had to realize that there had been no massacre in Jenin.

Sharon, however, refused a commission of inquiry point-blank, after a bitter meeting with Kofi Annan. Sharon knew from experience that such a commission would judge Israel guilty, regardless of the facts. Had not the American administration, and notably the State Department, already implied that Sharon had gone too far in his counteroffensive? Secretary of State Colin Powell had arrived in the region to act as intermediary between Sharon and Arafat and to try to obtain the support of the Egyptian president, in an attempt to get Arafat to be more moderate. In the helicopter, Sharon whispered in my ear, "The Israeli-American crisis is getting worse and worse. The Americans have demanded that the Egyptian minister of foreign affairs meet Arafat to bring him up to speed about the meeting between Powell and Mubarak. The Israeli cabinet has protested, saying that Israel should have been informed first."

Sharon saw this as an attempt on behalf of the Americans and the Egyptians to break the isolation that he had imposed on Arafat, but Sharon also knew that he must not go too far with Washington. He therefore received Colin Powell in Jerusalem; the two men already knew each other, and the tone of the meeting was friendly. "Powell was overwhelmed when I showed him the lab photos of the victims of the last attack on the Netanya bus," Sharon told me later. That the United States eventually came to understand that no massacre had been perpetrated was due largely to the behind-the-scenes work of Arieh Genger, who was in constant touch with the White House,

Sharon told me. Although the Israeli media widely credited Dov Weisglass, chief of the prime minister's bureau, because of his constant visits to Washington, it was Genger who truly was responsible for the breakthrough.

The helicopter landed outside Jenin. As soon as he was among the soldiers seated on the ground in front of him, Sharon was in his element: "We are the only democratic country forced to fight against the terrorism of the 'islamikazes' without repaying them in kind. You know as well as I do that there was no massacre in Jenin."

A soldier spoke up: "Why didn't we bomb the terrorists from the air? That operation cost the lives of more than 20 of our comrades!"

"That is the painful and inevitable price that those who refuse to abandon their humanity have to pay—precisely because they are the target of the cruelest of their enemies—human bombs."

Before leaving Jenin, Sharon stopped for a moment to answer the questions of Dan Rather, and he invited Rather to a longer interview in Jerusalem. Given the extent of the campaign of lies about the "massacre of Jenin," it was vital to clarify the facts. At that later meeting in Jerusalem, I chatted with Rather for a few minutes before he went into Sharon's office. We talked about the fierce competition in the media world. In the twentieth century, Rather said, every reporter, however well-known, was only as good as his last story, as the saying went; today, he is only as good as his next story.

Rather did not realize how right he was. He had barely emerged from the prime minister's office when he learned that there had just been a suicide bombing at the entrance to Mahane Yehuda, the biggest market in Jerusalem, and he hurried there with his cameramen.

JUNE 24, 2002
ARAFAT OUT

On the morning of June 18, 2002, while Sharon was getting ready for a long day at work, his military secretary told him that a Palestinian had just blown himself up in a school bus in Jerusalem. Sharon decided to go immediately to the site. The security men tried in vain to delay his visit, fearing a second explosion. When Sharon arrived at the smoking bus, he surveyed the place and saw schoolchildren's burned faces; 19 were dead and about 50 wounded. The prime minister walked among the black plastic bags of the men of Zaka, orthodox volunteers who, following Jewish ritual, undertook to gather the scattered remains to give them a decent burial. "I've seen the horrors of the battlefield. You, too, have seen shocking scenes of war, but these burned bodies will be stamped on my memory forever," Sharon commented in an almost inaudible voice.

Unlike his predecessors, Sharon rarely went to the site of an attack or visited the victims in the hospital, and he gave few public pronouncements after this kind of tragedy. "I prefer to invest my time in finding ways to reduce the number of attacks and of victims," he explained. That was why he would personally ask military commanders and Shin Bet leaders about different opportunities of attacking terrorist targets. "I have to push them to action!" Sharon complained often, when he still had time to call me from the "Tower"—the nickname given to the glass-walled office that he had built on top of Sycamore Farm that allowed him to see the fields all around.

At the same time, Sharon informed the White House of the situation, adding that he did not hope for a turnaround in Arafat's deadly strategy. "So far as I am concerned," he explained to Condoleezza Rice, "Arafat is over." Sharon never tired of repeating that statement, and it was time that the message got through to the American administration. George W. Bush was about to make an important declaration on the Israeli-Palestinian issue. A draft containing its main points had been given to Sharon: the president confirmed his position of supporting the creation of a Palestinian state under certain conditions. But after the carnage in Jerusalem, Sharon was expecting a strong gesture from his ally—and he didn't hesitate to make that known to Bush.

On the evening of June 24, 2002, a week after that disastrous morning, Sharon was in his office in Jerusalem watching the televised broadcast of President Bush's press conference held in the rose garden of the White House. Sharon's prayers were answered. He heard Bush say,

> For too long, the citizens of the Middle East have lived in the midst of death and fear . . . Peace requires a new and different Palestinian leadership, so that a Palestinian state can be born. I call on the Palestinian people to elect new leaders, leaders not compromised by terror . . . And when the Palestinians have new leaders, new institutions and new security arrangements with their neighbors, the United States of America will support the creation of a Palestinian state.

In brief, Bush was saying, "If you want a country, replace Arafat." Bush also outlined other nonnegotiable conditions: the complete cessation of terrorism and the dismantling of terrorist infrastructures, economic reforms aimed at wiping out the corruption within the Palestinian Authority, the holding of "fair and pluralistic" elections and the creation of democratic institutions.

Ariel Sharon finally allowed himself a smile. The United States had come around to his point of view—and, above all, the president was definitively excluding Arafat from the deal. Arafat was out of the picture, not just "over," as Sharon had said. Bush had clearly called on the Palestinians to get rid of him. This was only fair: Arafat had duped Yitzhak Rabin, Shimon Peres and Bill Clinton on the lawn of the White House on September 13, 1993. Sharon had immediately renamed this "peace of the brave" the "peace of the graves." Now the man who had been awarded the Nobel Peace Prize in 1994 with Rabin and Peres, the terrorist that Sharon had chased from Beirut 20 years earlier, had fallen from his pedestal on the international scene, thanks to a historic speech. One evening shortly thereafter, Sharon said to me in a voice full of sadness, "How much innocent blood was shed before Washington understood what had to be done! And in Europe they still haven't understood."

This change in the American position on June 24, 2002, was essentially the result of the intervention of Arieh Genger. He had been in Crete when he received a call from Sharon asking him to make contact with the White House to discuss the draft of the presidential announcement. Each word was the subject of long hours of telephone negotiations before Genger went to the American capital to put the finishing touches to the final text and to the concessions demanded of the two sides. In the end, the speech that Sharon heard in his office was identical in every detail to the version negotiated by Genger.

JULY 2002
THE LIQUIDATION
OF HAMAS LEADERS

On Tuesday, July 23, 2002, at 1 A.M., the telephone rang. "Turn on the news," the prime minister said. "We have just liquidated a murderer in Gaza. Write an article for your newspaper in New York. Well, that's the gist of it; I'm in a hurry. I've still got a lot of work."

Ariel wanted to share this good news with a friend, particularly since that friend was someone who had pestered him for a long time to know when he was going to get rid of these assassins. I immediately switched on the television, where a special bulletin announced that at about midnight, Israeli bombs had struck the house in Gaza of one Salah Schade. My sources, whom I then called (and woke up), confirmed that this was the leader of the armed branch of Hamas in the Gaza Strip, long sought by the Israelis for his involvement in several suicide attacks and the firing of Kassam rockets.

I called the *New York Post* and reported the news that I had heard from the mouth of Ariel Sharon himself. I was told that it would be on the front page the following day, but the official announcement of the Israeli army spokesman was late in coming. Going by the images of devastation on the TV screen, I saw that there was heavy damage in the Darej district. To my astonishment, I heard the Palestinians announcing that Schade was not dead. Could the prime minister have been misinformed? At about 2 A.M. I phoned Sharon back. Was Schade only wounded? Sharon confirmed that he was dead: "It's one of our greatest victories against those bastards," he added. "The air force and Shin Bet invested huge resources in this operation. We knew of Schade's planned attacks; tonight we've saved many innocent lives. I'm going to bed," Sharon ended, with a satisfied air.

The New York office contacted me: the international press agencies were not confirming Schade's death. I didn't reveal the fact that my information came from the most reliable source there was, but I repeated that the operation had been successful. To put their minds at rest, I suggested that, for form's sake, they state that Schade's home had been targeted with the intention of killing him. The same evening the Palestinians announced that there had been 12 victims in the strike but that Schade was still on the operating table. I did not go to bed, of course, and I followed all the news bulletins. At seven o'clock in the morning local time—midnight in New York—the Palestinians finally announced Schade's death.

Hamas had been dealt a tough blow. Schade had known for a long time that he was being tracked down, so he frequently changed homes and met his four wives and children in secret. Schade had recently bought the house that was destroyed by a one-ton bomb released from an F–16. Minister of Foreign Affairs Shimon Peres and Defense Minister Benjamin Ben Eliezer had both approved the mission.

✡

Sharon did not give up now that he was successful. Throughout the summer of 2002, Israel continued its struggle against terrorist cells, sometimes without the approval of public opinion. Sharon's political opponents criticized him for the collateral loss of human life. Journalists compared "Palestinians who kill Israelis and Israelis who kill Palestinians" and spoke of an endless cycle of violence, failing to mention Sharon's promise to stop the targeted killings the very instant that the Palestinians put down their weapons. Left-wing members of the Knesset even went so far as to accuse the air force pilots of war crimes, and they threatened to drag the pilots before the international criminal court in The Hague.

Sharon did not listen to these criticisms; he concentrated on the mission that he had undertaken, relying on Israel's intelligence services. Anxious to improve Mossad's efficiency, Sharon nominated Reserve General Meir Dagan as the head of Mossad. In the early 1970s, Sharon had encouraged Dagan to set up the Rimon unit, with the mission to neutralize terrorists in the Gaza Strip. The initiative was wonderfully successful, and for 15 years the region experienced relative calm. General Aaron Zeevi, the director of Aman (the army's intelligence department), later said to me, "Sharon's contribution to the war against terrorism was exceptional. With him, there were no long speeches: first we considered the objective, and then simply the possible pitfalls. And when we warned him of the repercussions of a decision on a Palestinian or Arab street, he would stop you with a brusque, 'Think less about the Arabs and more about Jews!'" The dynamic that Arik had initiated proved extremely effective. Targeted executions increased.

✡

Around 6 A.M. on March 22, 2004, I was woken by the telephone. "Get up!" ordered the friend who had called. "Arik wants you to know that Sheikh Yassin was brought down a few minutes ago. Turn on the radio. It was a real feat." Kol Israel was indeed announcing that the spiritual leader and founder of Hamas in 1988, Ahmed Yassin, had just been killed as he was leaving the mosque in his wheelchair and about to get into his car. His two bodyguards died with him. I immediately called the *New York Post*, which was already going to press.

I soon found out why this had been described as a real feat. To execute Sheikh Yassin without involving innocent people, Shin Bet calculated that we had a window of ten seconds in which to fire—ten seconds in which the Hamas leader and his guards would be isolated from his supporters. Sharon decided to use those ten seconds. Yassin's successor, Abdel Aziz al-Rantissi, survived only a month. On Saturday, April 17, 2004, at about 8:30 P.M., missiles hit his car, and he died instantly.

NOVEMBER 2002– DECEMBER 2003
ARIK CORRUPTED?

If Ariel Sharon had a single fear, it was that his integrity or that of his family would ever be questioned. If he suspected a colleague of dishonesty, he quickly cautioned or dismissed him. And so when Sharon and his sons were accused of corruption, and his opponents in the media described them as a "criminal family," I know that he was deeply hurt, although we spoke about it very little. My friend's only comment on the innumerable headlines like "Sharon suspected of corruption" was, "There's nothing in it." I thus had no reason to discuss the matter further.

It was not the first time that Ariel had faced such accusations. In 1999, when he was minister of foreign affairs, he had been subjected to a similar police inquiry. The government's legal adviser and district attorney Elyakim Rubinstein had dismissed the case, but Sharon's reputation was damaged nonetheless. The electoral campaign of January 2003 had unleashed a new avalanche of accusations of electoral fraud against Likud candidates—allegations freely disseminated in the press. The leader of the Labour Party, Reserve General Amram Mitzna, had also tried to stigmatize his opponent with a propaganda video that hammered out the corruption allegations to the theme song from *The Godfather*. Then television channels attacked Sharon's sons and broadcast clips that had been filmed with a secret camera in the office of private detective David Spektor, who called himself a "strategic adviser" of Ariel's in the 2001 election campaign. In these clips Gilad Sharon worried about the repercussions of the so-called "Greek island affair" in which he was said to have received the enormous sum of $600,000 for assisting the tourist development of an island in the Aegean Sea. The press added that the Israeli businessman David Appel had "greased Sharon's palm" through his son. During the summer of 2004 the government's legal adviser, Menaham Mazouz, said, "the case is nonexistent."

I went to great lengths to try to convince Sharon to refute these accusations, which were nothing but out-and-out lies fabricated by the Labour Party. Sharon agreed to do so, and during an important television program he stated that he would set up procedures to eliminate corruption from Likud. Thanks to this interview Sharon managed to stop the trend of accusations, and Likud again shot ahead in the polls. The press, however, was far from accepting defeat and began hounding Sharon with a campaign similar to that of Sabra and Chatila. The rumors multiplied. It was claimed that Omri Sharon had financed the election campaign with dubious money and that he socialized with disreputable characters. I encouraged Sharon to remove his son from his position as a Likud candidate. "Abraham was prepared to sacrifice his son Isaac," I wrote to Sharon in a fax, "and he was saved; it would be much easier for you to sacrifice Omri, with his consent, so as to win the election."

On January 5, 2003, a television program in which Amram Mitzna called the Sharons a "mafia family" was interrupted by the announcement of a double suicide bombing in the old central bus station of Tel Aviv. I quickly made my way to the site, to see with my own eyes the death and destruction that had been wrought in this deprived area. There were 23 dead and more than 100 wounded—most of them immigrant workers. Once again the Zaka volunteers were collecting human remains in plastic bags. Sharon called me from his car.

"I'm at the site. It's terrible," I said.

"I am going to the defense ministry to discuss our options in dealing with those bastards. I'm going to stop this wave of terrorism." He was silent a moment and then he added, "I just wanted to tell you that we've studied your proposal about Omri, and we've held a poll on it; it seems that his removal would be considered an admission of guilt and would harm us politically."

Two days later, another bombshell—this time, political—exploded. Three weeks before the elections, the newspaper *Haaretz* announced in a front-page exclusive that the police were holding a secret inquiry into Ariel Sharon and his sons on the transfer of $1.5 million said to have been given to Sharon by their friend the South African business-man Cyril Kern. In support of these claims the newspaper quoted an official but secret Israeli letter asking the South African authorities for permission to interrogate Kern. *Haaretz* then referred back to the events of summer 1999, when Omri Sharon, in violation of the law on electoral finance, had collected $1.5 million to support his father dur-ing the Likud primaries. When the general auditor had disclosed this fact after he interrogated Ariel and Omri Sharon, Ariel announced that he would return the money to its donors. Following the lead, newspa-pers announced that the attorney general suspected that Sharon or his son had used Cyril Kern's gift to repay the money. Gilad Sharon was suspected of being the main author of this transaction.

One of Arik's close collaborators called me; he sounded desperate: "It's an Israeli Watergate! Worse than Watergate! Arik is finished!"

"No way. Nothing is lost. I know nothing about the affair, but Ariel will explain himself," I retorted, although deep down I was very worried for my friend.

The press attacked Sharon. He had gone to the worksite of the se-curity fence meant to protect the country from terrorist attacks, but the press was more interested in Cyril Kern's dollars than in the mur-derers. A poll carried out by *Haaretz* gave Likud no more than 27 seats, while the Labour Party's share had risen to 23. The election that had seemed certain to be a victory now threatened to be a resounding defeat.

On Wednesday afternoon I learned that Sharon planned to re-spond in person to the accusations; he planned to respond both in the daily newspapers *Yediot Aharanot* and *Ma'ariv* and also in television in-terviews. Thinking this a disastrous strategy, I spoke to Sharon's ad-viser, the publicist Reuven Adler, and told him that rather than speaking to journalists who were just waiting for an opportunity to de-clare that "Sharon is finished, he looks old and pale," Sharon should hold a televised press conference to address the nation directly. My ar-guments won out, and the interviews planned for the following day were canceled. Ariel called me from his farm, having returned well after midnight. He seemed preoccupied and tense: "First and fore-most we must win the election. We can deal with this business afterward." He did, however, promise me that he would hold a press conference the following evening. At 3 A.M. I sent him a fax setting out some talking points for his televised address.

At 8 P.M. on January 9, 2003, journalists crowded into the prime minister's residence in Jerusalem. The atmosphere was lighthearted. Some journalists openly mocked Sharon, talking about his "last press conference" and predicting that it would be his political funeral. It took a lot of strength for Sharon to confront the journalists that evening.

Accompanied by his aides and by his secretary Marit Danon, Sharon answered questions about Gilad—who was, he said, "at 37, capable of defending himself"—and about his own actions. Sharon accused the Labour Party of having told outright lies. The president of the electoral commission, Judge Michael Heshin, a member of the supreme court, then ordered that Sharon's microphone be cut, because he said that these words constituted propaganda, forbidden during election campaigns. Coming out of the room, Sharon said to Marit, who seemed critical of his performance, "What do you think will happen to me? At worst, I'll return to my farm."

I rejoined Ariel and shook his hand, clasping him to me. He was clearly touched; he was barely successful in hiding his concern. I said to him, "You should award Judge Hesin the Jabotinsky prize.* By cutting the mike, he saved Likud. Tonight, most Israelis were dying to hear you address the accusations. Now they will be blaming the judge for undermining your freedom of speech and gagging you. You won the election tonight."

"You think so?"

"Absolutely! You're in the middle of the action and so you don't see it, but I've got more distance and I'm sure that Judge Heshin, without meaning to, has ensured your victory."

In fact, Likud immediately rose in the polls to 30 seats, and this trend increased when the attorney general Elyakim Rubinstein re-

---

* Prize awarded for services to Israel. Zeev Jabotinski (1880–1940) was one of the fathers of Zionism.

leased the results of the inquiry on the leaked confidential letter to the South African authorities. The attorney dealing with the case, Liora Glatt-Berkovitch, revealed during questioning that she had given the document to the journalist Baruch Kra because she was politically opposed to Sharon. This was an unprecedented illegal political act on the part of a state attorney.

The affair was not closed, however. Ariel Sharon's name was entirely cleared in June 2004, but the case against Omri continued. Accused on August 28, 2005, of illegal financing of an electoral campaign, Omri pleaded guilty at his trial and resigned from his Knesset seat on January 3, 2006. On February 14, Omri was sentenced to nine months in prison; because of his father's health, the sentence was reduced to six months.

JUNE 2003
THE ROAD MAP

On June 4, 2003, King Abdullah of Jordan organized a summit in Aqaba at which President Bush and prime ministers Ariel Sharon and Mahmoud Abbas were present. Under the scorching midday sun and before the world's press, who had descended upon the Gulf of Eilat, they solemnly declared the adoption of the "Road Map," Bush's statement of June 24, 2002, setting out his vision of "two States for two peoples, Israel and Palestine, living side by side in peace." Several minutes before this declaration, Sharon had obtained Bush's commitment that he would emphasize in his speech that Israel, the Jewish state, would coexist with a Palestinian state.

Starting in 2003, the idea of abandoning certain territories to advance the cause of peace was gaining ground with Sharon. On Friday, May 23, at midday, he said to me, "Tomorrow morning, between eight and 9 A.M., Washington time, the White House will publish a press release declaring that the United States will take serious account of Israel's grave concerns expressed in the 14 comments and reservations on the Road Map. I can then immediately submit the Road Map for the government's approval, which I am sure it will receive."

Sharon had the serenity of a man at peace with himself, ready to carry out a difficult decision. In his dark blue suit, he seemed to me like the grave, solemn Sharon of the battlefield, on the eve of a new offensive—this time, one of peace. On the solid basis of his relationship with George W. Bush, Prime Minister Sharon had accepted Bush's Road Map. The steps leading to its acceptance by the government of Israel reached their culmination in the third week of May 2003.

Did the United States put pressure on you?
No pressure, although there was coordination on our respective positions.

What made you accept the Road Map?

Several things. First, the desire to support the Bush administration in its difficult struggle to create peace and democracy in the Middle East, just as it was waging an uncompromising war against terrorism—these are aims that Israel shares. Second, the desire to avoid at all costs a situation in which Arabs and their sympathizers in the United States could blame Israel for the failure of the Road Map. Third, and most important, I was given the promise—officially—that Washington would take serious account of our reservations about the proposal, for the entire duration of its effective application.

✡

Ariel Sharon seemed absolutely determined to pass the ball to the new Palestinian prime minister, Mahmoud Abbas, called Abu Mazen, and put him to the test. If Abbas demonstrated a real commitment to the enterprise, the Palestinians would soon realize that they could have no better partner than Sharon in making progress on the path set out under the Road Map. But when another act in the Israeli-Palestinian drama was played out during the evening of Saturday, May 17, Sharon considered canceling his meeting with Abu Mazen, planned for 9:30 P.M. in Jerusalem. A Hamas terrorist blew himself up in a Hebron street, killing two Jewish pedestrians, the Levi couple. The prime minister decided to honor his appointment and left his farm for his office in the capital.

Abu Ala and Mahmoud Dahlan accompanied Abu Mazen to the meeting. As soon as they arrived, Sharon expressed his outrage at this latest attack and demanded the dissolution of terrorist organizations, as well as the confiscation of illegally held weapons, all as laid down under the first phase of the Road Map. For the whole three hours of the meeting, Abu Mazen and his two colleagues repeated the same refrain time and again: Israel must first officially adopt the Road Map— *haritat at-tarik*, in Arabic.

"Why do you keep repeating that?" Sharon asked. "I have officially declared that I accept Bush's project of June 24, 2002, that provides for a peace process leading to 'two States for two peoples.'" But the Palestinians remained obstinate. Sharon was due to go to Washington on May 20 to meet George W. Bush, but he promised Abu

Mazen that he would continue the discussion on his return. Events, however, decreed otherwise. Several hours later another Hamas suicide attack, this one on a Jerusalem bus, killed seven people and wounded dozens of others. This time Sharon did not hesitate, and with the approval of the White House, he postponed his visit to the United States. Sharon did not want to be abroad while another terrorist wave rocked his country. And, indeed, the afternoon of Monday, May 19, a Palestinian blew himself up at the entrance to a shopping mall in Afula, killing 3 people and wounding about 50.

As soon as he heard of the carnage, George W. Bush telephoned the Palestinian prime minister for the first time, demanding that he put an end to the attacks. Mahmoud Abbas promised to do so if Israel would first accept the Road Map. The American president informed Ariel Sharon the same day. So on May 20, Sharon sent his bureau chief Dov Weisglass to Washington for 24 hours, to finalize the conditions for Israel's acceptance of the Road Map: the dismantling of Hamas, Islamic Jihad and other terrorist organizations. Abu Mazen was given no alternative.

Weisglass was still in the United States when Israel's naval forces boarded the fishing boat *Abu Moussa*, which was sailing from Lebanon to the Gaza Strip with a Hezbollah bomb expert on board. The marine intelligence service rapidly discovered that Yasser Arafat's agents had organized this expert's trip—further proof that Arafat was determined to sabotage Abu Mazen's chances of success by continuing to support terrorist activities. This information, which was transmitted to Washington and confirmed by the CIA, intensified the atmosphere of urgency: Arafat, the al-Aqsa Brigade of Martyrs, Hamas and Islamic Jihad were on the verge of demolishing the chances of the Road Map to peace.

In his exchanges with the White House, Sharon was promised that the United States would supervise the implementation of the Road Map and ignore the interventions of the European Union and the United Kingdom, which clearly supported Palestinian demands. The Americans also kept control of all security matters and would not allow international interference in this area. The American president undertook the rapid organization of a tripartite summit meeting with Ariel Sharon and Abu Mazen. Because of the continuing war in Iraq, George W. Bush wanted his name to be associated with a peace initiative between Israel and the Palestinians.

On May 25, the Israeli government approved the Road Map by 12 votes in favor, 7 against and 4 abstentions. For the first time in its parliamentary history, the Jewish state had consented to the principle of the establishment, after due process, of a Palestinian state. Ariel Sharon agreed to be interviewed by me and received me in Jerusalem. He was in his second mandate as prime minister of Israel after his reelection on January 28, 2003. According to a public opinion poll published by *Ma'ariv* and *Yediot Ahronot*, Israeli heads of government had rarely enjoyed the popularity and trust of the people that Sharon did. For more than 50 years, after a long military career, Ariel Sharon had held various ministerial posts at the most critical times in the development of the Jewish state. Armed with this vast experience, for the past two years he had fought Palestinian terrorist organizations with unprecedented toughness. And from now on he would do all that he could to get Israel out of the long war imposed by the enemy and to set Israel on a course that would ensure security, as well as ensure peace, with its Palestinian neighbor and the whole Arab world.

Have you won the battle against Arafat and terrorism but lost it in terms of the Palestinian state and the Jewish settlements? In the end, it's the Road Map—which is not very advantageous for Israel—that holds sway.
Our government supported the principles outlined by President Bush in his speech of June 24, 2002. So long as the scope of the Road Map does not exceed the terms set out in that speech, we accept it, along with 14 reservations that we communicated to the White House.

What are your main reservations?
The central issue is security and the way in which the struggle against terrorism is implemented. Everyone agrees that there is a need for security, but there is a difference of opinion in terms of how things are formulated. Then there is the question of the stages of the peace process. We have agreed with the United States that we cannot proceed to the next phase until the previous one has been fulfilled, so with this system, deadlines are less important than the complete fulfillment of each phase. That is why the succession of the phases is to our mind of vital importance. Our third reservation concerns what Palestinians call the "right of return"; this issue poses a real problem.

They demand that Israel agree to the return of Palestinian refugees to what is now Israel's territory.

I am not opposed to the creation of a Palestinian state that welcomes the Palestinian people and refugees. In my view, that is the best solution for both us and the Palestinians. We should not continue to dominate another people. It's bad for us and for the Palestinians. How long can we stay in some of their towns? However, the Palestinian state must resolve the problem of refugees. A situation in which the Palestinian people actually have two countries to return to is unacceptable. Let us be clear: that is in essence what the Palestinians want, and we are not prepared to agree to it. The return of Palestinian refugees to our land would spell the end of Israel as a Jewish state. We will therefore never allow it. That has to be absolutely clear: Palestinian refugees, now in the third generation, cannot settle in Israel.

Does that also apply to family reunification?

Our previous governments committed a grave error. In order to disguise the return of Palestinian refugees to Israel, they widened the criteria for "family reunification" beyond the case of marriage. Since 1994 almost 130,000 Palestinians have entered Israel thanks to these measures. I put an end to that dangerous process.

Is your recognition of the existence of a Palestinian state—which you have said is your intention—dependent solely on the condition that the Palestinians give up on the right of return?

To put an end to the conflict, Palestinians have to recognize the right that every Jew acquires at birth (what the French call *droit du sang* and the English call *birthright*)—the right to an independent Jewish state in the historic birthplace of the Jewish people. That is, so far as I am concerned, the nonnegotiable condition for the end of the conflict. Despite their great importance, the agreements signed with Egypt and Jordan did not bring an end to the conflict. The end of the conflict will come about only with the recognition of this inalienable right of the Jewish people.

Do the Palestinians first need to give up the right of return?

No one in Israel, and that goes for all political parties, will accept the return of Palestinian refugees within our borders; I repeat, that would mean the destruction of the Jewish state.

Would you be prepared, perhaps as a gesture to the Americans, to freeze the development of the settlements or to evacuate the unauthorized settlements?
That is a sensitive issue. It will be tackled in the final phase of the negotiation, and it is not appropriate to discuss it at the moment.

If George W. Bush had to choose between two men that he respects, Ariel Sharon and Tony Blair, do you not fear that, despite his esteem and friendship for you, he would choose Tony Blair?
We are not under pressure. We are in dialogue. There are occasional differences of approach, but our relationship is very close. We have never before had such good relations with the White House. I want to emphasize this: we are not in conflict with the United States. I don't have the feeling that I am under any threat whatsoever.

What do you think of the strained relationship between London and Jerusalem before and during the Iraq war?
It's very serious, particularly the comparison between Iraq and Israel, which is disgraceful and inappropriate. I had always considered Tony Blair, whom I met several times in London and in Jerusalem, a friend of Israel. He perhaps still is, but his words and comparisons, accompanied by the demands he makes of us, smack too much of interference in our business.

Why does he have that attitude?
Difficult to say, but it is perhaps related to domestic difficulties. Tony Blair needed the support of the British parliament for the war in Iraq, and perhaps he obtained it at Israel's expense. The Jewish people should remain vigilant to this kind of thing. Blair won't be the one to pay the price for it.

Some commentators believe that the Road Map is even worse than the Oslo Accords and that the Americans have deceived you; after having led you to believe that the Road Map was not a serious document, they presented it to you as a fait accompli. Do you feel that you were tricked?
No. Israel is not a pawn that everyone can move around at will. We live here. It would be impossible to weaken our position on the vital issues of our existence.

Do you believe that the violence of the last three years is coming to an end?
I will use all the means at my disposal to achieve peace. As soon as the
new Palestinian prime minister was in place, I opened a dialogue with
him. But I am not holding my breath.

*Do you see in Abu Mazen—Mahmoud Abbas—a leader with whom you
could come to an agreement?*
Mahmoud Abbas knows that it is impossible to get the better of Israel
through violence.

*If the Americans told you that they have begun a revolution in the whole re-
gion and that it is now for you to do your part by dismantling the settlements
in Judea-Samaria and the Gaza Strip, what would you do?*
We would be prepared to make very painful sacrifices in certain areas.
I have, however, said repeatedly to George W. Bush that in matters af-
fecting Israel's security, I have never made concessions in the past, I
won't make them now and I never will. I explained clearly to him that
the historic responsibility for the future of the Jewish people rests
squarely on my shoulders. We ourselves are the only ones in a position to determine what is and isn't dangerous for Israel.

Does this include Netzarim, in the Gaza Strip?
I would rather not talk about specific places for now. One should not
concentrate too much on this sensitive issue. But if it turns out that we
can have a real dialogue with the Palestinians and that they understand that peace excludes terrorist activities and attempts to destabilize Israel, I would declare the necessity for every Jew, and for me in
particular, to take painful measures.

*You use general terms such as "concessions" or "painful measures"; isn't that
just a way of dodging the issue?*
Absolutely not. I speak from the bottom of my heart. We are talking
about the birthplace of the Jewish people; our whole past lies in historic places such as Bethlehem, Shiloh and Beth-El, and I know that
we will have to give some of them up. We will have to separate from
places that are linked to every stage of our history. As a Jew, I find that
extremely painful. But I have decided to make maximum effort to

come to an agreement—rational necessity has taken priority over feelings. I have, however, explained to President Bush and the European heads of state that, although we are willing to make painful concessions, Israel will not agree to any compromise that undermines the security of its citizens or that undermines its very existence.

Are you saying that the settlements of Siloe and Beth-El are possible candidates for evacuation?
No, no, I have not mentioned them as such.

So what exactly do you mean?
In speaking about painful concessions, I'm trying to explain what kind of pain I am referring to. The Tomb of the Patriarchs, a tomb that is unique in the world; Shiloh, a great Jewish political and spiritual center for 369 years; Beth-El, or Rachel's Tomb beside Bethlehem—these are all places that, as a Jew, I am linked to, body and soul.

What will happen to these places?
I haven't said that anything will happen to them. We will discuss each issue as it arises—not now. I am talking about pain in general. Hebron, where King David reigned for seven and a half years, is part of the patrimony of the Jewish people. Do places such as the tomb of Makhpelah, where the fathers and mothers of the nation—Abraham and Sarah, Isaac and Rebecca, Jacob and Leah—are buried, exist anywhere else in the world? I read the Bible often, and I feel a deep spiritual attachment to those places. Before and above all else, I am a Jew. My thinking is dominated by the Jews' future in 30 years, in 300 years and in 1,000 years. That is what preoccupies and interests me first and foremost.

Do you still intend to bring a million new immigrants to Israel over the next ten years?
Absolutely. I consider the immigration of Jews from all over the world to Israel a vital objective, perhaps even the most vital at the current juncture. We should facilitate the entry of Jews who want to settle in Israel as much as possible. Of course, I am not talking about bureaucratic procedures. For me, a Jew is any individual who comes to Israel, feels a sense of belonging to the Jewish people, does his military ser-

vice and fights for the country. As a former commander of paratrooper corps, I want to point out that today half of all our soldiers, both officers and privates, are new immigrants. Despite all the difficulties, these newcomers integrate well into Israeli society, at all levels.

When Bush and Blair ask you to implement the Road Map, what will you tell them?
That's not how it happens. That notion is based on a misunderstanding of our relations with the United States. I feel that I have been invested with a historic responsibility toward the Jews. Everything that happens here influences the lives of Jews around the world. At the same time, I will not miss the opportunity before me to come to a political agreement. I have been accused of having no plan of action. In reality, I am the only one who has formulated a political plan, which was submitted to Washington, was eventually endorsed and was included in the president's proposals, after our seven meetings at the White House.

Martin Indyk, the previous U.S. ambassador to Israel, proposed to President Bush that, rather than implementing the Road Map, the Palestinian territories should be placed under international stewardship. What do you think of that idea?
I see no reason to abandon Bush's plan. No stewardship or intervention, whether American or international, is a solution to our problems. Such an arrangement would only limit our ability to defend ourselves against terrorist activities.

What if you were pressured to accept it?
If you believe the press, Israel is under terrible pressure; we are terrified from morning to night. Frankly, I smile when I read the headlines. Israel has never had better cooperation with the United States than during the war in Iraq and even now. We don't agree on every point—today as in the past—but the basis of our relationship remains the strength of the dialogue established between us; the Americans are very clear about what we are and are not prepared to accept. I repeat that I am ready to accept large-scale concessions, but nothing that affects the security of the state and its citizens. Despite the friendship that links us to the Americans, something that I will not do and that I

recommend my successors not do is to entrust the security of Israel to others.

According to British and American reports, there are more than 1,000 illegal settlements. Why don't you evacuate them, as the British government proposes, for example?
I am not ready to accept vague figures. I have already said that what is legal is legal and what is illegal is illegal. One must distinguish between what is legal and what is not.

Have you thought of acknowledging the inauguration of the Abu Mazen government with an official gesture of some kind?
There is no reason to do anyone a favor. Things were agreed on between Israel and the United States before George W. Bush's speech in 2002. We agreed on the way in which the negotiations would be carried out. Our goal is to reach an agreement. The plans are in place; everything now depends on their implementation. There is no question of going back on the smallest point—everything must be fulfilled.

The Oslo Accords were destined to fail from the outset because of their complexity. They could have succeeded only if their terms had been scrupulously carried out. But the Israeli governments preferred to look the other way; they were too attached to appeasing the other side— and all they received in return was an increase in terrorism. Thanks to an extreme effort, we managed to stop that breaking wave. More and more Palestinians realize that it is impossible to break Israel with terrorism and that Yasser Arafat is responsible for the suffering they endure.

But will Abu Mazen be able to free himself from Arafat's grasp?
The struggle over that point is not a simple one. If Abu Mazen does not display the necessary competence and if Arafat continues to pull the strings, the chances of reaching an agreement will be minimal, even nonexistent.

In his doctorate, obtained at Moscow University in 1980, Abu Mazen denied the Holocaust. Have you forgiven him for that?
I haven't forgiven anything, but for the moment I am not concerned with that question. Abu Mazen seems to have understood that he will not conquer us by the use of force and that he must accept a compromise. That said, neither he nor the majority of Arabs in the region

have recognized the inalienable right of the Jewish people to establish our nation here. The conflict will truly end only when the Arabs recognize that right. Because it is impossible to achieve such recognition immediately, we have to progress toward a solution in stages.

But you wanted to be remembered as someone who engineered a spectacular about-face in our relations with the Palestinians.
I chose to make a real effort to reach a true agreement. Anyone who has seen, as I have, the colossal undertaking involved in the creation and consolidation of Israel will better understand the problems and the path to follow. This mission seems to have been the responsibility of my generation, who had the privilege of living through one of the most exciting periods in Jewish history. At my age, I don't have political ambition beyond the role I occupy. My objective is to bring peace and security to the people of Israel. I will use all the means at my disposal to work toward that end.

You have really accepted the idea of two nations for two peoples?
I think that that is what will happen. One has to be realistic. The creation of a Palestinian state seems inevitable to me. I repeat that in my view it is not appropriate for us to dominate another people or to control their lives.

And yet, under your leadership, Israel once again has direct control over Palestinian towns.
Our presence in Jenin and Nablus is temporary. It arises solely out of the concern to protect our citizens against terrorist activities. It is a situation that will not last.

After having established, believed in and developed the settlements, you now envisage the evacuation of isolated populations.
For a real, concrete and durable peace, we must make painful concessions. Not in exchange for promises, but for actual peace.

Some people claim that the security fence you are building is designed not only to stop terrorists from getting into Israel but also to fix the country's borders unilaterally.
It is neither a political border nor a security border; this wall is designed purely and simply to stop terrorists from getting into Israel.

The construction is being carried out very rapidly, thanks to an enormous fleet of heavy construction vehicles. I believe that the section between Gilboa and Elkana will be finished around the end of the year.

Will the wall also enclose big settlements like Ariel and Emmanuel?
As a general rule, the wall will not determine the fate of settlements. It is in our interest for the wall to surround as many Jewish towns, and as few Arab ones, as possible.

But what will happen to the specific towns of Ariel and Emmanuel?
I think that they will be surrounded from our side.

Some people want to see you acting like an Israeli de Gaulle—a national leader who realizes at a certain point that reality has changed.
In making that comparison, one must not forget a vital point: our Algeria is here, not overseas. Therefore we need to be far more cautious.

In the past, you spoke about long-term transitional agreements. You did not believe in the possibility of a permanent solution or an end to the conflict.
The change that the Arab world in general and the Palestinians in particular have undergone has created circumstances that did not exist before and that make it possible for us to reach agreement more quickly than we believed.

The Israeli public elected you twice with a large majority so that you could defeat Arafat and get rid of him. Have you succeeded?
In my view, one of our greatest successes is to have opened the eyes of many groups of people, in Israel and elsewhere, to the truth about the Palestinian Authority and its leader, who has been declared out of the game. I shocked a lot of people when I first used that expression, but when all is said and done, Yasser Arafat is now out of the game.

For years you said that Israel should keep its territories to prevent an Iraqi invasion from Jordan. With Iraq now under American control, isn't it time to reevaluate the concept of the Jordan Valley as a buffer zone?
We have to confront a world that is full of danger. Certain Israelis are filled with an ardent desire to be smaller, more dependent on others

and less capable of defending themselves with their own resources. But national defense is not a matter of guesswork. We don't know how things will evolve in Iraq and what sort of government will be established there. The Americans are not going to stay there forever. And we have other enemies—for example, Iran, a country in which even moderates call for the destruction of Israel and which is actively trying to obtain weapons of mass destruction and develop ballistic missiles that could reach our towns. Not to mention the role that Iran played with Syria in activating Hezbollah in Lebanon, or Iran's subversive intrigues among Arab Israelis to incite them to terrorist action against the country. Lebanon is also strongly determined to obtain nuclear weapons. We don't know what side Saudi Arabia will take. And then, of course, there is Syria. In other words, the war in Iraq has created a new situation in a world that has otherwise stayed the same.

Were you surprised by the speed with which Iraq collapsed?
No. I didn't give much credence to the dramatic and alarmist media commentaries at the beginning of the war. The United States is powerful but circumspect. Perhaps they don't have the charisma of those who make no bones about decrying their supposed failures, but they know how to work seriously, in an organized way. And they know how to prepare a military offensive.

The transition to democracy in Iraq does not seem certain. I would have liked Israel to be surrounded by democracies, but unfortunately that's not going to happen tomorrow. Today, the United States is paying the price for its lack of interest in facilitating democracy in the Middle East—there is no comparison with the resources that were invested in preparing the people of the former Communist bloc, for example, for democracy. This form of government cannot just be imposed in every country. In terms of our region, the Islamic factor obviously doesn't help.

Why is it that to this day the Americans still haven't found proof that there are weapons of mass destruction in Iraq?
You have to remember how vast the country is. The Iraqis had a lot of time to hide these weapons. We know that Iraq possessed chemical and biological weapons and that Saddam Hussein was trying to get nuclear weapons.

Does Syria have nonconventional weapons?
Yes. It has a large arsenal of chemical weapons, as well as the means of deploying them. However, I don't think that the threat of a Syrian attack is plausible at the moment because of the very inadequate state of its army.

In that case, why fear Syria?
Because it is dangerous: Damascus possesses chemical weapons, is trying to develop biological weapons and has a terrorist organization under its control: Hezbollah. Add to that its poor capacity to evaluate situations—for example, why, when it was clear that Iraq would be defeated, did President el-Assad think that the United States would lose the war? He welcomed key figures in Saddam Hussein's regime, and we know that the Iraqis have transferred military equipment to Syria, either to hide it or to arm Hezbollah.

What do you plan to do about all this?
The Americans must pressure the Syrians. They must make clear and specific demands: the disbanding of the Palestinian terrorist organizations that operate out of Damascus; the expulsion of the Iranian Revolutionary Guards Corps from the Lebanese Bekaa Valley, a territory entirely under Syrian control; the end of cooperation between Syria and Iran; the deployment of the Lebanese army in southern Lebanon and the withdrawal of Hezbollah, as well as the withdrawal of the missile batteries directed against Israel. The pressure should be political and economic, not necessarily military.

After Iraq, do you think the United States will turn to Iran and Syria?
Both Iran and Syria harbor terrorists. The Americans should concentrate on these two countries.

Using military means?
It's not for me to make recommendations to other countries. However, Syria will not readily accept the changes that I have just outlined.

What threat would Israel be under from Syria if Syria were attacked by the United States?
Israel will defend itself. It is futile to indulge in declarations and warnings on this subject. Reacting calmly is the most effective form of threat.

People say that Israel's image in Europe has never been so bad.
That can be explained by the growing incidence of anti-Semitism in European countries. We are aware of the danger posed by anti-Semitism dressed up as opposition to Israel's justified self-defense.

Has not Israel been partly responsible for its negative image in Europe?
How? By not giving in to Yasser Arafat's terrorism?

Is the new picture in the Middle East created by the Iraq war good or bad for Israel?
Iraq was under a terrible, bloody dictatorship. Let's not forget that when the Iraqi president realized that no one was going to sell him nuclear weapons, he decided to make his own bomb. Saddam Hussein's downfall is an undeniable relief, but the removal of the Iraqi threat doesn't mean that all our problems have disappeared.

Does this mean that what happened in Iraq should also happen in one form or another in Iran, Libya and Saudi Arabia?
In terms of Iraq, the United States demonstrated a keen sense of responsibility. I don't think it realistic to envisage a new intervention so soon after this one. Even superpowers have their limits. Victory comes at a high price. It is, however, possible that a new era is beginning. The traumatic effect of the Iraq war on the Middle East could bring about big changes. Israel has the opportunity to establish new relations with the Arab states and the Palestinians, and we should not pass up that opportunity. I intend to look at that opportunity with the utmost seriousness.

Do you think that we might reach an agreement in the near future?
That depends above all on the Arabs. A change of direction is called for, involving the fight against terrorism, a number of reforms, the total end to subversive incitement and the dismantling of all terrorist infrastructures. With leaders who understand the need for these measures and who seriously put them into practice, we could reach an agreement.

Despite your optimism about the possibility of a future agreement with the Palestinians, your agenda has been overturned by new terrorist attacks. In the space of 48 hours on May 17–19, 2003, five terrorists murdered 12 Jews and wounded dozens of others in Jerusalem, Afula and Hebron.

In all the battles in which I fought, I have never despaired, not even in the most difficult moments. The losses that we are currently experiencing are particularly heavy and cruel because it was mainly civilians—men, women and children—who were deliberately targeted. Nonetheless we must keep struggling, despite the pain. In the war of independence in 1948, even though I was seriously wounded in the battle of Latrun, I didn't despair. During the Yom Kippur war in 1973, I was certain of victory after we crossed the Suez Canal, and I am equally sure that we will win again today.

What is your optimism based on?

More than anything else, on the Israelis' ability to resist. Would the citizens of other democratic countries have shown the same endurance that the Israelis have shown in the ruthless war imposed on us since September 29, 2000? My compatriots refuse to give in to terror; they carry on with their normal lives. They work, they produce and they develop the country in every area. Our soldiers show as much courage on the battlefield today as soldiers from previous generations did. Civilians demonstrate a determination, responsibility and cool nerve that are truly worthy of praise. Terrorism has therefore failed to break either our morale or our democracy—the first and only democracy in the Middle East.

After the last attacks, President Bush called and asked me to pass on his condolences to the people of Israel. I told him that the terrorist acts committed in Israel, as well as those committed by Islamic extremists in Saudi Arabia and Morocco, would reveal to the world the cruelty of the enemy we face. I am determined to take the initiative in trying to introduce peace, security and tranquility between our people and the Palestinian people. To make progress, however, we have to beat terrorism and reestablish peace.

SEPTEMBER 2004
A PLAN FOR ISRAEL

In September 2004, Ariel Sharon gave me an official interview to discuss his plans for the future of Israel. He was eloquent, but I felt that he wasn't showing his whole hand. "A true secret is a secret that one doesn't tell anyone, even oneself," he liked to say.

Sharon had occupied his post of prime minister for much longer than either of his two predecessors, Benjamin Netanyahu and Ehud Barak. These two men, both much younger than Arik, were waiting impatiently for him to cede his place. Sharon, however, convinced that his policy was the only one that combined history and reality, had no intention of disappearing quietly. In the absence of a viable Palestinian partner, Sharon advocated a strategy of separation that would reduce friction as much as possible, in the hope of seeing the emergence of a Palestinian leader with whom Israel could live peacefully. At 76, Ariel Sharon was preparing to face his biggest test since coming to power. His unilateral plan of separation—which included the dismantling of all Jewish settlements in the Gaza Strip and of four others in northern Judea-Samaria—was due to be executed in the summer of 2005.

This plan had a strong impact on the Middle East and throughout the world, and, of course, provoking great political stir in Israel. Within Likud there was violent opposition to it. In a referendum on May 2, 2004, militants decisively rejected Sharon's plan. Arik again failed when he tried to win the support of the Likud central committee for his proposal to include the Labour Party in the government. Yet the more Sharon experienced political failures, the more opinion polls showed that the majority of Israelis approved of the plan. The prime minister didn't budge and kept repeating, "I'll put this plan into operation and that's the end of it!" Would he succeed? Would he be forced to call for a referendum—a national one this time—or to hold new elections?

A year ago, your government made the decision to isolate Arafat because he constituted an "obstacle to peace." What are your precise intentions toward Arafat?

We eliminated the leaders of Hamas—Sheikh Ahmed Yassin, Abdel Aziz al-Rantissi—and other terrorist heads when the time was right. The same principle goes for Yasser Arafat. We will treat him like the others. I see no difference between him and Yassin: they both murder Jews. For Arafat, we will choose the time that suits us best. Everyone will receive his due. The question will be debated when the time is right, as it was for the leaders of Hamas.

The Palestinian terrorist offensive is entering its fifth year, and Yasser Arafat continues to lead it.

The IDF and the security forces have made enormous progress and have had numerous successes in the fight against terrorism. I do not see the Palestinians abandoning that approach; however, despite their loyalty to Arafat, some Palestinians have realized the extent of the damage caused by their strategy of terror.

I insist: will Arafat be expelled?

I repeat that it's useless to go into details at the moment. We will choose the right conditions and the right time. We categorically reject the European suggestion that we end Arafat's isolation on the pretext that he is the most powerful man on the Palestinians' side. Such proposals do nothing but delay possible solutions to the problem.

Even in your own camp, people are speaking out against liquidating or expelling Arafat.

It is my responsibility. No external person will influence my decision. I might listen to the opinion of my son Omri, who is on the Knesset's foreign affairs and defense committee, or consult various experts. But I alone will make the decisions, in the solitude that is the lot of every political or military leader.

How have you managed to reduce the number of suicide attacks, and with that the number of deaths? No democracy in modern times has resisted a terrorist war for so long.

It's the work of a team and not of an isolated individual. I cannot claim all the success. The internal security forces, the army, Mossad and the police have made enormous progress, and I am in permanent contact with all the Israeli services involved in the fight against terrorism. Together, we are using new methods that have enabled us both to stop the increase in attacks and also to strike at terrorist leaders. We have to continually surprise them. The intelligence services play an essential role in this complex struggle, and the construction of the security fence represents only one way to prevent the terrorists from reaching our people. But it isn't the only solution. The eradication of terrorism necessitates a dynamic and constant offensive on our part.

Before you became prime minister, the security forces had almost totally failed in their fight against the "industry" of Palestinian human bombs. What is your secret?

Let's not discuss that; it's futile to talk of their failures. Let them take the credit for the fruits of my action—it doesn't matter to me. Only results matter.

According to the head of Shin Bet, Avi Dichter, Jewish extremists are planning an attempt on your life. Do you fear a violent act against you?

Not against me personally. I don't fear for my life. I proceed on the basis that those responsible for my security know their job.

These threats come from extreme right-wing Jews. In the past they came from left-wing extremists.

I have protected Jews all my life. It's bizarre to think that in addition to ensuring our defense against the Arabs, the security services have to worry about defending me against the Jews!

The banners proclaiming you a traitor don't frighten you?

I trust those responsible for our security, but I keep my eyes open.

The situation has become so strained that it is said that these extremists might use, not a pistol, as they did for the assassination of Rabin, but a bazooka!

I am sure that all the necessary precautionary measures have been taken. In any case I can tell you that these threats have no affect on my work or my plans.

Do you fear a civil war?

No, thank God. That would be terrible. Everyone must remain conscious of his obligations to his country, and even if there are differences of opinion, we must do all that we can to prevent civil war. There are also responsible people in the settlements who know the disaster that would strike Israel in such a situation—which is why it is so important to stop the calls to violence. I certainly am aware of the seriousness of the situation. When I learned that a senior officer and his family had to leave their house in Karnei-Zur because of threats coming from the neighboring settlement, I made it clear to my cabinet that I have no intention of allowing this kind of thing.

In November 2000, I accompanied you to Kfar Darom, in the Gaza Strip, where you went to comfort the inhabitants after an attack on a school bus. Can you understand that today these people feel betrayed by you?

I have only carried out my responsibilities as the head of the government for the good of the whole population of Israel. We risked having other plans imposed on us, such as the Saudi Arabian plan or that of the German minister Joshka Fischer. Without an initiative on my part, Israel would have had to enter into negotiations that would have ended in an agreement imposed on us from the outside.

You have been called a "dictator" who "doesn't give a damn about anyone." Some think that the IDF soldiers will be very badly received in the settlements. A family man has declared that he will open fire on anyone, even a soldier, who attempts to dig up his daughter's body.

Those are serious, dangerous and unacceptable words. I have asked ministers to denounce this kind of threat with the utmost force. However, in Judea-Samaria and the Gaza Strip as elsewhere, people still fear a civil war, which would be disastrous for Israel. So long as the calls to violence continue, the danger that extremists will commit irrevocable acts increases. I understand what the inhabitants of the settlements feel. Some have been there for three generations and have accomplished great, sometimes even extraordinary, things—in agriculture, for example. But the government has decided on a course of action. My task now is very difficult: on the one hand I have warm feelings for individuals, and on the other, I have the resolve to act in the people's best interests. If someone thinks that he can stop the government's decisions from being implemented by using force, he is wrong. They will be implemented according to the timetable that I have fixed, and they will be carried out to the letter.

Will you meet the inhabitants of the settlements that will be dismantled, to try to convince them?
Yes, of course. A few days ago I had a very serious meeting with one of their representatives, and I will meet others. During these interviews I emphasize the benefits that this separation plan has already given us. The plan will allow us to harmonize our position with that of the United States. We have only one friend in the world capable of preventing, for example, a vote for sanctions against us at the United Nations. We mustn't forget that. President Bush's letter of April 14, 2004, contains fundamental points: the refusal of Palestinian refugees' right of return to Israel; the recognition of "large blocs of Jewish settlements"; the rejection of any plan other than the Road Map, and the recognition of Israel's right to defend itself and to exercise its power of dissuasion in the face of regional threats.

*Is the construction of the security fence going to continue in spite of the criticism of the International Court of Justice at The Hague?**
We are trying to inconvenience the Palestinian population as little as possible, while ensuring that Israeli citizens have maximum security against attacks; 200 kilometers of the fence are already standing, 75 are under construction and work is beginning in the region of Lakhish. It's an enormous worksite that has 400 heavy machines and

---

* On June 9, 2004, the International Court of Justice declared the construction of this fence illegal and demanded its destruction. The United Nations General Assembly followed suit.

huge amounts of imported material. In the beginning we thought about making openings for every *fellah*[*] who wanted to work his fields or for every Palestinian child going to school. That didn't work. If the wall is to succeed in preventing terrorism, you cannot open doorways.

Other factors get in the way of a normal life. The Palestinian population has suffered a lot, and that has provoked protests around the world and even here. I have therefore decided to amend certain things; the number of Palestinian enclaves, for example, has been reduced. If the wall had followed its original course, hundreds of thousands of Palestinians would have found themselves in enclaves, and thousands of them would automatically have been absorbed into Israeli territory.

Nonetheless, we are carrying out the basic plan. We have come to the conclusion that, in certain sectors, the wall will stick closely to the Green Line, which remains a geographical reference. Some settlements, or groups of Jewish settlements, will now be east of the wall, but they will themselves be enclosed for their protection. The Gush Etzion bloc will doubtless be inside the designated area of the wall, as well as Ma'ale Adumim and the region of Ariel.[†] We consider the Jordan Valley a security zone.

So you will continue to build?
Absolutely. Everyone talked about it and made promises, but I am the only one to actually build it. I have documents here on the decision made by Yitzhak Rabin, on January 23, 1995, to construct a separating wall after the suicide bomb of Beit Lid, which killed more than 20 Israelis. During a televised interview, Rabin announced this detailed plan and spoke of the need to separate Palestinians and Israelis. I quote: "The government is following a policy that will end the domi-

---

[*]   Agricultural laborer.
[†]   The Gush Etzion bloc is a bloc of settlements between Jerusalem and Hebron; one of the largest settlements on the West Bank, Ma'ale Adumim is a town of about 30,000 inhabitants at the eastern edge of Jerusalem, where it is considered part of Greater Jerusalem; and Ariel is a large town in the West Bank, 43 kilometers from Tel Aviv.

nation of another people and that will introduce a partition, but not following the demarcation lines of 1967. Jerusalem will still be unified, and the security border of the state of Israel will be fixed along the length of the Jordan." Rabin thought that the wall could be built in a year, but nothing was actually done. Ten months later Rabin was assassinated. Finally, after lots of false starts, I took it over and made the project a reality.

What did you feel when you read the letter denouncing your dismantling of the Jewish settlements, written by Meir Har Tzion, the living legend of Unit 101 and of the 890th Paratrooper Battalion, which both had been under your command?
Har Tzion and I have always been on friendly terms, and he came to see me several months ago. But despite all the respect I have for Har Tzion, the officer, heroic fighter, agriculturalist and great Zionist, I have to assume responsibility for the destiny, the security and the very existence of our people.

Were you right in the past, when you strengthened the settlements, or are you right now, when you are dismantling them?
I was right at the time and I'm right now.

Meaning?
That the situation is not the same. That's all there is to it.

Some of your ministers, including some of the most important ones, are not in favor of your initiative.
Personal considerations and political ambitions are also involved. Some ministers suggested dismantling the Palestinian Authority—dismantle, destroy, liquidate. This would be a mistake in my view. If one of those ministers was elected head of state, he would soon realize that it's impossible. There are 3.5 million Palestinians in the territories of Gaza and the West Bank. Is he going to look after them, feed them, educate them, give them social benefits, take care of everything from medical care to sweeping the streets? Is Israel in a position to take on that responsibility? The Gaza Strip alone includes 1.2 million Palestinians.

When you take on the role of prime minister, you see things you don't see from the opposition benches. Some people advised me to do

nothing and to wait quietly for the next elections in 2006. But after
the fall of the Palestinian prime minister Abu Mazen on September 7,
2003, we risked an avalanche of new "suggestions" from the international community. We couldn't stand by and do nothing, arms folded.
The United States agreed to help us on condition that there was a
process and that something happened.

In the beginning, my plan for a unilateral withdrawal from the
Gaza Strip and evacuation of the settlements surprised the Americans.
I presented it in broad terms to the White House envoy Elliot
Abrams, during a secret meeting in Rome in November 2003. He had
come to discuss the situation in the Middle East and Syria, which
seemed ready to enter peace negotiations with Israel—or at least that
was the impression given by the propaganda campaign launched by
Damascus on the subject. I stated that I was ready to undertake such
discussions if the Syrians ceased supporting terrorism, which wasn't
the case and still isn't. I emphasized, however, that it was better to
concentrate, above all else, on a single problem, that of the Palestinians. After that meeting Washington didn't bring up the question of
negotiations with Damascus again.

Don't you think you let an opportunity slip?
That wasn't the case. In reality, Syria was in an awkward position. Its
president, Bashar el-Assad, wanted to free himself of the pressure exerted by Washington in order to win time and to elicit Washington's
sympathy and support. For him, the best way of doing that was to declare himself ready to negotiate with Israel. But I didn't see any real
change in the Syrians. If there had been, they would have eliminated
the leaders of terrorist organizations and closed those leaders' offices
in Damascus, expelled the Iranian Revolutionary Guards Corps,
helped deploy the Lebanese army along the whole border with Israel
and so on. Now everyone knows that we are far from that. Negotiating with Arab countries is not a problem for me—on the contrary—
but it will happen only on condition that they are serious.

*Bashar el-Assad said, "When Sharon is ready to negotiate, I will be too." Are
you ready?*
Once again, Damascus must first of all prove its sincerity. As well as
the measures I've already outlined, Syria must destroy its supply of

rockets and missiles in southern Lebanon—13,000 items—and forbid Hezbollah from supporting Palestinian terrorists in the territories. Israel will not be used as Syria's pawn in its power game with the Americans.

If Bashar el-Assad fulfilled all these conditions, would you be prepared to negotiate with him?
In any event, we would need to wipe the slate clean in terms of previous promises that might evoke associations with the three Israeli governments—two Labour under Yitzhak Rabin and Ehud Barak, and one Likud under Benjamin Netanyahu—who held talks with Damascus in the past. The two parties should meet and outline their demands. It's the only way to negotiate and the only way to reach an agreement.

Your decision to withdraw from the Gaza Strip and to dismantle the Jewish settlements has often been compared with General de Gaulle's decision to give Algeria back to the Algerians.
I don't like to compare myself with anybody, but I feel closer to Winston Churchill or Georges Clemenceau. And in terms of a parallel with French Algeria, let me just point out that unlike the *pieds noirs*,[*] Israeli citizens do not have the option of repatriation with their mother country, and they have no intention of leaving.

On September 21 of this year (2004), the International Herald Tribune *published a long article by Jean Daniel. He wrote, "We cannot accept a war against terrorism led by a Bush-Putin-Sharon alliance." The editor of* Le Nouvel Observateur *added that the violent criticism of Israeli policy expressed in France cannot be attributed to anti-Semitism.*
I haven't read the article. The anti-Semitism that is currently spreading in Europe arises from the fact that almost 15 million Muslims now live in the European Union. Since it is not acceptable to be explicitly anti-Semitic, anti-Semitism is dressed up as anti-Zionism. In other words, European anti-Semitism is concealed.

---

[*] People of European descent living in North Africa.

We have suffered Arab and Palestinian attacks for more than 100 years. The terrorism that has overrun us and that has also struck the United States, Russia, Spain, Turkey and Indonesia is identical. There can be no compromise with these assassins. It is the biggest danger threatening the world today. Of course, despite the horror of the suicide attacks, we're still dealing with conventional weapons—but terrorist leaders are doing all that they can to obtain weapons of mass destruction.

Do you have information on this?
We know that they are trying to get their hands on these kinds of weapons.

Are Islamic extremists involved?
Oh yes! For years we had trouble persuading the world of the nature and danger of terrorism. Thinking that one can put an end to terrorism with reassuring words is a mistake.

Does that "we" include the United States, Europe and Russia?
Europe is threatened. After the attacks in Spain and Turkey, we saw the barbarism of which this terrorism was capable in Russia as well. We should confront it together. Assigning to mediators the task of dealing with the terrorists would only encourage the terrorists. We have to act together in sharing intelligence and, if necessary, on an operational level. The free world must wake up. We simply cannot go on swallowing all these tall tales.

So it was important to intervene in Afghanistan and Iraq?
Very important. George W. Bush neither withdrew nor wavered. If the free world does not want to be under the thumb of a fundamentalist Islam imposing its values on us all, there is no other solution.

The Europeans are urging you to speak with Arafat and not to isolate him.
A serious mistake. That would only delay the possibility of an agreement between Israel and the Palestinians. Certain European countries continue to engage in dialogue with him, to send him delegations and reinforce his position, but nothing good can come of it.

What will the next step be, after the withdrawal from Gaza?
President Bush promised me that no pressure would be put on us to accept a plan other than the Road Map. But I have no illusions about the intentions of the Palestinians: I do not expect that they will call a halt to the violence. It is therefore very possible that after our retreat from Gaza, there will be nothing else for a very long time.

For many years?
That's hard to say. Any additional measure would demand a spectacular reversal in the Palestinians' strategy, and for the moment, nothing allows us to predict that that will happen. Israel will pursue its fight against terrorism and maintain its presence in the territories, which will remain under its control after the withdrawal.

Would you describe President Bush's attitude toward Israel as positive?
Our relations with the United States were already friendly and have strengthened even more since his election. The level of cooperation between our two countries has never been so high. George W. Bush is a friend of Israel, and our personal relationship is very close.

And yet in his speech to the General Assembly of the United Nations on September 21 of last year (2003), Bush did not mention your withdrawal plan, but he criticized Israel's treatment of the Palestinians.
He was talking about the security fence. On other points the president repeated what he had already said on other occasions. We must accept the fact that our two countries can disagree in certain areas. The main thing is that we each respect our obligations to the other.

American headlines occasionally accuse Israel of carrying out acts of espionage in America.
I can declare in the strongest possible terms that Israel does not spy on the United States. In any case, we have no need to do so.

Could the backlash created in Israel by your withdrawal plan lead to an early election?
That would not be wise. If the implementation of the plan were delayed or interrupted, Israel would suffer greatly as a result. We must

avoid an early election at all costs. I hope that my government will survive until the next election, planned for November 2006. But if the election has to be pushed back, I strongly intend to run, and I think I have a good chance of being reelected. Israel needs unity, and it's important to form a government of national unity. I don't reject any party in principle, and certainly not the Labour Party.

According to the New York Times, *Israel will undertake military action against the Iranian nuclear threat.*
There is no question. We would engage in dissuasive force, and we have the capability of self-defense. We will act in strategic cooperation with the United States. The whole world should be concerned about the Iranian threat. Iran, which already possesses ballistic missiles with a range of 1,300 kilometers—capable, therefore, of reaching Israel—is developing missiles with a range of 2,500 kilometers. This danger does not affect just our country, it affects European and other countries as well. Once again, it is the role of the international community to block Iran's nuclear capability, and it is the role of the U.N. Security Council to take the necessary measures. I am very concerned about the voices saying that we have to resign ourselves to the idea that one day Iran will inevitably join the club of nuclear countries.

Aren't Europeans aware of the danger?
Their primary consideration is their economic interests.

And the Americans?
They understand the danger presented by nuclear weapons in the hands of a regime like that of Iran. The tight control exercised by the International Atomic Energy Agency has led to an interruption, or at least a delay, in the Iranian nuclear program. But Iran is a huge country in which it is easy to hide installations, and the Iranians are masters in the art of double-dealing.

What is Russia's attitude?
I began speaking about the issue years ago with Viktor Chernomyrdin, Boris Yeltsin's prime minister, and I continue to do so with President Putin. They take it seriously.

Is Iran the most serious strategic threat that Israel faces today?

Yes, it is. Aside from their nuclear ambitions, the Iranians are actively involved in terrorism. From their regional base in Lebanon they support the Tanzim—the armed branch of Fatah—financing its missions and paying terrorists on pro rata according to the number of attacks against Israel. That is in Judea-Samaria. In Gaza the Iranians help Hamas and provide them with smuggled weapons. More serious still, the Iranians try to recruit Arab Israelis, the great majority of whom want, however, simply to live in peace.

But whatever the problems Israel faces, I remain—as I have always been—a born optimist.

NOVEMBER 2004
ARAFAT'S DEATH

On April 14, 2004, Sharon was finally able to extricate himself from the promise that he had involuntarily made to the American president in March 2001—not to touch Yasser Arafat. Sharon was at the White House; George W. Bush advised him to leave the destiny of the Palestinian leader in the hands of divine providence, and Sharon replied, half joking and half serious, that providence sometimes needs a helping hand. Without giving Sharon the green light to eliminate Arafat, the president didn't try to impose a further commitment on him, either.

In any case, George W. Bush had already "let go" of Arafat in political terms when he had mentioned, in his speech of June 24, 2002, the urgent need for a new Palestinian leader who would not be "compromised by terror." When he came out of the White House, Sharon told Israeli journalists that he thought that he would now have some elbow room with regard to the president of the Palestinian Authority. Sharon publicly declared his intention to act, perhaps issuing a last warning to Arafat.

In Israel and abroad, many commentators then started talking about a "war between two irritable old men." According to these savants, it was high time that Sharon and Arafat left the political scene and be immediately replaced by leaders determined finally to bring peace. This attitude irritated Sharon beyond measure, particularly because the Israeli intelligence services were very clear on the issue and could back it up with proof: Arafat continued to finance terrorist organizations and even directly sponsored attacks. Although he bore the title of President of the Palestinian Authority, the former Fatah leader had never renounced his strategy of terror.

As for Ariel, he still held the view that he had expressed in 1988, during the first Intifada: "There is a difference between an enemy and a criminal. You make peace with an enemy, but you hunt the criminal until the very end, as the Allies did during World War II with Hitler, driving him back into his bunker in Berlin, even after the Nazi chief of staff proposed a cease-fire."

Strengthened by the support of his transatlantic ally, in September 2003, Sharon reacted vigorously to an attack on a bus in Tel Aviv that killed four people by dispatching bulldozers to destroy part of the main building of the Mukata'a. Left-wing idealists like Uri Avneri immediately rushed to Ramallah to act as Arafat's "human shield." At the time, the Palestinian leader also still enjoyed the support of the European Union and of the U.S. State Department. American diplomats worried about rumors of a plan to capture Arafat in his headquarters.

During the first three years of war against Palestinian terrorism, Sharon sometimes said that he would like to become a simple commando leader again and deal with the Mukata'a himself. After a particularly bloody Palestinian attack, I asked Sharon why he didn't expel Arafat once and for all, or at least bring him to justice for his terrorist activities.

"Do you want a troop of European lawyers landing in Jerusalem to defend that criminal?"

"So what can we do? We can't kill Arafat, and we can't expel him. Do we just let him enjoy total immunity?"

"Let me deal with this my way!" This was an untypically abrupt ending to our conversation, for which Sharon later apologized.

No sooner had Sharon been given greater room for maneuver after his interview of April 14, 2004, with President Bush, than Arafat's health declined. Taken to the Percy Military Hospital in Clamart, near Paris, Arafat died there on November 11. He returned to Ramallah only to be buried. The Palestinians immediately accused Israel of having poisoned Arafat and announced that there would be an inquiry into his death. My article for Ma'ariv began, "Ariel Sharon will go down in history as the man who liquidated Yasser Arafat without killing him."

SEPTEMBER 2005
AFTER THE DISENGAGEMENT

Palestinian terrorism did not disappear with Yasser Arafat. Almost a year after the Palestinian leader's death, I discussed with Sharon how the situation had evolved.

Given the chaos reigning in the Gaza Strip, exemplified by the assassination on September 7 of Mussa Arafat, Yasser Arafat's nephew, what do you expect from the president of the Palestinian Authority, Mahmoud Abbas?
I can say what he should do, not what I expect of him, because in our region declarations, speeches, promises and even written agreements count for nothing. Only their implementation matters. In order to start negotiations based on the Road Map, Abu Mazen (Mahmoud Abbas) must put an end to terrorism, violence and incitement. He must dismantle terrorist organizations and confiscate their weapons. He must completely reorganize the security services, which are also terrorist devices. They are all implicated in terrorism. Drastic reforms are necessary: the security forces need to be trained in peace. Abu Mazen is certainly conscious of the dangers lying in wait for him. Though he does not belong to a Zionist organization, he is aware that the Palestinians' suffering—impossible to ignore—is the result of terrorism, of a policy and strategy of terror. He understands it, and I'm sure that he wants terrorism to be eradicated. But he binds himself, so to speak.

And traps himself?
Yes, by signing a cease-fire with terrorist organizations and by promising, particularly with regard to Hamas, not to dismantle it or disarm it and to award it political status, which will allow Hamas to take part in the elections and undoubtedly to form part of a future government. I imagine that Abu Mazen, bound by his promises, will not act and will

not fulfill the conditions necessary to the implementation of the Road Map. As a result, it will be impossible to engage with the heart of the matter.

The Palestinian state can form itself only according to the Road Map, which in turn will be executed only if adequate measures against terrorism are taken. But Abu Mazen is bound hand and foot. His explanation is that he has made commitments so he cannot act immediately, but that he promises to act when he is stronger. Is he doing everything in his power? I don't think so. He has deployed military force and managed to stop people from firing during the evacuation of the Gaza Strip, but he hasn't stopped the Hamas leaders. If there is relative calm at the moment, it's because Hamas wants to enter politics, so it's in their best interest.

What if Hamas took part in the parliamentary elections planned for January 25, 2006?
I am strongly opposed to it, and I have made that clear. I have said that I would be ready to consider it on two conditions. The first is if Hamas is effectively disarmed before the elections; we would not be satisfied with a promise that they would disarm afterward. Second, Hamas must declare the abolition of its 1988 charter that calls for the destruction of Israel.

To whom have you made these two conditions known?
To everyone. To the Americans and, very clearly, to the French.

Why? Did either country urge you to accept Hamas's inclusion in the election?
No. I keep asking the Europeans to declare Hamas a terrorist organization. Silvio Berlusconi agreed when Italy had the presidency of the European Union. However, each country in the union must make a separate declaration. Germany, Holland and Italy have already done so. If Hamas took part in the elections, that would mean that we no longer considered it a terrorist organization. Stretching the concept of democracy like that worries me a great deal.

Like Hezbollah in Lebanon?
Absolutely. That is why I clarified my position to European representatives who come to Jerusalem.

This is a position that the Americans understand?
Although they seem conscious of the risks, I'm not sure that they understand the situation in its entirety. Their passion for democracy is so fervent, some of them believe that the simple fact of holding elections is enough to found a democracy. The Americans have never said that they disapprove of my position, but until they respond to it, I will continue to explain it. We will not give Hamas freedom of movement between Gaza and Judea-Samaria.

And if a Hamas activist still traveled between Gaza and Judea-Samaria?
If he dared, he would end up in prison.

What of international cooperation against Islamic terrorism?
That cooperation is tight. It goes beyond the normal bounds of relations between secret service agencies, and it involves a very large number of countries. Four years ago—knowing that information doesn't always reach a head of state and that even intelligence services have trouble identifying the vital facts among the mass of data they receive—I took an unprecedented measure by setting up a direct link between my cabinet and that of my foreign counterparts. We are in daily communication with the White House, and also with 10 Downing Street and with the Elysée Palace. We are also in contact with Moscow and Berlin. There are barely any important issues that are not shared with, for example, a member of Tony Blair's cabinet.

And the Iranian nuclear threat? Who should be responsible for neutralizing it: Israel, Europe or the United States?
Israel of course cooperates with the United States, Great Britain, France and Italy. We have close relations.

What is the extent of the Iranian threat?
Iran is trying by every means to equip itself with nuclear weapons— truly by every means.

Even its new president Mahmoud Ahmadinejad?
Even more so under him.

At this moment, Ariel Sharon's secretary entered and gave him the text of a news bulletin released by the radio station Kol Israel. He read it aloud, with obvious pleasure: "The most expensive bull ever offered at auction has just been bought by the prime minister's two sons. They paid 17,400 shekels [about $4,000] for this pedigree Simmental bull . . . The Sharon family offered for sale seven breeding bulls, and sold five for a total of 60,000 shekels. The minister of agriculture, Israel Katz, who attended the sale, declared that this bovine competition can be compared to the one going on for the leadership of Likud, with the difference that the owner of the winning bull pockets his check and disappears from view, whereas in politics, there is always another round."

To go back to the Iranians, they have developed their own missile, the Shihab–3, they possess cruise missiles and they are now trying to acquire longer-range missiles as well. They are working furiously in the nuclear domain but are still coming up against technological obstacles. The point of no return will be reached the day that they manage to overcome those obstacles.

The General Assembly of the United Nations, which has often condemned Israel for your military operations or settlement drives, is now being very considerate toward you. In France, President Chirac, who until now you thought of as a "slab of concrete," received you at the Elysée with all honors. What is behind this sudden change?

There are probably several factors, but principally my decision to leave the Gaza Strip and to guide the state of Israel through an extremely tough political process. Perhaps people did not really believe me or doubted that I would be able to pull it off, because of the extreme difficulty of the task. I think, however, that France and the United Nations saw it as an opportunity to restart the political process.

So long as this disengagement is not interpreted as a weakness that would allow the United Nations or France to maneuver against Israel to the advantage of the Arabs, as was the case for a long time?

I don't think that my action is interpreted as a sign of weakness. In my discussions with various heads of state, I explained very clearly what I was and was not prepared to do in terms of our relations with the

Palestinians. I think they realize that Israel has shown itself ready to make a sacrifice that would allow us to pursue the political process, despite all its difficulties.

But what does the political process mean in their view and in yours?
For me, it's the possibility of reaching a situation where we can begin negotiating. We are at the pre–Road Map stage, not yet at the Road Map itself. If the Palestinians do what they are supposed to do, we will be able to discuss things further. This process should lead to an unprecedented situation, a more peaceful one, in which there will perhaps be cooperation, not only with the Palestinians but also with other Muslim countries—those who are, of course, interested in cooperating.

What were your feelings before you made your speech to the United Nations General Assembly, where so many resolutions against Israel have been passed and where you were personally attacked after certain military operations and political acts?
In 77 years of my life, I have seen and lived through all sorts of situations and turnarounds. I am not touched by displays of affection any more than I am downcast by attacks. I have said clearly to everyone— the Americans, the French, other Europeans, Russians, Turks, Indians and many others—that Jerusalem is a place of pilgrimage for the planet's heads of state. They can channel their personal and national interests into it. I have always said that I was ready to make painful concessions but that I would not accept any intervention from anyone in decisions linked to Israel's security needs. I have just repeated this to the Spanish foreign affairs minister, Miguel Moratinos, after having said it a few days ago to General Omar Soliman, head of the Egyptian intelligence services. We have deployed an artillery unit, and once we have completed withdrawal from the Gaza Strip, we will react in the most vigorous fashion to any offensive action.

What does "we have deployed an artillery unit" mean?
At the first shot from Gaza, our artillery units will respond in the harshest manner. I have said as much to the Arabs, so there is no secret about it. I have also explained it explicitly to the Americans and to all the Europeans, and I am firmly resolved to go through with it if

need be. How can one claim that the withdrawal has no consequences for Israel? There is no slander, verbal abuse, insult, slight or slur that has not been made about me. My opponents say that I signed an agreement with the Americans, not the Arabs. It's true that I trust the Americans more than the Arabs. We have never obtained before as much as we have obtained now, thanks to this agreement. Not that it has been easy. I went to the United States a good dozen times for some very stormy talks.

However, you cannot build between Jerusalem and Ma'ale Adumim.
Leave that to us. The construction is going well almost everywhere, and I can confirm that we will continue to build in the large settlement blocs.

You don't fear confrontation with the American administration over your often-repeated declaration—notably in April 2005 in Crawford, Texas, in front of President Bush—that as head of the Israeli government you will maintain the big blocs of settlements that have a continuing territorial link with Israel?
No, on the contrary. That's very clear. Moreover, we are continuing to build.

But the risk of tension between Israel and the United States?
Every time that high-ranking members of the American administration come to Israel, the media talk about the strong pressure that we will be subjected to. During those visits, I have never felt the slightest pressure, either in the words or in the opinions expressed by the people I was talking to. These armchair analysts don't seem to understand that an envoy does not necessarily come to pick a fight. These gloom-and-doom articles have always made me smile.

Perhaps the Americans were waiting for the disengagement they wanted so much before resorting to pressure?
Why does a serious journalist like you, who understands the issue well and has written about it for years, let himself get caught up in such pessimism? No pressure is being exerted on Israel. Do the Americans like us building settlements? No. I have discussed it more than once with them. The first construction in the territories goes back to 1968.

The Americans remind me that they have opposed it since the end of the Six Day War, and that every Israeli government has ignored them even when they continued to express their disapproval. So, they say to me, what do you expect? That Washington suddenly gives us its blessing and declares that we can do what we want? The position of the United States remains unchanged.

Where is construction going on today?
Hundreds of apartments are being built in Ariel, a thousand housing units in Beitar Illit—a little construction is going on everywhere. There is nothing to prevent us from building in the big settlement blocs. Will the Americans be enthusiastic about our large-scale construction? I don't think so. Will they take measures against Israel? I don't think so, either.

No measure?
No.

All the same, if pressure were exerted, would you be able to resist it?
First, I am capable of resisting pressure. Second, there won't be any pressure. The answer to the question is therefore "yes."

Some enemies of Israel are undoubtedly delighted to see the country begin to look like a Lego set. Sharon has dismantled whole settlements, they say— something that never happened before in the history of Israel—we will continue to dismantle as we wish, and the left will come to power after Sharon.
For me, the real danger lies in the right.

Will the supporters of the settlements favor a left-wing government?
No, not necessarily.

Yitzhak Rabin and Shimon Peres declared that they signed the Oslo Accords on the basis of the Camp David agreement in 1978 between Sadat and Begin, which recognized the rights of Arabs and allowed the dismantling of the settlements in the Sinai. In the future, another left-wing government will say that Sharon has taken the state of Israel apart.
The right is going to dismantle the settlements. The left is incapable of it; people on the left say it themselves. They have never evacuated

settlements anywhere, except in Jordan. By signing the peace agreement with King Hussein in 1994, Yitzhak Rabin gave back the territories of Arava,* occupied since I had conquered it in 1970, as head of the southern command. I stress that there is something that I will never go back on; as I have stated unambiguously, I have no intention of discussing Jerusalem.

Do you have the feeling that Jerusalem is truly unified and does not run the risk of being divided?
I do not intend to discuss the question of Jerusalem. Period. I have said that hundreds of times. But I am surrounded by a group of provocateurs. I repeat my intentions, but it does no good—they keep on saying that I'm going to break up Jerusalem. And other fortune-tellers claim to know that another disengagement is planned. Another lie. The withdrawal from Gaza is an isolated act. If the Palestinians respect their commitments, it will be possible to initiate talks, under the Road Map. For the moment, I don't see that happening.

What did you get from the Americans?
In the beginning, they wanted to pursue the process initiated in 2000 by Bill Clinton with Ehud Barak and Yasser Arafat, which would have left 4 percent of the West Bank in Israeli hands. Barak was ready to give the Palestinians part of the Halutza dunes.† Where are we today? First, on the question of Palestinian refugees and their right of return, Israel has signed an agreement that is of considerable importance, that no Labour or Likud government was able to obtain until now: the United States has declared that the Palestinian refugees will not return to Israel. The second advantage concerns the settlements. Third, we will adhere to a single plan—the Road Map.

Then there is the right of self-defense. Nearly four years ago, almost the entire world was rocked with indignation at an Israeli military incursion 300 meters from Beit Hanun, north of the Gaza Strip.

---

* A region of the Negev.
† An area in the Negev bordering the Gaza Strip and offered to the Palestinians in exchange for an equivalent area in the West Bank for the Israelis.

Now, no one interferes in the military measures that we take to defend ourselves. I also consider it an extremely important improvement that the United States has firmly recognized the existential threat that hovers over Israel and recognizes our need to defend ourselves by our own means, not only against regional, but also against extraregional—particularly Iranian—threats. In other words, the Americans are saying, "Don't touch Israel or its powers of dissuasion." We live in a world governed by pressures: pressure on Gadhafi's Libya, and now pressure on Iran.

Israel has therefore won important advantages. I think that we will keep them if we don't go back on them. I will not go back on any of the points in this agreement. President Bush has publicly told the Palestinians, three or four times, that they must break up terrorist organizations and their infrastructures.

What is the secret of your friendship and understanding with President Bush?
On his first visit to Jerusalem, in 1998, when he was governor of Texas, I took him to visit Samaria and the valley of Jordan; our helicopter flew just over the rocks. That was the beginning of our relationship. On February 6, 2001, President Bush, who had just been elected the previous month, was the first head of state to call to congratulate me on my own victory.

Since then, you have fought suicide attacks, there was the war in Afghanistan and the Iraq war, and your bond is still strong.
The White House seems to appreciate Israel's efforts against terrorism. George W. Bush believes that Islamic terrorism represents the greatest existing threat to the survival and culture of our democracies.

Do you agree?
Yes. I have always had the sense that the president thought highly of our active resistance against terrorism, for so many years.

Sixteen years ago, you said in an article published by the New York Times *that the road to peace in the Middle East would occur through a democratization of the region. President Bush's intervention in Iraq was also in the name of democracy. Can we talk about the failure of this aim?*

Saddam Hussein's regime was despotic, dangerous and bloodthirsty, because of the man's character. The bodies of all those who were assassinated have not yet been exhumed—not to mention the massacre of thousands of Kurds or the use of toxic gas against them. Which is why the American intervention was so important; it has also shaken up the region.

What are the effects of the war?
Countries like Syria now realize that there are limits that must not be crossed.

However, Syria allowed all sorts of terrorists to enter Iraq via its borders.
Exactly. I believe that Iraqi and other terrorists are also being trained in Syrian camps.

So have things changed?
The changes have already made themselves felt—for example, American and above all French pressure on Syria concerning Lebanon, and now the pressure put by numerous countries on Iran. The process is slow, but something is shifting. However, the transformation will not be quick. Iraq faces the problem of how Sunnis, Shiites and Kurds will coexist.

Is the exercise worth it for the United States?
In my opinion, yes—in the long term. The Americans must stay in Iraq for several more years; they can't leave immediately. However, the shock waves have been set in motion, including in Lebanon, and democratization is underway.

Is there proof that President Bashar el-Assad was involved in the assassination of the Lebanese president Rafik Hariri?
He seems to have had a hand in it, but the only source for that information is the Syrian officer who deserted and gave details of the affair to the French.* At any rate, assassinations are commonplace in this region; we are surrounded by murderers.

---

* This interview took place before the conclusions of the U.N. inquiry, which incriminated the Damascus regime, were made public.

If proof of Bashar el-Assad's responsibility in this crime were made public, is it possible that the dictatorship in Syria would fall?
So long as the voices advising Israel to enter negotiations with Damascus are ignored. The Syrians would love to go through the motions of negotiating peace with Israel, which would immediately release the pressure they are under from the Americans and the French. We must not let up or assist them in any way. We must concede nothing—nothing at all!

In your view, the war in Iraq has created greater shock waves than we can imagine.
It is a process. Will it be short-lived? That will depend on the Americans' capacity to resist—and on their willingness to resist. But something is happening with Syria. And now there are talks with the Lebanese about disarming Hezbollah.

Who is talking to the Lebanese?
The French are talking to them, and the Americans are expressing their views on the subject as well, because of Iran. Apart from the issue of nuclear weapons, which is obviously the biggest one, the Iranians are implicated in terrorism. They are even agitating the Arab Israeli population, through the Islamic Movement; at the moment they have recruited just a small minority, but the group is growing. They transfer money through Lebanon and fund Palestinian terrorist organizations. They are in permanent communication with Islamic Jihad, and they also help Hamas. The Iranians are implicated in everything concerning the training, preparation and activation of local terrorist networks.

Were you disappointed when, after the withdrawal from the Gaza Strip, President Pervez Musharaf declared that Pakistan would establish diplomatic relations with Israel only after the creation of a Palestinian state? Were you hoping that other Arab or Muslim countries would establish open relations with Israel?
Israel already has links with countries like the Gulf States, Morocco and Tunisia. I was even invited to Tunisia for an international conference, but not everyone is comfortable with the idea of this visit, because Tunisian law does not allow visitors to be accompanied by their

own security service. As for Pakistan, I have met Pakistani representatives—which fortunately does not prejudice our excellent relations with India. I have never asked anyone to establish relations with Israel or even to recognize our state. Take the meeting in Istanbul between the Israeli and Pakistani ministers of foreign affairs: the Turkish prime minister called me one evening to tell me that Musharaf had asked him to arrange the meeting. Everyone wants to get involved in our affairs. It gives publicity to these characters and increases their stature.

You have to understand that Israel is thought to have universal power; Israel is taken to be a country that pulls all the strings in every area. Musharaf wants to be invited by Jewish organizations in the United States and, of course, is trying to create closer ties with Washington. He thinks that the Jews have great influence in the United States. Arabs and Muslims think of Israel as a serious, strong country that is capable of carrying out a policy as complex as withdrawing from Gaza—and this facilitates the possibility of agreement because it can no longer be claimed that Israel is opposed to peace.

Do you mean that this policy has led to the strengthening of official ties between Israel and Muslim and Arab countries?
Absolutely.

2004–2005
A MOTHER'S ADVICE

Whenever the prime minister had a falling out with me, he would ask our friends to intercede. He did this, he explained several times, in honor of a promise that he made to his mother on her deathbed. Vera, whose influence never faded, had urged him never to break off with old friends or relations because of an argument. She knew her son well and was aware that over the course of his stormy career he had frequently made provocative or slighting comments about the army's general staff or those in power. After he took office as prime minister, Ariel followed her last piece of advice, particularly in his relations with political or media opponents.

In 2004, however, the announcement of his plan to withdraw from the Gaza Strip almost caused the end of our old friendship. As soon as I got wind of his intentions, I pressed him to go to see the inhabitants of the settlements in their homes: "You really owe that to the 8,000 Israelis who courageously resist the Palestinians!" When I saw him hesitate, in hopes of avoiding a heated confrontation with the settlers, I decided to issue a public appeal to him through the columns of the daily *Ma'ariv* in an article entitled "Go to Gaza!" Unfortunately, my editor, in an attempt to be sensationalist, changed the title without telling me to "Go to the Devil!"

A mutual friend told me that Arik was not pleased. Nonetheless, he called me in Tokyo, where I had gone to cover a news story, and did not even mention it. "I've just had an operation on my urinary tract," he told me. "Everything went well, and I'll be fully recovered in a few days. But I asked the two White House envoys who were coming to postpone their visit until next week, because I want to tell them how I see the future of Jerusalem, whatever agreement is reached. In that regard, I don't delegate to anyone—no one!"

Then he bombarded me with questions about Japan. "Senior government officials in Tokyo told me that they are very much looking forward to your coming here," I told him.

"I long to go, but I'm very busy with the disengagement. It's been 30 years since I last went to Japan. So what has changed?"

"Aside from the Kabuki theater, it seems that they have planned for you to visit a sumo training center. In spite of your size, you'll look puny next to them!"

"What? Are they that fat?"

"Very fat, but incredibly strong."

"In that case, I prefer them to Israeli politicians. Here, the fight has only just started."

Shocked, the inhabitants of Gaza refused to believe that Sharon was going to raze their houses. Some of their spokespeople were already calling him a traitor; had he not been their champion only yesterday? Some accused him of having come up with this plan to distract attention from the inquiry into his and his son's dubious funding of the electoral campaign. It was also said that these accusations were coming from sympathizers of the left and that Sharon was trying to buy their good will, even their inertia, by turning against the Jews in the Gaza Strip. Faced with this flood of invectives, which spread to the benches of the Knesset and made headlines in the press, Sharon retired behind a wall of silence and refused to speak to the settlers.

Although there was the likelihood of violent confrontation between the population of Gush Katif and the forces of law and order, Sharon's coldness toward our compatriots surprised me very much. In March 2004, after we commemorated the fourth anniversary of Lily's passing, seated on the lawn of Sycamore Farm, I repeated to Sharon that I thought it wise to talk to the settlers. "They deserve a personal explanation," I said.

"We're only talking about 400 agricultural plots! We will give them others in compensation." He paused, and then he added, "Every day, between 5:30 and 6 in the morning, I fear that my military secretary will call me to announce that more soldiers or civilians have been killed in Gaza."

Very concerned by this media storm, Sharon spoke to Yaacov Nim-
rodi, the owner of *Ma'ariv*, in plain terms: "You played a dirty trick on
me!" He was referring to a piece of around 20 pages that the paper had
devoted, the previous day, to the accusations of corruption. In addition,
Ma'ariv rode its hobbyhorse about the supposed financial and personal
links between the prime minister and the family of businessman Elhanan
Tanenbaum,* who had been kidnapped and then released by Hezbollah.
It was pure invention; Sharon did not even know Tanenbaum.

In May 2004, Sharon organized a referendum in Likud to approve
the disengagement plan in Gaza. His entourage had led him to believe
that the ideological support of the majority of his party's members
would make the affair less dramatic. Sharon had promised to respect
the result, whatever it was, his advisers having convinced him that he
would win the vote. After all, had he not obtained from President
Bush on April 14 a vital agreement guaranteeing Israel's continuing
hold on the majority of the settlements? This did not take into account the determination of the settlers and of Sharon's rivals for the
leadership of Likud, who were uniting in an effort to sideline him.

This also did not take into account the relentlessness of Israel's
enemies: the very day of the referendum, May 2, 2004, Palestinian
terrorists entered Gush Katif and assassinated the Hatuel family—a
mother and her four girls—who were just setting out for Ashkelon. It
was proof of the violence to which the Jewish state was exposed at all
times—and against which the settlements in the Gaza Strip formed a
shield. Sharon had lost. I urged him to organize a national referendum, which would allow him to benefit from the caution of most of
the population and wipe out the defeat that he had suffered within his
party. In addition, I told him, if he won public opinion, it would remove the risk of a devastating schism.

When he failed to react, I published an article in *Ma'ariv* entitled,
"We warned you!" in which I went over my argument point by point.
Several toadies whispered in Sharon's ear that I had harmed him, both
with this article and also by appearing every Friday night in a weekly

---

*   This businessman and Israeli reserve colonel was kidnapped by
    Hezbollah at the end of 2000 and released thanks to German media-
    tion, in exchange for the release of terrorists imprisoned in Israel.

news program on TV's Channel 1. The prime minister gave me his response in person when—having freed himself of official engagements for the evening—he attended a surprise party organized for my birthday by my family and friends on May 19, 2005. In front of 200 guests, he gave a long speech about our friendship and its history.

That did not stop him from getting angry, two months later, about one of my television commentaries and complaining to the friend with whom we had planned his visit to the Temple Mount on September 28, 2000: "Uri is a disaster! He keeps putting his foot in it!"

Maybe I was always putting my foot in it, but Sharon never missed the political debates broadcast on Friday evenings. He returned to his farm for Shabbat every weekend; this weekly break in the Negev allowed him to recharge his batteries by surveying his land and watching over his flocks of sheep and herds of cattle. If he managed to get away earlier on Friday, he would have lunch with neighboring farmers. He often called me just after the program, while I was driving back to Tel Aviv. Or else he would call me the following day to congratulate me on a position I had taken on the Jewish state or on the importance of Eretz Israel, on my justification of the systematic elimination of terrorists—or even on my sartorial choices.

On Thursday, August 11, 2005, we had just returned from Paris, where Sharon had met President Chirac, who supported his disengagement plan. I had taken advantage of the trip to buy an orange tie from an exclusive Parisian shop—orange being the rallying color of the people who opposed the withdrawal from Gaza, in honor of the oranges grown in the estates of Gush Katif and of the Ukrainian revolution.

That Thursday, the settlers had mobilized some 250,000 people in a giant demonstration against the expulsion of Jews from the Gaza Strip. The moment of withdrawal—of the "uprooting" as we said in Hebrew—was approaching. The media talked about tens of thousands of men and women in uniform—police and army mixed together—ready for the evacuation. Omri described the scene for his father: "Everything is under control," he said, using his favorite expression.

The whole country—on balconies, car mirrors, T-shirts and hats—was decked out in a strange mixture of orange and blue (the color favored by those Israelis who agreed with disengagement), when the leaders of Likud and their entourages announced that Sharon was creating his own "big bang"—namely, his departure from Likud and his founding of a new party.

That evening, on Channel 1, Yigal Ravid was moderating the debates. My colleague Ayala Hasson caught me unawares by revealing that I had turned down the post of Israeli ambassador to Paris. "Is it true?" she asked.

"Would you be prepared to give up your career as a journalist?" I replied. "Well, neither would I."

Attention then turned to my orange tie.

"It's a sign of solidarity with the uprooted, with the pain and suffering of the people who are being torn from their homes," I explained.

"And what about the big bang? What about the party that Sharon wants to create?"

"The real big bang is the mammoth demonstration yesterday in Tel Aviv that gathered 400,000 people. It's the big bang of the settlers who are defending their country on the front lines. We must do everything to avoid a civil war. And the expression that I most detest is, 'Everything is under control.'"

Finally, Yigal Ravid asked me about Ariel Sharon's chances in the next election.

"Those who didn't want him as prime minister a second time will have him as prime minister a third time," I declared.

Right after the interview I went to the King David Hotel, where I was to dine with Patrick Wajsman, founder and editor-in-chief of the French magazine *Politique Internationale*. A mutual friend of Ariel's and mine called me on my mobile. "You can't imagine how angry Arik is with you," he warned me. "He was so beside himself that he switched off his television. He said to me, 'Our friend—our friend doesn't miss an opportunity to screw me! There weren't 400,000 people on the Kings of Israel Square in Tel Aviv yesterday—there were only half as many.' I tried to calm him down and explain that it was just a figure of speech, but it was no good. He is really angry with you."

This time I awaited his phone call in vain. Ariel was beside himself with anger. It was doubtless the wisdom of his mother, Vera Scheinerman, that saved our friendship, which has endured through all our differences of opinion.

SEPTEMBER 2005
WITHDRAWAL FROM GAZA

August 15 and 16, 2005, were agonizing days for Sharon. He went to see the president of Israel, Moshe Katsav, to discuss the unprecedented act of the unilateral withdrawal from Gaza. Journalists had already reported the threats made by settlers to soldiers. People were talking about civil war. Sharon exclaimed to the press, "If they want to attack someone, they should attack me, not our soldiers!" President Katsav, conscious of the threats to the prime minister's life, immediately changed his tone. But Sharon couldn't care less about the danger to himself.

Holed up in his Jerusalem office, Sharon followed the events hour by hour, via official reports and television coverage. He never participated in the obvious joy of his advisers when they came to tell him that the withdrawal was taking place calmly and without victims. He did not seem happy; rather, he seemed somehow cut adrift.

What was the hardest moment for you in the evacuation of the Gaza Strip?
It was terrible for me—terrible. I cannot highlight a particular moment. The decision itself was the most painful thing.

But you saw the pictures.
Of course. The sight of soldiers gathering up children's toys and helping to pack them particularly touched me. I shared their pain and their heartbreak. The dishonorable behavior of certain adults also angered me—to see them insult and humiliate those young policemen and soldiers.

It was only a minority. You had feared the beginnings of a civil war. Was it mainly thanks to the army and the police that no blood was shed, or to the settlers as well?

The hardest thing was tearing these people from their homes and villages. For me, the credit goes to the 11,000 families who packed up their possessions and obeyed the order to evacuate; despite their pain, they accepted the decision of the government and the Knesset. But there were others—those adults, and thousands of young people recruited and sent there by the regional council of Yesha [Judea-Samaria] to try to prevent the evacuation by force. We witnessed very serious acts, including calls to revolt by some rabbis. As for those who sent their children out, decked with orange stars, their hands raised . . .

These cases were a minority.
You have no idea how many cases there were, or what revoltingly crude insults were spat in the faces of young soldiers. The inquiry on this issue is underway, and we are collecting statements from witnesses. These rioters deserve no indulgence.

You're talking about a small number of people.
You're the one who says it was a small number.

No, I'm asking you the question.
It was not a small number. They hurled degrading and incredibly brutal insults at the soldiers and police. There were many such extreme cases during the evacuation. It was painful for all the inhabitants of Gush Katif, but there are limits that should not be crossed. A close friend wrote to me that we should grant an amnesty to all rioters. He is wrong. None of them should be granted an amnesty.

Don't you feel somewhat isolated in your office in Jerusalem, as though you are living in a bubble? There are death threats against you and you cannot move freely.
I feel absolutely in no way isolated or cut off from people.

I'm talking about what you feel in response to these death threats.
I have often confronted danger, including in your company. It has no effect on my plans or on my behavior. It's true that my presence at certain events has become complicated by the fact that one cannot ask the impossible of the security services. Every trip has become very expensive because of the insane climate of hatred that surrounds me.

Are there concrete threats against you?
The security services are dealing with that; I don't get involved. They
know what they need to do, and I make sure that I don't make their
task even more difficult.

*You are accused of now wanting, after so many wars, to appear like a man of
concessions to atone for the dismantling of the Jewish settlements in the Gaza
Strip and to ensure your place in history.*
I do not act out of personal interest, and I have nothing to be forgiven
for. I have worked all my life for the defense of Jews and Israel. I have
actively participated in everything that has happened here since the
creation of the state. I have nothing to atone for.

*Nonetheless, it is the first time that the head of the government has disman-
tled settlements in the entity that we call Eretz Israel. It is an extraordinary
and cruel step.*
Yes, a very difficult step. I am accused of so many things—I am aware
of all the condemnations, insults and lies against me.

Is it a lie to say that you want to enter the annals of history?
To tell you the truth, I don't need to. Over the years I have reached all
sorts of goals, and I would still like to reach a few more.

To run for reelection, for example?
Of course.

And do you think you will win?
I think I can win and be reelected.

For the third time and within Likud?
I belong to Likud. After all, I invented the creature. My struggle to establish Likud succeeded. During the summer of 1973, after selling a
ton of hay produced by my farm, I rented the hall of Beit Sokolov [of-
fice of the Israeli Association of Journalists] for a press conference and
to announce my intention of creating that party, destined to replace
the Labour Party, which had been in power for decades. For me, it
was a major contribution to Israeli democracy.

You are now accused of being antidemocratic. Do you regret not having held a referendum on the withdrawal from the Gaza Strip?
I think I did the right thing, because a referendum would have unleashed a huge wave of animosity.

But a democracy would require it.
I made the biggest possible contribution to Israeli democracy by creating Likud—the first real alternative to a Labour government.

Maybe you ruined that contribution by not consulting the people before withdrawing from Gaza.
For some, democracy consists of spreading oil on roads, scattering nails on them and committing other acts of violence.

Not everyone took part in such demonstrations against the withdrawal.
I wasn't talking about the majority. Indeed, the majority of people don't think my policy was wrong.

Another reason to hold a referendum, since you would have won.
That referendum would have opened up internecine hatred and maybe caused terrible damage to the country. That was why I decided it was not necessary.

What would happen if Hamas took power in Gaza and started a new war?
Israel would react relentlessly.

Isn't Israel's security largely under the control of the Egyptian army, now that the IDF is abandoning the Philadelphia axis and leaving Cairo the job of curbing the arms smuggling between the Sinai and the Gaza Strip?
Our presence there unfortunately did not put an end to trafficking. My predecessors as head of state demonstrated an almost criminal naïveté. The Oslo Accords allowed us to control a narrow band, 200 meters wide and 14 kilometers long, between Egyptian Rafah and Palestinian Rafah. By accepting that, Israel committed an error of judgment that cost us dearly. Keeping control of that strip of land when we have left the Gaza Strip would mean putting soldiers lives' at risk for no reason.

But doesn't allowing Egyptian forces to be deployed there threaten our peace agreement with Egypt?
It's just a case of limited action replacing several hundred Egyptian policemen with several hundred . . .

Soldiers.
Border police!

The border police are accountable to the Egyptian army.
So? That doesn't make any difference.

Now that the withdrawal is completed, will you allow Palestinians from the Gaza Strip to come and work in Israel?
No. Under the law that has been in force for a long time, the number of Palestinian workers in Israel must gradually decrease until 2008.

How many are there at the moment?
About 15,000, I think.

Do you believe in the economic recovery plan for the Gaza Strip under the authority of Shimon Peres and James Wolfensohn, delegates of President Bush and the Quartet [the United States, the United Nations, the European Union and Russia], or do you fear that yet again enormous sums of money intended for Palestinian development will find their way into the pockets of Palestinian leaders?
Peres is doing important work in this area. His brief is to bring an end to Israel's responsibility in the Gaza Strip. The area must be opened up because its current status prolongs Israel's responsibility.

Open it in what direction?
Toward Egypt and toward the sea. Not toward Israel; access toward us should be totally blocked, except for commercial transactions, which will continue. Israel sells many things that cannot be bought in the Gaza Strip, and traders can travel freely. I think it vital that we free ourselves of our responsibility toward Gaza.

Did the Palestinians recognize that the occupation is over? Is there a debate about this with the Americans or the Palestinians?
I have not discussed it with the Americans.

With whom, then, since the Palestinians are demanding more territories in the Gaza Strip and are saying that the evacuation is insufficient?
Let them say it. There will not be the slightest movement on the issue of the border. The borders have been fixed once and for all on that side.

Are the Palestinians ready to declare that the occupation is over and that Israel is no longer responsible for the Gaza Strip? Who should announce it, and what have you demanded?
It is not for us to demand that the Palestinians announce the end of the occupation. We will announce it. I think that the Quartet or another organization will announce it.

Are you waiting for an announcement? Are you asking for one?
I can't in fact remember where we are on that point—who is asking or not asking—but the occupation is over.

That is what you say, but not what the Palestinians say. Do they have other demands with regard to the north or east of the Gaza Strip, as the media are reporting?
Such a demand would be completely unjustified. They can make it, but it won't count for much.

[Concerned by my question, the prime Minister called his political adviser, Shalom Turgeman, then replied . . .]
Okay, this is the situation: Israel is announcing not the end of the occupation but the end of its responsibility for the interior of the Gaza Strip—and we are not discussing the issue with the Palestinians.

So it is Israel who is announcing it.
Yes, because the concept is very complex. International law also involves negotiations on the West Bank, and the Palestinians are not going to consider that a resolved issue.

Is Cairo prepared to accept free movement into Egypt from the Gaza Strip?
Yes. We, on the other hand, are not prepared to accept free movement into Israel. Palestinian goods can travel through Nitsana, and people can cross via Kerem Shalom, probably within the next six months.

Hasn't the withdrawal led to a certain weakening of Israel's ability to fight terrorism?
On the contrary, we are now in a much better position, in terms of quality and experience.

SEPTEMBER 2005
SPEECH TO THE
UNITED NATIONS

In September 2005, Ariel Sharon went to New York to represent the state of Israel at the General Assembly of the United Nations, which was meeting on the sixtieth anniversary of its creation. It was during this trip that he showed the first signs of physical ailment. On the day of Shabbat, freed from his numerous official obligations, he welcomed three old friends into his suite at the Palace Hotel. Despite the obvious pleasure that he derived from their company, Arik could not hide his weariness. Pale, his voice hoarse, he complained of his heavy schedule and the problems that awaited him on his return because of Netanyahu, who had called a meeting of Likud's central committee to threaten Sharon's position. Sharon had personally called hundreds of influential members to get their support. He spoke bitterly about "Bibi" and was furious about what he thought was a useless confrontation—since the next general election would not be held until November 2006.*

But Sharon was receiving increased backing from the leaders of the Jewish communities in America and Europe, who were now unanimous in their support, even if they had previously been hostile to him. In addition, the speech that he gave on September 15 to the General Assembly of the United Nations was well received by the heads of state and governments of the entire world and added to his international status. In his address, Sharon spoke about the withdrawal from Gaza: "Israel has shown that it is ready to make painful

---

* Sharon's creation of the new Kadima Party shortly thereafter involved a dissolution of the Knesset and an election planned for March 2006.

concessions to bring an end to the conflict with the Palestinians. It is now for the Palestinians to prove their desire for peace. Until that happens, Israel will defend itself against terrorist groups. The successful implementation of the disengagement plan creates opportunities for progress toward peace, under the stages set out in the Road Map. I am among those who believe that we can come to a balanced compromise and that Jews and Arabs can live together as good neighbors."

During the dinner organized in his honor by the media magnate Rupert Murdoch, Sharon discussed ways of improving Israel's image in the world. The withdrawal of Jews from the Gaza Strip was Sharon's entrance ticket to the world's club of socially acceptable heads of state. His country had been struck off the list of undesirables. What a powerful message was sent out by Israel's willingness to tear homes away from thousands of innocent citizens in the name of peace! And who had accomplished that? Ariel Sharon, the man who until then had been identified with the settlement movement.

Sharon did not conceal the pleasure he felt at this adulation, sincere or otherwise, but he was well aware of the ephemeral nature of this state of grace. He had experienced it often enough. Showered with praise after a brilliant military victory one moment, he would be called an "aggressor" or a "bloodthirsty warmonger" the next. People expected him to destroy the enemy, only to slander him when he did so. Sharon the realist savored the moment of glory before the inevitable return of criticism that occurred when he refused to compromise on Israel's total control of Jerusalem or on continuing the development of settlements in the West Bank. Upon Sharon's return from the United Nations, Shimon Peres, the deputy prime minister, told him: "You're in an ideal situation. Bush is caught up in Iraq, Blair is under fire in his country, Chirac is at rock bottom in the polls, while you, Arik, are enjoying the support of the whole world."

"Yes, but for how long?"

NOVEMBER 2005
KADIMA

In his speech to the United Nations, Ariel Sharon had given a caveat to his overtures toward the Palestinians: "There will be no compromise on Israel's right to exist as a Jewish state with defendable borders, safe, free from threats and terrorism." The antiterrorist struggle would therefore continue.

General Gadi Shamni interrupted an interview of ours to hand the prime minister a note informing him of the liquidation of some terrorists. A fleeting smile lit up Sharon's weary face; he asked his military secretary to verify their identity and to prepare a summary of their crimes. He had just been commenting that even if Arafat's successor did not want to carry out attacks against Israel, he was clearly incapable of stopping them.

At 4 P.M. on that Tuesday, November 1, Gadi Shamni interrupted us again to give Sharon further information. He read aloud: "Hassan Madhun and Fawzi Abu Kara, both members of Hamas, were killed by an air-to-ground missile while they were driving in the Djebaliah camp." Madhun was responsible for the deaths of at least 20 Israelis—he had organized, among other attacks, a double attack on the port of Ashdod and an attempted suicide attack in a hospital. A 21-year-old woman who had been treated at the Soroka hospital in Beersheba for serious burns caused by a domestic accident was due to return there for more tests and so had a pass to cross into Israeli territory. This female terrorist was apprehended in the Erez passage, north of the Gaza Strip, thanks to electronic devices. On being discovered, she attempted—unsuccessfully—to activate the ten-kilo explosive belt that she was wearing, before being blocked by IDF soldiers.

Sharon asked his military secretary to ensure that these names were published at once: international opinion had to know that Israel did not kill Palestinians indiscriminately, but only those with blood on their hands. Arik also wanted to reassure Israelis, because rockets were still being fired into Israeli territory in spite of the evacuation of Gush Katif. He was being criticized by ministers and Likud members opposed to the unilateral withdrawal, which, according to them, would have the inevitable consequence of an increase in terrorism and the transformation of the Gaza Strip into "Hamastan"—just as, several decades earlier, southern Lebanon had been nicknamed "Fatahland." Led by Netanyahu, these rebels did not hesitate to use the most ignoble methods to humiliate Sharon. And so, not content with their refusal to ratify the nomination of two new ministers, they arranged for his microphone to be turned off during a meeting of the party's central committee. But none of these maneuvers seemed to upset him.

Things were not going well between Ariel Sharon and Likud, the party that he had created more than 30 years earlier. He thought seriously about leaving it to create a new party, one more in line with his current thinking. Arik knew that he needed at least 14 of the 40 Likud members to come over to his side in order to obtain the necessary financing that would allow his new party to be included in the electoral race (the equivalent of $250,000 per member).

I was opposed to the idea of Sharon leaving Likud to create a new party. Realizing that I was getting nowhere in our conversations, I decided to bring him to his senses on a television program. Forty-eight hours before he slammed the door on his party, the prime minister heard me stating on live television, "Ariel Sharon is the master of Likud. He is the only person capable of putting its house back in order. What does it matter if some of its neighbors are noisy?" I was hoping to silence his rivals in the party, who were already spreading the rumor of a split, while at the same time urging Sharon to stay at the helm. The following day, a Saturday, someone complained at Sycamore Farm of the "stupid things" that I had said. Sharon took him to task: "Uri Dan doesn't say stupid things!"

I wasn't the only one who wanted Sharon to stay in Likud. But certain party apparatchiks, including several ministers who had no hope of political advance without Sharon's help, hoped that he would leave. They detested Benjamin Netanyahu and feared that he would become prime minister before them or in their place. Surprisingly, the big shots of the Labour Party added their voices to the chorus of toadying. After all, the polls predicted a tidal wave in favor of Sharon and any party that he led—they predicted 40 or so members of the Knesset, representing a third of the total seats, which would guarantee control in a coalition government, in which thwarted members of both right and left hoped to play a role.

One of the advisers who was encouraging Sharon to leave Likud took me aside on the morning of Sunday, November 20: "Listen, he's old now. He cannot bear the attacks of those revolting against him anymore. Not only did they cut his mike when he won the election of the Likud central committee against Netanyahu, they are also insulting him on a personal level."

On August 22, during a meeting of the Knesset's foreign affairs and defense committee after the disengagement from the Gaza Strip, two members of the Knesset even accused Sharon of having made Israel "one of the most corrupt countries in the free world." Ariel was so visibly shocked that his friends feared that he would suffer a stroke. "Remember," my confidant continued, "when Sharon asked Michi Ratzon, a Likud member, why he was against him, Michi replied, 'I am opposed to everything you support.' Sharon is no longer up to leading his party."

I explained to this adviser, one of the few to profess a sincere affection for Ariel, that it was precisely because of the prime minister's age—he was almost 78—that he couldn't launch into a new adventure. "It's an enormous task, even for a young man," I went on. "But for someone nearly 80 . . . It's true that so long as Arik heads the new party and decides the candidates for the next election, he will continue to lead the country in his own way. He will strengthen the settlement blocs and establish Jerusalem's sovereignty as the capital of Israel. But I think that the new party will be taken over by opportunist members, at the risk of breaking national unity and isolating Sharon in the face of the threat from the Islamists and Hamas."

On that decisive Sunday, the adviser went to see the prime minister and spoke to him for a long time; when he left his office in the afternoon, he still didn't know what Sharon had decided. I learned afterward that Rafi Eitan had also tried to convey his reservations to Sharon by fax. In vain. That same evening we heard Sharon announce on the radio that he was leaving Likud to create a new party, Kadima ("moving ahead"). I admit that I was extremely worried. This announcement rewarded a swarm of traitors for their efforts—people about whom I had tried, by every means, to warn my friend.

I remembered Sharon's reaction to one such warning during Sukkot, the feast of tabernacles, in October 2005. Simha Stern, a devoted friend of Lily and Ariel's, had invited us to lunch at her home in Caeseria. "Don't be so extremist!" Sharon had exclaimed, while trying to calm me down with a hand gesture. Then, as if giving me a consolation prize: "And what if we shut ourselves away on the farm for six months, so you can write my biography?"

For some time I had been urging him to give me a certain number of hours of his time so that I could progress with this biography. An account of his life was necessary, if only to sate the curiosity of the international public. The withdrawal from Gaza, carried out in defiance of all the dire predictions about its consequences, was in itself reason enough to assess the character of Ariel Sharon. In the months that followed, we discussed his life whenever he had the time. I would have loved to reflect on his memories with him at his home for six months, but that never happened—Prime Minister Ariel Sharon would not give himself a break. He still had so much to do.

DECEMBER 2005–
JANUARY 2006

On Sunday, December 18, 2005, at around 8 P.M., Sharon called his son Gilad from the car that was taking him from his office in Jerusalem to Sycamore Farm. Worried by his father's labored speech, Gilad alerted the security team, who stopped the caravan as it was leaving the capital. A nurse hurried to the prime minister, who was confused; she tried to give him an oxygen mask, but Arik refused. When asked to smile, he did so.

Meanwhile, Gilad had joined his father's personal doctor, Professor Boleslav Goldman, who ordered his patient to be taken immediately to the Hadassah Ein Kerem Hospital. At around 9 P.M. the news was released to the press. Sharon's advisers flocked to the hospital. Two hours later, it was announced that Sharon had had a stroke but that he had survived, his faculties unimpaired.

The cabinet secretary Israel Maimon declared, in agreement with the government's judicial adviser Menahem Mazouz, that Finance Minister Ehud Olmert would temporarily take over leadership while Sharon recovered. Others, like Sharon's bureau chief Ilan Cohen, offered themselves as spokesmen to the press. In hindsight, this tragicomic spectacle of a media pantomime makes me think of a satirical program on Israeli television called *What a Wonderful Country!* Even the prime minister was forced to take part in it; he was urged to talk on the telephone to half a dozen journalists that evening: "I feel well. Everything is fine. *Ani mamshikh kadima*"—which means both "I'm forging ahead" and "I'm going on with Kadima."

Even in his hospital bed, Sharon didn't take it easy—and indeed, no one suggested that he should. He left the hospital 36 hours later, all smiles and appearing impressively fit in front of the cameras. "Arik wanted to give an image of stability," a close colleague told me. "He feared that his attack would spoil his party's chances."

The energy that Sharon put into defending his project would soon provoke a second, terrible, stroke. As a member of his inner circle whispered to me in a phone call from the hospital that evening of December 18, "Those bastards around Sharon are going to take him away from us."

On January 2, 2006, at 5:15 P.M., my friend called me for the last time from his car. He was going to Sycamore Farm, where he was to dine with his family. Arik was still shuttling between his office and Jerusalem and his farm in the Negev, despite the advice of his doctors, who urged him to stay near the Hadassah hospital. He detested his official apartment, where he felt like he was suffocating. "Get well soon!" I said to him. "Forty cretins are waiting for you to get them elected to the Knesset!" Instead of losing his temper or trying to calm my "extremist" fervor, Ariel broke into the thundering laughter that so many Israeli comedians liked to imitate. No, he wasn't fooled by the political maneuvers of his current allies. That laugh still resonates in my ears, like a cry of truth.

"How was New York?" he asked.

I had come back the previous day. I couldn't help telling him that the hot dogs at Nathan's, which he loved, were as delicious as ever; he laughed again, but without real enjoyment. With an operation planned for January 5, his menus were subject to strict scrutiny. He joked a lot about his first stroke, however, and the comments that it had caused. I told him that I had considered writing an article panning the members of his entourage and drawing parallels with the sketches of *What a Wonderful Country!* but that I had not gone ahead with it so as not to offend him.

"No, no!" he protested. "Write it; that's really funny!"

✡

Until his last moment of consciousness, Ariel Sharon did not spare himself. His doctors had told him to work for no more than four hours a day—impossible for a man used to 15-hour workdays. And it was useless to try to reason with him: on January 1, the Palestinians had inaugurated 2006 by firing Kassam rockets from dismantled localities in the Gaza Strip—Elei Sinai, Nisanit, Dugit—onto Jewish towns in the Negev, and their missiles were threatening the coastal town of Ashkelon. Nothing was working—neither the Israeli artillery canons, which targeted wasteland territories in the Gaza Strip, nor the seal-ing-off by the air operation "Sky Blue," ordered after Sharon left the hospital.

Having built all his arguments for withdrawal on the promise of greater calm and increased protection of Israeli territory, Sharon could not tolerate such hostilities. He had won over the majority of the public to his cause by convincing them that dismantling settle-ments in the Gaza Strip would solve the root causes of the problem. If the rockets reached the Jewish state or led to human losses, Likud and the extreme right would rub their hands at the prospect of the ap-proaching election. Despite the state of his health, Ariel Sharon was incensed: he ordered the immediate liquidation of the commandos re-sponsible for the attacks. In this kind of operation, the combined ef-forts of Shin Bet and the air force usually produced spectacular results. There was just one problem: the information from Palestinian sources did not reach the prime minister's office quickly enough. Had the targets been neutralized? To put his mind at ease, Ariel met our friend, the expert on Palestinian affairs, on Monday January 2, 2006, at around 9 P.M.

"What do the Arabs say?" Sharon asked.

The expert consulted his sources and confirmed the news: Sayid Abed-El Fatah Ibrahim Judyan, 41, head of the al-Qods brigade, the armed wing of Islamic Jihad and instigator of rocket attacks and sui-cide attacks, had indeed been liquidated. A missile had struck his car at Jabalya in the Gaza Strip, killing him with one of his lieutenants. A third individual, himself implicated in terrorist activities, had been se-riously wounded (he eventually died of his wounds).

A statement from Islamic Jihad announced, "We will avenge Judyan. Our reaction will be swift and painful. Sharon should know that Judyan's liquidation will not win votes for Kadima."

Satisfied with the turn of events, Sharon said mockingly, "Good, the Arabs know that I'm working." And then he added, "I'm getting stronger and stronger."

Nothing could have been further from the truth. The incessant comings and goings of secretaries, advisers, bodyguards, doctors and nurses around him created an impression of dynamism that masked

his weakening health. Everyone thought that he was invincible—
above all me, who had seen him survive so many personal, military
and political fights, even if I had detected signs of weariness in him.
Scorning the most basic caution, Sharon devoted what remained of
his energy to protecting his land, his country and his people. Perhaps
he also threw himself into work in this manner in order to silence the
anxiety that welled inside him.

The prospect of surgery under general anesthetic on January 5
hardly pleased him, but the doctors assured him that the operation
would last only three hours. His habitual optimism reigned. He was so
sure that he would be able to carry out his mission that he never
thought of designating an "heir," whether moral or political.

On Wednesday January 4, 2006, Sharon spent the evening at
Sycamore Farm with his son Gilad, his daughter-in-law Inbal and his
three grandsons. He spoke on the phone with chief of staff General
Dan Halutz, and they discussed how a Hamas terrorist training camp
in the Gaza Strip could be neutralized. His voice was weak, and the
general thought that his words were confused. At around 10 P.M. a
mutual friend called me in alarm: "Arik was taken by ambulance to the
Hadassah Ein Kerem Hospital. The neurosurgical department is on
alert."

Horrified, I turned on the television. They were showing the ambulance driving toward Jerusalem. Through the vehicle's rear window,
one could discern Ariel Sharon's face, recognized by everyone: the
face of the formidable prime minister of Israel, his head crowned with
a white mane, the great leader of the Jewish people and the man I had
known for 52 years.

The hospital announced that he had had a stroke. The operation
lasted several hours and was followed by another. And yet another.
Seven operations in total. "The doctors have killed Arik," my wife
Varda said in a strangled voice.

I didn't try to hold back the tears that were streaming down my
face. They have not yet dried.

CHRONOLOGY

November 1917: Balfour declaration in favor of the establishment of a Jewish national homeland in Palestine.

1920: San Remo Conference; Palestine placed under British Mandate. *Ariel Sharon's parents, Shmuel and Vera Scheinerman, emigrate to Palestine.*

1922: *Shmuel and Vera Scheinerman settle in the Kfar Malal moshav.*

July 1922: The Allied Supreme Council confirms the British Mandate over Palestine.

February 26, 1928: *Birth of Ariel Sharon at Kfar Mahal.*

November 29, 1947: United Nations Resolution 181 proposes the division of Palestine into two states, one Jewish and the other Arab.

May 14, 1948: Declaration of independence of the state of Israel.

May 15, 1948: Start of the first Israeli-Arab war.

May 26, 1948: Sharon seriously wounded at Latrun.

1949: Israeli-Arab armistice treaty.

October 29, 1956: Start of the Suez campaign.

May 29, 1964: Creation of the PLO.

June 5–10, 1967: Six Day War and reunification of Jerusalem.

September 1970: Yasser Arafat and the PLO expelled from Jordan ("Black September").

September 1973: *Begin and Sharon create Likud.*

October 6–25, 1973: Yom Kippur war.

January 1974: *Sharon elected a member of the Knesset.*

1977: *Sharon named minister of agriculture.*

November 19, 1977: Anwar el-Sadat visits Israel.

September 17, 1978: Signature of the Camp David agreement between Israel, Egypt and the United States.

December 1978: Nobel Peace Prize awarded to Menachem Begin and Anwar el-Sadat.

March 26, 1979: Peace treaty signed between Israel and Egypt in Washington.

July 30, 1980: Jerusalem is declared by the Knesset to be the "eternal capital of the Jewish people."

June 7, 1981: Bombing of Iraq's Osirak nuclear reactor.

1981–1983: *Sharon becomes minister of defense.*

October 6, 1981: Assassination of Anwar el-Sadat.

June 6, 1982: Start of operation "Peace in Galilee" in Lebanon.

August 1982: Arafat expelled from Beirut.

September 16, 1982: Lebanese Phalangists massacre Palestinians in the Sabra and Chatila refugee camps.

1983: *Sharon dismissed from ministry of defense.*

1984: *Sharon becomes minister of commerce and industry.*

December 1987: Start of the first Intifada, known as the "war of stones."

1990–1992: *Sharon becomes minister of construction and housing.*

1990–1991: First Gulf war.

1992–1996: *Sharon member of the Knesset's defense and foreign affairs committee.*

September 13, 1993: Signing of Oslo Accords in Washington.

July 1994: Arafat returns to Gaza.

December 1994: Nobel Peace Prize given to Yitzhak Rabin, Shimon Peres and Yasser Arafat.

November 4, 1995: Assassination of Yitzhak Rabin.

January 20, 1996: Yasser Arafat elected president of the Palestinian Authority.

1996: *Sharon becomes minister of national infrastructure.*

1998: *Sharon becomes minister of foreign affairs.*

October 1998: Signing of the Wye Plantation agreement.

September 1999: *Sharon becomes leader of Likud.*

July 11–25, 2000: Israeli-Palestinian summit at Camp David, which ends in failure.

September 28, 2000: *Sharon visits the Temple Mount.*

September 29, 2000: Beginning of the second Intifada.

February 6, 2001: *Ariel Sharon elected prime minister.*

September 11, 2001: Attacks on the World Trade Center and the Pentagon.

October 2001: American intervention in Afghanistan.

December 3, 2001: Start of the blockade of Arafat's Mukata'a in Ramallah.

April 30, 2002: Publication of the Road Map developed by the Quartet (United States, United Nations, European Union and Russia).

June 2002: Plan to construct a security fence between Israel and the West Bank adopted.

November 11, 2004: Death of Yasser Arafat.

May 9, 2005: Announcement of the disengagement from Gaza.

August 15–September 12, 2005: Evacuation of the Gaza Strip.

September 15, 2005: *Ariel Sharon speaks at the General Assembly of the United Nations on the sixtieth anniversary of its creation.*

November 21, 2005: *Sharon resigns from Likud and creates the Kadima Party.*

December 18, 2005: *First stroke.*

January 4, 2006: *Second stroke.*

March 28, 2006: Israeli elections; victory of Kadima.

April 6, 2006: Ehud Olmert officially invested as prime minister.

INDEX